BLACK POLICE IN AMERICA

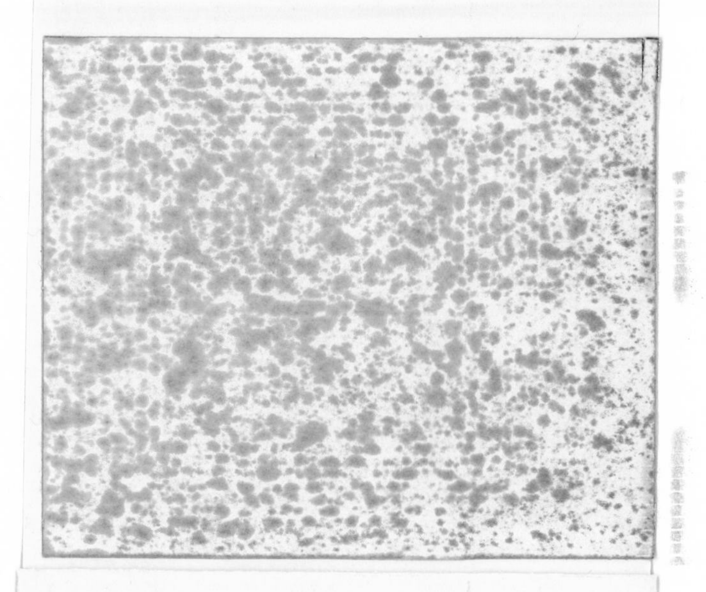

Blacks in the Diaspora

Darlene Clark Hine, John McCluskey, Jr., and David Barry Gaspar
GENERAL EDITORS

W. MARVIN DULANEY

Indiana
University
Press
BLOOMINGTON AND INDIANAPOLIS

The paper used in this publication meets the minimum requirements of American National Standard for Information Sciences—Permanence of Paper for Printed Library Materials, ANSI Z39.48-1984.

Manufactured in the United States of America

Library of Congress Cataloging-in-Publication Data

Dulaney, W. Marvin, date
Black police in America / W. Marvin Dulaney.
p. cm. — (Blacks in the diaspora)
Includes bibliographical references (p. -) and index.
ISBN 0-253-33006-8 (cl : alk. paper). — ISBN 0-253-21040-2 (pa : alk. paper)
1. Afro-American police—History. 2. Police—United States—History. 3. United States—Race relations. I. Title. II. Series.
HV8138.D85 1996
363.2'089'96073—dc20 95-19359

1 2 3 4 5 01 00 99 98 97 96

To strong African-American men

Willie Frank Dulaney
Raymond Jones
Dr. Joseph D. Lewis

CONTENTS

TABLES

FOREWORD

REUBEN M. GREENBERG, CHIEF OF POLICE, CHARLESTON, SOUTH CAROLINA

Recent history might lead someone who is unfamiliar with the topic to assume that African Americans have long served as police officers in America. After all, in recent years blacks have held the top positions in police departments in most of the largest cities in the nation: New York, Chicago, Houston, Dallas, Washington, D.C., Los Angeles, Philadelphia, Detroit, Miami, New Orleans, Baltimore, Oakland, Atlanta, and Memphis.

Blacks have been installed as chief executives of a number of state law enforcement agencies as well. They also have been elected or appointed to head a large number of sheriffs' offices. In addition, there are numerous small and medium-sized law enforcement agencies where blacks serve as chief executives.

Blacks have headed police departments in cities whose history would indicate that an African American would be unwelcome and strongly opposed in such a high position. This might be expected especially in the southern states. Nonetheless, the departments in such cities as Columbia, Charleston, Orangeburg, Florence, and Andrews, South Carolina; Mobile and Birmingham, Alabama; Greensboro and Durham, North Carolina; Richmond and Petersburg, Virginia; and even Jackson, Mississippi, have all had black chief executives.

Two African Americans have served as president of the International Association of Chiefs of Police. But all of this is indeed recent, and everywhere that African Americans serve as chiefs, ranking officers, or ordinary patrolmen, that service has been hard fought and hard won. Indeed, the experience of African Americans in law enforcement parallels the history of black participation in almost every other form of governmental service in North America. African Americans were only grudgingly accepted as police officers. Even after they were hired, they were still denied equal authority with white police officers, discriminated against in promotion and assignment, segregated, expelled, banned, and even prevented from wearing their uniforms. In some cities they were denied the right to carry arms and to arrest whites.

Entry into law enforcement has long been a means by which impoverished immigrant groups have attained economic and political power. But in their efforts to pursue this same avenue of socioeconomic advancement, African Americans have had to overcome obstacles that no immigrant group encountered. Blacks had to acquire political power first before they could achieve meaningful participation in law enforcement.

There have been two distinct periods during which African Americans participated in law enforcement: the post–Civil War period and the post–World War II period. These two periods were separated by more than half a century during which blacks were virtually excluded from the field of law enforcement. This exclusion was not caused by poor or disreputable service by black law enforcement officers. Instead, it was a result of the reimposition of Jim Crow statutes, and a conscious decision to exclude blacks from participating in the organized, coercive power of the state.

The black community itself was forced to confront a troubling dilemma with respect to its participation in law enforcement. White police and the nation's judicial establishments displayed little interest in protecting black citizens from the crime and violence directed against them by either black or white criminals. The established law enforcement agencies acted only to punish, deter, and arrest blacks when they transgressed or violated laws in cases where the victim was white. This left black communities subjected to criminal activity by black and white criminals from which there was inadequate or nonexistent protection or relief.

The dilemma faced by the black community was to continue to be victimized by black and white criminals, or to agree to support, endorse, endure, and recognize a race-based system where the position of black police officers was inherently inferior to that of white police officers. Black police officers were restricted to quasi-officer status, official impotence, and mandated inaction on their part with respect to violations by white offenders. This meant that black officers exercised limited geographical authority, and for the most part they were required to remain anonymous outside the black community.

This book is the only comprehensive study of the origin, role, accomplishments, and experiences of African-American police officers throughout the United States. While there have been a number of books outlining the participation of blacks in specific law enforcement agencies, this is the first study to examine the history of black police in this country.

W. Marvin Dulaney introduces us to pioneering blacks such as Charles Allegre and Constant Michel, who served on the city guard in New Orleans as early as 1814, as well as to the exploits of Ira L. Cooper of the St. Louis Police Department and W. E. "Ned" Jones of the Houston police force. All of these men were active during what Dulaney calls the "crime fighter" era of the African-American experience in policing, when police officers often had to use physical force to enforce the law.

According to Dulaney, the crime fighter era was followed by the "reformer" era. This period is represented by police officers such as Buster Landrum of Galveston, Texas, who sought to provide the black community better police protection without the use of physical force. Currently we are in what might be called the "professional" era of the African-American police experience in America, represented by black police chiefs such as Lee Brown, formerly of Atlanta, Houston, and New York City; Willie Williams, formerly of Philadelphia and presently of Los Angeles; and Hubert Williams of the Police Foundation.

While little evidence exists to indicate that black police officers are more skilled either in preventing or in solving crime, a great deal of evidence, empirical and otherwise, exists to suggest that African-American police officers can markedly improve the overall relationship between the police department and the African-American community, and, more important, that they can reduce the number of shootings by police as well as cases of alleged police brutality. With few exceptions, the race riots of the mid- and late twentieth century resulted not from direct conflicts between black and white citizens, but instead from direct conflict between police departments and black citizens.

It is for these latter two reasons that black police chiefs are sought and selected today. Many of the improvements that have been achieved in American race relations to date can be attributed to a reduction in the violence between the African-American community and the police forces that were, in many cases (especially in the South), organized to control the black population.

The inclusion of African Americans in the ranks of law enforcement officers has improved the profession. As Dulaney points out, most of the blacks recruited into law enforcement were much better qualified than their white counterparts—black recruits were *required* to be more qualified in order to be accepted in the first place. Many of the black recruits were college graduates, while many of their white colleagues had not graduated from high school. This was especially the case during what Dulaney calls the "second coming" phase of black participation in law enforcement in the southern states. The presence of black college graduates on police forces made it possible for police work to attract white college graduates, and it stimulated both black and white officers who were already on the job to improve their education.

The extent of black participation in American policing historically has been closely associated with the presence or absence of African-American political power. During the period that Dulaney calls the "first coming" of African-American police officers—the Reconstruction period—as black political power increased, African Americans became involved in the enforcement of the law and even controlled it in some areas. When the brief period of Reconstruction was over, African-American participation in law enforcement, like black political power itself, virtually disappeared.

Even today, with very few exceptions, blacks have served in significant numbers as members and chief executives of law enforcement agencies only in those cities where the appointing authorities are black, or where significant and even overwhelming African-American political power or populations exist. Thus, even though African Americans have made tremendous progress since the first blacks began serving in the New Orleans Gendarmerie in 1805, the foundation of their participation in law enforcement remains essentially the same. African Americans are represented in law enforcement agencies because of black influence or control of executive and legislative positions in political entities.

W. Marvin Dulaney's book highlights this important fact. Moreover, it takes us on a journey through the origins and dynamics of black policing in America. Dulaney escorts us through that uniquely American, self-made quicksand that uses race as the determinant of all aspects of life.

As a black police officer, I can understand the essence of the race problem within American law enforcement agencies. I can also see how this problem has been spawned by labor unions and fraternal and benevolent organizations within the law enforcement establishment.

I personally experienced just how negative an impact racism can have on law enforcement as a black officer visiting Johannesburg, South Africa, in 1986. After witnessing firsthand the abysmal relationship between South Africa's white supremacist police agency and that nation's black majority, and after being made aware of the fact that black officers always served at the lowest police ranks and supervisory levels, I suggested to a high-ranking South African police official that many of their problems could be alleviated if they promoted black officers to the highest ranks and gave them command authority to fully police the areas assigned to them. The response was that such action would not solve the problems, but would create a new and greater problem—white police officers would have to obey black police commanders! At that time, the white supremacist government had been neither willing nor forced to confront the critical issue of eliminating racism in law enforcement. As has been the case in the United States, unless and until that issue was resolved, black participation in policing could not be fully and equitably implemented.

It will be interesting to read the book written about the African-American experience in policing that continues W. Marvin Dulaney's work to the year 2025. The accomplishments of the next generation will inform us as to whether service in law enforcement has provided the African-American community the same political, economic, and social uplifting and fulfillment that it has provided other minorities when they had their turn in law enforcement.

PREFACE

On September 10, 1899, detectives George Gaston and Abe Kleeman of the Columbus, Ohio, Police Department were patrolling an area in the central part of the city. They were looking for Charles Dumont, who was wanted for grand larceny in several cities. The two detectives encountered the suspect at the corner of Poplar and Harrison avenues. Dumont fired at them, striking both officers. Kleeman died immediately from his wounds, but Gaston returned Dumont's fire, killing him. Gaston sustained two wounds in the encounter, one in the shoulder, the other in his forehead. Gaston subsequently served with distinction for thirty-two years on the Columbus police force. He carried Dumont's bullet in his forehead for the rest of his life. Gaston was one of the first African-American police officers appointed in Columbus. His encounter with Dumont became part of the department's official lore because Detective Kleeman was the second police officer, white or black, in the city's history to die in the line of duty.[1]

Gaston's presence on the Columbus police force at the turn of the twentieth century was a unique phenomenon. During the first three centuries of their presence in North America, few African Americans had the opportunity to serve in the police or constabulary forces organized by Americans to preserve the peace and maintain order. Moreover, during the colonial and antebellum periods of American history, when most African Americans were slaves and were considered to be a threat to the public order, some of the earliest police systems were organized to patrol their activities and regulate their behavior. According to several scholars, African Americans have been patrolled and policed throughout their history in the Americas and have had to endure both legal and extralegal police methods as a consequence.[2] Given this legacy, it was rare for African Americans, "the policed," to become members of the patrols and forces organized to suppress them.

In antebellum New Orleans, "free men of color" served on the city guard and constabulary forces as early as 1803. It was clear, however, that these men held their positions because of their status in the city's unique multiracial society and because they wanted to establish their loyalty and ties to the city's white population rather than its black slave population. Their service as "policemen" in New Orleans contradicted one of the prevailing legacies of American law enforcement, namely, suppressing the activities of people of color.[3] One of the objectives of this study is to examine in more detail the circumstances surrounding the entrance of these "black pioneers" into American law enforcement.

Today there are African-American police chiefs in such cities as Philadelphia, New York, Chicago, St. Louis, Baltimore, Washington, D.C., Los Angeles, and Atlanta. The fact that African Americans now hold some of the top police jobs in American cities necessitates an examination of the long African-American experience in American law enforcement in order to explain and understand how blacks progressed from being objects of policing to becoming some of the leading police administrators and reformers in the American police establishment.[4] Some obvious questions, then, are the following: How and why did some African Americans become law enforcement officers? Were men such as Gaston pawns, or simply dedicated law enforcement officers? How did racial segregation affect the police authority of African-American police officers? Who were these law enforcement officers? What impact, if any, did they have on American law enforcement policies for African Americans?

Although a wealth of literature on African Americans in law enforcement exists, only a few select articles and monographs examine the phenomenon from a historical perspective. Studies that address the specific history of African Americans in policing exist for New York City, Philadelphia, St. Louis, Los Angeles, St. Paul, Minnesota, New Orleans, Houston, and Memphis.[5] One of the shortcomings of these studies is that they address only the experience of African-American police officers in a single city and lack a comparative perspective. Another shortcoming is that the time perspective for each study is usually limited. The studies by Homer F. Broome, James N. Reaves, and James S. Griffin provide the most comprehensive analyses of the careers of individual police officers because of their intent to highlight the positive contributions of African Americans to the Los Angeles, Philadelphia, and St. Paul, Minnesota, police forces, respectively. Nevertheless, all of these studies are valuable for the insight that they provide on African Americans in policing for their time period. In this study I synthesize some of the findings from these earlier studies with my own new research to present a broad, comparative analysis of the African-American police experience from a national perspective.

Unfortunately, American historians who have examined the role of police in urban American society have paid little attention to the importance of race. This omission is stunning when we note the huge literature on racism in American history. The major histories of the earliest formal police departments in American cities either ignore the issue or mention only the "first Negro" in a given police department.[6] My study not only fills this gap but also shows how race has been an important aspect of American policing since African Americans began to enter American police forces in the nineteenth century.

This study will also make use of the extensive literature on black police officers provided by the fields of sociology and criminology. Unlike historians, scholars and writers in these fields have made the greatest efforts to examine the status and role of African Americans in law enforcement. They have proposed theories about the "marginal man" status of African-American police officers in American society; they have posed questions about the role conflicts that African Americans must have had when they assumed positions in agencies that historically sought to regulate the behavior of black citizens through force and intimidation; and they have gathered the survey research data to support theories that African-American police officers are/were "the men and women in the middle" of American racial conflict and oppression. In addition, scholars and writers in these fields have gathered many anecdotal data which can be utilized by historians who use oral history to supplement and highlight African-American police attitudes and views on the policies and issues that affected them at given points in history.[7]

These studies by criminologists and sociologists, however, pose another problem: they lack a historical perspective. Most of them examine the problems and issues confronting African-American police officers in a historical vacuum. My study contributes the historical analysis needed to tie together some of the theories about the status and role of African-American police officers in American society today with historical research on the past experience of African Americans in law enforcement.

African-American newspapers are a neglected source for the study of the African-American experience in policing, but they are a most important one. First, their editorials serve as definite proof that law enforcement and crime prevention in the black community have preoccupied African Americans from the Reconstruction period of American history to the present; second, they indicate that as early as the 1860s, African Americans believed that police officers of their own race would enforce the law impartially and even at times protect them from the racially biased system under which they lived in American society. These are two important perspectives. The first refutes the old notion that African Americans protected and provided solace to criminals in their community because they believed that black criminals were simply victims of American racism.[8] The second shows very clearly that African Americans regarded the employment of black police officers as a solid crime-prevention and community-relations measure much sooner than have most recent American police and crime-prevention experts. The latter did not accept this position until the 1960s, when urban racial violence appeared to mandate it.

I have relied extensively on African-American newspapers as a primary source not simply for the above reasons but, more important, because they provide much more thorough coverage of the employment of African-American police officers than does any other source. Four excellent clipping files provided the majority of African-American newspaper sources for this study—the Schomburg Collection in New York City, the Associated Negro Press Clipping File in the Claude A. Barnett Papers at the Chicago Historical Society, the Hampton University Newspaper Clipping File in Hampton, Virginia, and the Tuskegee Newspaper Clipping File at Tuskegee University in Alabama.

Chapter 1 of this volume provides a brief historical analysis of the African-American experience through the nineteenth century and the close relationship of black history to the development of the first formal American police organizations. Chapter 2 analyzes the origins of African-American participation in law enforcement and examines how "free men of color" became law enforcement officers in antebellum New Orleans. This chapter also explains how African Americans acquired and lost police jobs in the Reconstruction South. Chapter 3 examines the emergence of African-American police officers in the North; it shows how the political patronage system aided the "integration" of American police forces but still relegated African-American police officers to token positions. A second theme of this chapter is the impact of police reform on the status of African-American officers and the emerging color line in American policing. Chapter 4, returning to a discussion of black police officers in the South, analyzes the extensive and intense campaigns by African Americans to gain a foothold in law enforcement. Case studies on Louisville, Atlanta, Baltimore, and Dallas examine the arguments and pressure used by African Americans to regain police jobs in the South. The status of African-American police officers in the South prior to the civil rights movement is the focus of chapter 5. Chapter 6 traces the development of African-American police organizations from the 1930s to the 1970s and the rise of police unions advocating equal rights for black officers. Chapter 7 analyzes the rise of African Americans to administrative and even leadership positions in American policing in the 1970s and 1980s and investigates how the election of African-American mayors provided the opportunity for black control of the police. Finally, chapter 8 analyzes the three generations of African Americans who have served as police officers and assesses their contribution to American policing and to the black community.

In conclusion, this book provides an important contribution to three interrelated and overlapping subfields of American history. First, it chronicles the African-American experience in American police history and challenges the prevailing historical interpretations about twentieth-century police reform and the professionalization of American police forces. Second, it fills an important gap in African-American history by investigating a little-known field where blacks have made a significant contribution in spite of the odds and obstacles imposed against them by American racism. Third, it aims to contribute to the history of American race relations by tracing how, when, and why African Americans were able to achieve access to one of the most powerful (and dangerous) occupations in American society.

ACKNOWLEDGMENTS

This study of the history of African Americans in law enforcement began some twenty years ago as a master's thesis at Ohio State University. Then, as now, I was concerned about addressing one of the problems affecting the African-American community: urban street crime. Despite the public outcry against crime in African-American neighborhoods, there appeared to be little or no effort by national, state, or local authorities to resolve it. I became intrigued, however, by the call by many African Americans for more "race policemen" to solve the problem of crime in African-American communities throughout the nation. Indeed, after just some preliminary research, I found that there had been a perennial and consistent call for "colored police for colored people" by black leaders throughout the African-American experience in the United States.[1]

The events of the 1960s also spurred my interest in the history of blacks in law enforcement. Twenty-five years ago, the employment of African Americans as police officers was a "hot issue" because of the Kerner Commission's recommendation that American law enforcement agencies increase their number of black officers to counter the charge that predominantly white police forces constituted occupying armies established to police and oppress (not protect) African-American communities. The resulting recruitment and promotion of African-American law enforcement officers in the late 1960s and early 1970s forced police departments to attempt to reform long-standing policies that had denied blacks full access to police jobs and relegated them to virtually a second-class status as police officers. Needless to say, the attempt to reform the historically racial policies of American police departments only engendered more problems—especially when reform meant challenging the hegemony of white officers for positions and promotions in policing.[2]

By the early 1970s, racial conflict was the norm in most American police departments, and many scholars began to study the effect of increasing the black presence in law enforcement. The issue was first brought to my attention by a fellow graduate student and long-time friend, Stuart Holloway. He convinced me that the history of African-American police officers was a viable and useful topic that was complementary to my own interest in black community development. I am eternally grateful to him for turning my attention to such an important subject.

To study the phenomenon of the entrance of African Americans into American police departments, I have had to log more than thirty thousand miles of travel, talk to several hundred police officers and politicians, and consult a variety of archival and library sources. Along the way I have incurred an indebtedness to police officers from all parts of the country who met and talked with me while I was a graduate student at Ohio State University, and who continued to correspond with and encourage me for more than twenty years in my pursuit of this important story. I know that to name any of them is to leave out many of them. Nevertheless, I must give special mention to A. V. Young of Houston; Wilbert K. Battle of San Francisco; Homer F. Broome, formerly of Los Angeles; Harold James, James N. Reaves, and the late Al Deal of Philadelphia; Lynn Coleman, Boise Mack, and Jean Clayton of Cleveland, Ohio; the late Harvey Alston, James Jackson, Richard Hopson, and Jesse Brant of Columbus, Ohio; Jimmy Hargrove, William Johnson, and Harold Respass of New York City; the late Harold Martin of Washington, D.C.; Tyree Broomfield of Dayton, Ohio; Johnny Sparks, Paul Bowser, and Claude Dixon of Atlanta; Howard Saffold and Renault Robinson of Chicago; Harry Gardner of Peabody, Massachusetts; Robert Ingram, George Adams, and Otis Davis of Miami; and James Taylor, Eugene Reece, and James Buchanan of St. Louis.

A number of individuals at the various libraries and archival collections that I consulted were also very helpful. They include Daniel Williams of the Washington Collection of Tuskegee University, and Ethel Brown of the Peabody Room at Hampton University. The staffs at the Schomburg Collection in New York City, the Moorland-Spingarn Research Center at Howard University, and the Chicago Historical Society also provided me invaluable assistance.

During the course of this project, I have also relied upon the selfless support of my colleagues in the history profession. My mentor, Joseph Lewis of Central State University, was always there when I needed encouragement and support. Robert Edison of Dallas, Kenneth M. Hamilton of Southern Methodist University, and Harry Robinson of the Dallas Museum of African-American Life and Culture have always been supportive friends. Buzz Anders, Kathy Underwood, and Bob Fairbanks of the University of Texas at Arlington; George Wright of Duke University; Alwyn Barr of Texas Tech University; Barry Crouch of Gallaudet University; Howard Jones of Prairie View A & M University; and Louis Marchiafava of the *Houston Review* believed in and supported my work when no one else did. I am especially appreciative of the faculty development leave from the Department of History and the College of Liberal Arts at the University of Texas at Arlington that enabled me to complete the bulk of the revisions on the manuscript.

Finally, I am especially indebted to two special colleagues and friends: Stanley Palmer, my colleague at the University of Texas at Arlington, and Darlene Clark Hine, John A. Hannah Professor of History at Michigan State University. Professor Palmer read the first drafts of the manuscript and offered numerous suggestions for improving it. In 1990, Professor Hine visited Dallas to lecture at the African American Museum, and during the course of her stay she provided me the heartfelt encouragement needed to begin revising and completing the manuscript.

BLACK POLICE IN AMERICA

ONE

AFRICAN-AMERICAN HISTORY AND AMERICAN POLICING

You see de City policemen walkin' his beat? Well, dats de way de patty-rollin' was, only each county had dere patty-rollers, an' dey had to serve three months at a time, den dey would gib you thirty-nine lashes, 'ca'se dat was the law. De patty-rollers knowed nearly all de slaves, an' it wurn't very often dey ever beat them.

—Frank Gill, Mobile, Alabama

De Paterollers was de law, kind of like de policeman now.

—Polly Colbert, Colbert, Oklahoma

My father did tell some of the stories about how they had to get permission to go from one plantation to the other, and if they was out after a certain hour the patrols ... would catch them. And if they'd catch them, sometimes they wouldn't take them in but they would whip them every step of the way from there as far as they had to get back to their plantation.

—Marie Bing, Washington, D.C.[1]

African Americans in the U.S. have always been policed. Most Africans arrived on American shores as captives in the Atlantic slave trade, and the regulation of their behavior and the suppression of potential rebellions always preoccupied their captors. Indeed, the presence of Africans in America created a dual heritage for American police forces. Most northern police forces copied the "British model" of policing developed in London by Sir Robert Peel as Great Britain's answer to recurring street violence and urban crime. In the American South, however, police forces were formed not on the "British model" but on a model related to the existence of slavery and racial oppression.[2] While most northern police forces operated outside the system of slavery, they also developed a pattern of policing that targeted African Americans. Thus, African-American history has always been bound to the history of American law enforcement.

The policing of African Americans, of course, was linked to the nation's reliance on slave labor. Before the American Revolution and the founding of the United States, African slavery had existed in North America for nearly 150 years.

At the time of the first census in the United States, in 1790, there were 757,181 Africans in the country, constituting 19.3 percent of the total population. All but 59,557 were slaves. The bulk of this slave population was in southern states, where they had been used primarily to grow the staple crops of tobacco and rice.[3]

Africans enslaved in America were a troublesome presence. Belying their captors' claim that they were made for slavery, Africans rebelled against the institution in a variety of ways. They resisted on a daily basis by refusing to work, destroying crops and farm implements, and killing livestock. They poisoned their owners, destroyed property through arson, and fought with their owners and other whites. Some ran away from slavery; others cooperated with Native Americans or white indentured servants to resist through physical force. This resort to violence created the greatest problem for whites in the colonial period of American history. They lived in constant fear of slave rebellions, and as a result passed many laws to deter, control, and suppress such insurrections.[4]

By the beginning of the eighteenth century, most American colonies had enacted laws to regulate the behavior of African slaves. Labeled the slave, black, or Negro codes, these measures prohibited Africans from assembling in groups, possessing weapons, leaving the plantations where they worked, selling certain items, resisting punishment, and striking any white person. The penalties for these actions were extremely harsh and included castration, whippings, maimings, and hangings. The codes also established the slave patrol or "patterollers." The slave patrol was the first distinctively American police system, and it set the pattern of policing that Americans of African descent would experience throughout their history in America.[5]

By the middle of the eighteenth century, every southern colony had a slave patrol. Although in some communities *all* white males were required to serve some time as patterollers, their ranks were usually filled with poor whites. The patrols were authorized to stop, search, whip, maim, and even kill any African slave caught off the plantation without a pass, engaged in illegal activities, or running away. The patterollers policed specific geographic areas in southern communities called "beats." Paramilitary in nature, the slave patrol often cooperated with the militia in the southern colonies to prevent and suppress slave insurrections. To facilitate the rapid mobilization of the patrol and to ensure that every white man supported its activities in emergencies, colonial governments granted all whites the authority to detain, whip, and even kill slaves suspected of illegal activities or conspiracies. The colonial slave patrol exercised awesome powers which were often abused.[6]

The slave patrol was primarily a rural phenomenon since most African Americans worked as agricultural laborers. During the colonial period, however, some blacks lived in the small cities that were emerging as centers for commercial activity. Modest in size during their early development—in 1690 only 7,000 people lived in Boston, 3,900 in New York, 4,000 in Philadelphia, 1,100 in Charles Town—these cities facilitated the transfer of agricultural products and furs from the American hinterland to Europe. A diverse group of people settled in the cities: absentee planters from the rural areas, middle-class artisans, merchants, immigrants from Europe, sailors, vagabonds, runaway indentured servants, free African Americans, and fugitive slaves. As crime and disorder, licentious behavior, and arson became more prevalent by the late seventeenth century, many cities developed watches, city guards, or constabulary forces to control the "dangerous classes" that they attracted.

By the eve of the American Revolution, several cities had grown significantly. Philadelphia, with a population of 40,000, was the largest city in the American colonies. It was followed by New York with 25,000 people, Boston with 16,000, Charleston with 12,000, and Newport with 11,000. As crime and disorder increased with the growth of the population, city officials sought improved ways to handle the threat posed by the "dangerous classes." In most cases, the watches, city guards, or constabularies developed in the seventeenth century became better organized.[7]

For most American cities, these formal watch or city guard systems became the foundation for the American system of policing. Boston, for example, had had a city watch since 1634. The citizens of Boston reorganized their government in the nineteenth century and by 1838 had converted the watch into a full-time police force similar to the Metropolitan Police Force of London. In 1845, New York City also reorganized its watch into a police force based on the London model. Other cities followed the lead of Boston and New York. In 1821, Columbus, Ohio, established its first city watch, and within thirty years it had a formal police force. Philadelphia created its formal police force in 1845, as did Chicago in 1855. By the end of the Civil War, most major American cities had begun to organize formal police forces to control the crime, disorder, and recurring violence that continued to plague urban life.[8] (See table 1.)

The administration and composition of these early police forces became an important political issue. Although the elites in American cities created and commanded the police, immigrants and the lower classes usually staffed the lower ranks. But even before the Civil War, immigrants were challenging the elites for control of police forces. The Irish emerged as the most important immigrant group to occupy administrative and rank-and-file positions. Other nationalities, such as the Germans, competed with the Irish for police jobs, but the Irish eventually prevailed. Through their numbers and political influence, Irish immigrants were able to dominate the police forces in most American cities, including Boston, New York City, St. Louis, New Orleans, Milwaukee, and Philadelphia. During the antebellum period, the Irish tied police jobs to political patronage and made the police a significant part of urban politics.[9]

African Americans were unable to compete with the Irish for police positions in antebellum America, but they did compete with them in two other areas: jobs and neighborhoods. Competition between the two groups for jobs led to recurring race riots in Cincinnati, Philadelphia, Baltimore, and New York City. When the Irish had first immigrated to the United States, many of them had faced hostility and physical violence from the old-stock American immigrants. Now they were using the same type of violence against a group occupying a lower and more precarious position in society than they. In some of these race riots, Irish police officers were just as antagonistic and brutal toward blacks as the Irish workers that led the mobs. These conflicts fed an animosity that survived for generations.[10]

The failure of Irish police officers to protect African-Americans from antebellum mobs provided blacks in Pittsburgh, Pennsylvania, a rare opportunity to participate in law enforcement. In April 1839, blacks and whites fought in the streets of Pittsburgh. After the initial encounter, a mob of whites began to organize to attack the black community. In anticipation of this attack, African-American leaders Martin R. Delany and John B. Vashon organized and armed black men to defend the community. Delany consulted with Pittsburgh mayor Jonas R. McClintock to inform him that since the night police were unable and unwilling to protect black citizens, they would defend themselves. Mayor McClintock decided to deputize Delany and his men as special police officers. That evening an interracial police force confronted the mob that sought to attack the black community, disarmed them, and arrested their leaders. Although Delany and his men served only a short time, this was perhaps the first example of successful interracial law enforcement in American history.[11]

The situation in Pittsburgh was unique. Most blacks were prevented from advancing in antebellum America because of their status as slaves. Although the African-American population in the United States grew from 1,002,037 in 1800 to 4,441,830 in 1860, the free black population reached only 488,070 in 1860. Following the American Revolution, these free African Americans formed small communities in cities such as Philadelphia, New York, Charleston, and Baltimore. The free black communities in these cities usually consisted of first- and second-generation ex-slaves and, of course, fugitives who were subject to capture and return to their legal "owners."[12]

These "free" African Americans led precarious lives in racially segregated areas. In New York they lived in "Five Points," in Cincinnati in "Little Africa," and in Boston in "New Guinea" and "Nigger Hill." They could not vote, testify against whites in court, or hold any political office. They functioned entirely at the sufferance of the white community, and in some states, such as Ohio, they even had to post bonds or obtain white sponsors just to enter the state. Since they competed with white immigrant groups for jobs, African Americans also found that many occupations were closed to them. Thus, free blacks usually toiled in the lowliest occupations—literally the menial jobs that white workers did not want.[13]

African Americans in northern cities seemed to have a better lot than those in the South. Although they were disfranchised, confined to racially segregated neighborhoods, and subject to the often violent whims of local whites, they had more opportunities to develop productive lives. For example, African Americans in antebellum northern cities organized the first black churches, schools, and protest organizations. They also held protest meetings, petitioned the local government and state legislature about their grievances, and engaged in a number of activities to challenge the racial status quo and to improve the circumstances of their lives. In general, African Americans in northern cities exercised some of the basic rights of citizenship that local, state, and national laws allegedly guaranteed to all Americans.[14]

Conditions were much worse in the South. Living in a society dominated by slavery, free blacks in southern cities found that the institution severely limited their rights. They had to observe the slave or black codes, just as if they also were slaves. This hampered their ability to organize schools and churches, to assemble for meetings, and to travel from place to place. Agitation against repressive laws or abolitionist activities by free African Americans in southern cities was prohibited and would result in imprisonment, whippings, or expulsion from the state. Criminal acts could even result in their enslavement.[15]

These restrictions on free black life did not prevent some African Americans from becoming an indispensable part of the economy in these cities. Free blacks often held skilled jobs such as carpenters, bricklayers, ironworkers, and stonemasons. Many of them were second- and third-generation free persons, and they had established themselves in their communities by offering skills and services needed by southern whites. In contrast to the experience of free blacks in northern cities, they were not always confined to racially segregated neighborhoods. Despite their lack of political rights, free blacks in some southern cities—especially in Baltimore, Charleston, Mobile, and New Orleans—surprisingly held more wealth than those in northern cities. In general, while free African Americans in southern cities had less freedom than those in the North, they may have had better relationships with some whites because they lived closer to the whites and had some wealth.[16]

Free African Americans in southern cities were also closer to the black slaves. This proximity often determined the freedoms and rights that they could enjoy. Free blacks had to be able to prove their status at all times. Thus, they carried passes, certificates, and other documents issued by the local government verifying their freedom. Nevertheless, whites suspected that all blacks were fugitive slaves. As a result, free blacks in southern cities faced the same proscriptions, limitations, and harassments that the slave or black codes imposed on the slave population. As Ira Berlin defined them, they were literally "slaves without masters."[17]

The presence of an ever-increasing slave population affected the status of all African Americans in antebellum America. African Americans were held in bondage on the basis of their skin color, and white Americans developed racist justifications to keep them enslaved. Theories of race based on religion, science, and in some cases outright nonsense developed to justify slavery and the suppression of free blacks. The religious argument maintained that Africans were cursed, and that their dark skin was evidence of their cursed nature. Antebellum "scientists" argued that before Africans were enslaved in America, they had wandered through the "jungles of Africa" like wild animals without any social organization. Pro-slavery Americans, in general, believed that American slavery was the civilizing and socializing institution for Africans. When African Americans rebelled or resisted slavery, pro-slavery scientists diagnosed their actions as the product of such diseases as *dysaethesia aethiopica* (having a propensity to destroy farm implements and act unruly) in order to explain seemingly illogical behavior.[18]

Not all antebellum white Americans accepted the religious and scientific inferiority of African Americans. There were some who believed that all human beings were equal and deserved the freedom and opportunity to live to the best of their abilities without any restraints. By the 1830s, Americans who believed in human freedom and who wanted to purge the nation of slavery had organized the abolitionist movement. It consisted of free blacks and northern whites, many of whom—especially women—had undergone the religious conversion experience of the Second Great Awakening. The abolitionists began a great moral crusade—a minority movement in terms of the number of participants—to convince other Americans to support the elimination of slavery. They wrote pamphlets, held public meetings, gave speeches, and petitioned the United States Congress to act against the evil "peculiar" institution in the South. The abolitionists were successful in keeping the issue before the American public for three decades.[19]

Most antebellum white Americans, however, supported the status quo for African Americans. While they may have disliked slavery, they did not accept the notion of racial equality. They viewed all African Americans as inferior and wanted to keep them in their place. Thus, as the urban police evolved in antebellum America, part of their responsibility was to suppress blacks, to regulate their behavior, and to capture those suspected of being fugitives from slavery. Police forces in both northern and southern cities assumed these responsibilities. In southern cities, however, suppressing and regulating the behavior of African Americans—slave and free—became almost the *raison d'être* for the police forces.[20]

The antebellum policing of blacks in the South did not differ significantly from that which had existed during the colonial period. Patterollers continued to police the rural countryside and to use virtually the same tactics of physical abuse, intimidation, and cruel punishment. In fact, after slave insurrections such as Nat Turner's in 1831 in Virginia, the rural slave patrol became even more vigilant and organized. Patrols also developed in southern cities, and they were much more sophisticated than northern city guards and watches. Responding to the threat of potential slave insurrections, the patrol system in Charleston, for example, developed into an elaborate paramilitary force whose sole purpose was to intimidate the city's large black population. As in Charleston, all of the police forces in southern cities—such as Louisville, Mobile, New Orleans, and Richmond—had the direct responsibility of regulating the slave population. This function included capturing runaways and whipping belligerent slaves. The administration and organization of police forces in southern cities were directly related to the institution of slavery.[21]

The police in northern cities were not organized specifically to regulate blacks as they were in the South. Nevertheless, northern police forces also did their share of slave catching and regulating of black behavior. In Philadelphia, for example, by the beginning of the nineteenth century, African Americans were targeted and arrested by the city guard for minor crimes that were ignored when the culprits were whites. Blacks were also more likely to be successfully prosecuted. As a result, the Philadelphia jails always contained a disproportionate number of African Americans. Urban historian Leonard Curry has found a similar pattern of social control in other antebellum American cities, where African Americans were often arrested for minor crimes or for just being in the wrong place at the wrong time. According to Curry, the belief that African Americans were habitual criminals was implanted in the minds of white law enforcement officers well before the Civil War.[22]

As the antebellum period progressed, the policing of African Americans became even more rigorous. Southern police forces reacted to the challenge to the slave system by clamping down even harder on slaves and free blacks. In the North, the Fugitive Slave Act of 1850 forced northern police forces to adopt a more vigilant attitude toward the blacks who claimed to be free. Thus, the status of African Americans was not much different in the antebellum period of American history than it had been in the colonial period. They were still an outcast group—segregated and victimized by white violence in northern cities, and pursued and harassed in southern cities.

It was in this racist and hostile atmosphere in the nineteenth century that the first African Americans became law enforcement officers. They served in a racist, slave society and implicitly accepted the oppression of African Americans in order to carry out their duties. By accepting the racial status quo and the legal oppression of other blacks, these law enforcement officers became the first African Americans to confront the paradox of policing a society where the color of a person's skin often determined guilt or innocence. They also became the first to accept such roles because they believed that they could improve their own precarious position in a society where status was based on skin color.

TWO

BLACK PIONEERS

The first African-American police officers in the United States were members of the New Orleans city guard. We know little about these "free men of color," but we do know that at the time they accepted a job that other citizens did not want. In addition, one of their primary responsibilities was to serve as slave catchers and to police the behavior of "black" slaves in New Orleans. As the importance of policing increased in New Orleans, "free men of color" lost their positions on the city police force. African Americans did not regain this lost ground until the turmoil of the post–Civil War period allowed them to become law enforcement officers once again. By that time, black "pioneers" became members of police forces throughout the South, serving in one of the most violent periods in the nation's history. The "first coming" of African-American police officers in the Reconstruction South was short-lived, however. Redemption ended black political participation in the South and made law enforcement the exclusive preserve of white men.

It was not an accident that the first African-American police officers in the United States appeared in New Orleans. From the early eighteenth century, when the Orleans colony was under French and then Spanish rule, to the beginning of the nineteenth century and its acquisition by the United States, people of African descent played an important role in the colony. As part of that role they served in the militia with the French and the Spanish in several wars against the English and the Indians. As a result, many African slaves won their freedom and became "free men of color." New Orleans was also a unique colony because of the miscegenation and intermarriage that occurred there. Many women of African descent became the mistresses, concubines, and wives of white men because of the shortage of white women. The offspring of these relationships—individuals of mixed race who were classified as mulattos, quadroons, and octoroons—formed the largest part of the "free persons of color" who lived in New Orleans when the United States purchased the colony from France in 1803. By that time, these "free persons of color" had developed a fairly stable social and economic position in New Orleans and had formed two militia groups. Delille Dupard, a quadroon, was a member of the syndics, the law enforcement officers employed by the Spanish governor to police the city's periphery. The presence of Dupard and other "free men of color" under arms in the militia in New Orleans paved the way for their eventual entry into the city's first organized police forces.[1]

The first formal police force was created following the acquisition of New Orleans by the United States. From 1805 to 1809, the city council tried four police organizations—the Gendarmerie (1805–1806), the first city guard (1806–1808), the constables and lamplighter-watchmen (1808–1809), and the second city guard (1809 and after)—before settling on the latter organization as its permanent police force until 1836. All of these organizations were established on the "military model," and while their duties included maintaining order, patrolling the docks, and making an ineffective effort to fight crime, their chief function was controlling the city's substantial black slave population. Since there were never enough white men willing or able to carry out this vital police function, the task fell to "free men of color" by default.[2]

"Free men of color" served on all four of the city's early police organizations. In 1805, the council passed an ordinance that allowed them to serve on the Gendarmerie as long as they were commanded by white officers. In addition, the four police organizations established before 1820 were supported periodically by the militia. The two militia groups composed of "free men of color" patrolled and served along with other militia groups in the city—especially in emergencies such as the 1811 slave insurrection in the neighboring parishes of St. Charles and St. John the Baptist. The performance of one of these groups in suppressing the 1811 insurrection solidified the two militia groups' standing with the American governor of New Orleans, William C. Claiborne. Claiborne and other American officials had considered disbanding the militia groups of "free men of color" because, like most Americans of that era, they felt that armed black men were a threat to the colony.[3]

Despite the fear of their intentions, "free persons of color" were not a direct threat to white supremacy in New Orleans. Although their wealth and standing in the city clearly challenged the notion among whites that all blacks were inferior, these men were loyal citizens and sought only to enjoy the rights and privileges of American citizenship. If the duties of citizenship required patrolling, policing, and suppressing "black" slaves, the "free persons of color" in New Orleans were willing to assume such tasks in order to improve their own precarious position in a society where skin color usually determined status and condition of servitude. Under Spanish rule, "free men of color" had proven that they were willing to suppress other blacks, as, for example, when their militia assisted in subduing slave insurrectionists in the Cimarron War of 1784. Moreover, under both French and Spanish rule, "free persons of color" had served as a buffer between whites and the slave population. Some even owned slaves. Their intent was to assume the same strategic position under American rule. From 1805 to 1820, "free persons of color" held onto their privileged position by serving in the city's police organizations, participating in the suppression of the slave insurrection of 1811, and fighting under the command of Andrew Jackson in the Battle of New Orleans in 1815. After that high point, however, they disbanded their militia organizations, and their status in New Orleans declined to a point where they were no longer needed or wanted in the city guard.[4]

Who were these "free persons of color" who accepted the task of regulating the behavior of "black" slaves and putting down potential rebellions among them? A few of their names are known. Charles Allegre and Constant Michel served on the city guard in 1814. Very little information is available about Michel, but Allegre fought in the War of 1812 as a member of Fortier's Battalion of free men of color. Another member of Fortier's Battalion was Pierre Aubry, who along with Augustus Bolen was on the city guard in the 1820s. In addition, two African Americans, Ellidgea Poindexter and Douglas C. Butler, served for several years as turnkeys in the city jail. While we may know the names of these early African-American law enforcement officers in New Orleans, we have little information about their actual motivations for serving on a constabulary force that was clearly designed to regulate the behavior of blacks held in bondage. We can only speculate that, like the black men in the twentieth century who would become police officers in the South and enforce segregation laws, they were motivated by a combination of self-interest and a sense of service.[5]

The African-American presence on the city guard soon ended. In 1822, the New Orleans council directed the city labor manager to employ only white workers in city jobs. By 1830, this policy had eliminated all "free persons of color" from the city guard. Increasingly, immigrants, especially Irish immigrants, took over those positions. The police job also became part of the city's political spoils. Various political factions competed for control of the police and rewarded friends and supporters with employment on the city's police force. No faction sought the support of the "free persons of color." As a result, they did not receive the jobs and political appointments that other ethnic groups demanded and received. In fact, in the post-1820 period, the rights and status of free African Americans of all colors in New Orleans came under attack. As the number of Anglo-Americans in the city increased, there was a concurrent increase in the racial hostility toward the "free persons of color." One manifestation of this phenomenon was the implementation of segregation laws that applied to all "persons of color," regardless of status. Free African Americans would not regain their pre-1820 status until the catastrophic and revolutionary change wrought by the Civil War briefly improved their position in the city's civic affairs.[6]

The Civil War was a watershed in American history in many ways. Not only did it end African slavery in the United States, it also improved the status of free blacks in cities such as New Orleans, Mobile, and Charleston. More important, the entire nation had to adjust to the change in status of African Americans from slaves to free persons. For many southern whites, this was not an easy adjustment. They could not accept their former slaves as free persons or as equals. In the immediate aftermath of the Civil War, whites acted to reestablish the pre-war status quo by passing new Black Codes that sought to return African Americans to a status similar to slavery and to reassert the dominance of whites over their lives. In some cases, violence was used to achieve these objectives. In race riots in 1866 in New Orleans and Memphis, Tennessee, former Confederates carried out a reign of terror against African Americans and their white Republican allies. In both cities, African Americans found that the police were unwilling and incapable of protecting them from white violence. The police even participated in the riots by leading mobs to murder and intimidate blacks. As a result, one of the earliest postwar demands made by African Americans was for fair and equitable law enforcement. Given the complicity of white law enforcement officers in the terrorism against blacks in the post–Civil War era, African Americans came to believe that only police officers of their own race would provide them the protection of the law, and fair and equitable law enforcement.[7]

In May 1867, the *New Orleans Tribune,* the first daily African-American newspaper established in the United States, complained vociferously that city officials were still allowing racial prejudice to determine the composition of the police force. In the wake of the 1866 riot, and because the Confederate-dominated police force continued to harass blacks, the military governor of Louisiana, General Philip Sheridan, had ordered the mayor to reorganize the force and appoint former Union Army soldiers as one-half of its members. But even under Sheridan's orders, the first appointments to the police force did not recognize the rights of black citizens to serve as police officers. The editors of the *Tribune* let the mayor know their displeasure with his white-only appointments:

> What good and solid objection can be made to the appointment of colored police officers? Will it be said that the population of African descent does not bear a sufficient proportion to the whole population, to entitle them to any share on the police force? This would be absurd, since everybody knows that one-half at least of the inhabitants of the Crescent City have more or less African blood in their veins and moreover, three-fourths of the qualified voters of the city, as far as registration goes today, belong to the colored race. These three-fourths are deprived of their share of representation on the police force.

The *Tribune*'s editors further observed that the new police appointed under Sheridan's orders still included some members who had served under the Democrats and who had terrorized blacks in the 1866 race riot. The editors posed the threat that African Americans would elect a black mayor in the city in order to obtain recognition for public office.[8]

The complaints received almost immediate redress. On May 28, 1867, the *Tribune* reported that Governor Wells had appointed Charles Courcelle, a "newly enfranchised" citizen, to the Board of Police Commissioners. Three days later, the newspaper reported that two African Americans, Dusseau Picot and Emile Farrar, had been appointed to the police department. During the month of June, more than a dozen black police appointments followed—including the June 1 appointment of Octave Rey, who in 1868 would become the first African-American police captain in the nation. With the barrier to black participation in law enforcement removed, more black police appointments followed, and the "Africanization" of the police force stirred the resentment of the city's white population.[9]

For whites, the New Orleans police force was becoming too black. As historians Dennis Rousey and John Blassingame have shown, the whites in New Orleans were still adjusting to African Americans as free persons. White supremacy remained the norm in the city, and prior to May 1867, the members of the all-white police force still whipped and harassed African Americans as they had done before the Civil War. The appointment of black police threatened the racial status quo. For example, African-American police officers would not enforce the segregation of blacks on city streetcars.

Nevertheless, black police still faced paradoxical circumstances. In their first months of service, they were ordered by Mayor Heath to enforce racial segregation. On June 19, for instance, the *Tribune* reported that the mayor had issued a proclamation allowing New Orleans's merchants to bar blacks from patronizing their stores. On the same date, he sent a black police officer to guard a public ball that excluded African Americans. By December 1867, African-American police officers confronted another challenge when white officers rebelled against the presence of blacks on the force and denounced the Republican party for its recognition of "negro equality."[10]

In 1868, New Orleans's white citizens received an even greater shock. The state legislature passed a metropolitan police bill and placed the city's police force under state control. Under the new bill, legislators reorganized the city police force into a metropolitan force with authority over the three parishes contiguous to New Orleans—Jefferson, Orleans, and St. Bernard. This new district was under the control of five police commissioners appointed by the governor. Three of the new commissioners were African Americans, including the chair of the metropolitan police board, Oscar J. Dunn. Dunn was a former captain in the Union Army in General Benjamin Butler's Corps d'Afrique, and he also served as lieutenant governor. Under Dunn and the black-controlled metropolitan police board, more than 170 African Americans were appointed to the new metropolitan police force and they made up 65 percent of the men serving on it.[11]

Whites in New Orleans and its neighboring parishes strongly resisted this "Africanized" police force. The New Orleans and Jefferson city councils fought the bill and refused to obey the new police appointed by the board. Both councils objected to a police force on which, they said, blacks were overrepresented. After the metropolitan police bill passed in September 1868 and police superintendent J. J. Williamson assigned his men to duty, violence erupted in New Orleans and in Jefferson and St. Bernard parishes. Realizing that the racial composition of the metropolitan police was causing most of the hostility to it, in November Superintendent Williamson dismissed all of the black men on the force. After the federal military intervened, the hostility toward the metropolitan police force was quelled, and the local officials in New Orleans, Jefferson, and St. Bernard were forced to accept the authority of the new metropolitan police board. After this initial resistance to black police officers, African Americans would again be appointed to the police force. But their representation did not reach the percentage of 1868; by 1870, blacks held 28 percent of the positions on the 600-member force.[12]

Despite the reduced black presence on the metropolitan police force, its authority and its large African-American contingent remained a point of conflict in Reconstruction New Orleans. The metropolitans, as they were called, served to protect the "Radical" government and its black and white Republican supporters. In 1868, for example, the metropolitans battled white Democratic clubs that sought to intimidate and drive black voters from the polls. On several occasions, such as the Colfax, Louisiana, riot of 1873, the metropolitans were used outside of New Orleans to battle white terrorist groups that were intimidating and murdering Republican voters. In the now-infamous 1874 "Battle of Liberty Place," the metropolitans fought the White League, a white Democratic rifle club that sought to overthrow the "Radical" government in the city of New Orleans. The metropolitans lost the battle and retreated in disorder. The intervention of federal troops prevented the fall of the "Radical" government. This encounter, however, thoroughly discredited the metropolitans, and the poor performance of African-American members of the force received special condemnation and criticism from the New Orleans press. Despite its failure at Liberty Place, the metropolitan police force continued to exist; it was not abolished until 1877 with the overthrow of Reconstruction in Louisiana by politicians in Washington. Even then, African Americans continued to serve on the New Orleans police force until the turn of the twentieth century.[13]

Although no other city appointed as many black officers as New Orleans, the black police experience in other cities in the Reconstruction South was similar to that in New Orleans. By the 1870s, African Americans were serving as police officers in Montgomery, Mobile, and Selma, Alabama; Vicksburg, Meridian, and Jackson, Mississippi; Jacksonville, Florida; Charleston, South Carolina; Chattanooga, Tennessee; Austin and Houston, Texas; and Washington, D.C. African Americans Ovid Gregory of Mobile and Bryan Lunn of Raleigh, North Carolina were even appointed assistant chiefs of police. (See table 2.) In almost every case, black police officers were appointed by Republican administrations to protect African Americans from the endemic white violence and terrorism that characterized the Reconstruction era. Just as in New Orleans, their presence on police forces was resented by whites, and the exercise of police powers by African Americans became one of the most hated features of the Reconstruction governments.[14]

Despite the hostility toward them from whites, most Reconstruction African-American police officers patrolled their beats and performed their duties the same as other officers. Some were good police officers, and some were bad. Kenneth Alfers's analysis of the personnel records of the Washington, D.C., police force during Reconstruction found that there was no significant difference between the performance of black and white officers. It seems that District of Columbia police officers of both races could violate regulations and disgrace their uniforms by unbecoming conduct. Conversely, a proportionate number of black officers had careers as exemplary as those of whites. Alfers's analysis stands in sharp contrast to the allegations against black police officers made by Reconstruction historian Walter Fleming, who in 1905 wrote that black police officers in Selma, Montgomery, and Mobile irritated whites by discriminating in their arrests in favor of blacks. Fleming's charges are indicative of his biased perspective of black participation in Reconstruction governments in the South—especially since the *New Orleans Tribune* reported in July 1867 that the first black officers appointed in Mobile were restricted to policing black areas and arresting only other African Americans. The arrest powers of black officers were also restricted in New Bern and Raleigh, North

Carolina, and in Nashville, Tennessee. In most cities, however, African-American police officers had the right to arrest all citizens who broke the law.[15]

African-American police officers of the Reconstruction era seem to have exercised fairness in their arrests of all citizens. Their presence allowed some African Americans, especially in New Orleans, to experience equitable law enforcement for perhaps the first time in American history. Rousey's analysis of black and white arrest records in New Orleans during the period when the metropolitan police force patrolled the city indicates that black arrests were proportionate to the percentage of blacks in the population. Rousey attributes this finding to the fact that African Americans served on the city's police force, and the fact that black officers may have used the same discretion and standard in making arrests of blacks as white officers used in arresting whites. To Fleming and other whites who abhorred the presence of blacks on Reconstruction police forces, the treatment of African Americans by black police officers would appear to be unfair—especially if one believed that all crime was attributable to African Americans.

Despite the presence of black police officers, the criminal justice system was still used to regulate blacks' behavior and enforce the racial status quo. As Howard Rabinowitz has found, in the Reconstruction era the criminal justice system—the police, courts, and prisons—was used to punish, discipline, and control African Americans. Thus, minor crimes committed by blacks were punished to the full extent of the law, while the same crimes by whites were ignored or no-billed in the courts. From 1865 to 1900, in most southern cities the number of arrests of African Americans far exceeded their percentage in the population.[16]

Black police officers, although few in number in most southern cities, were a threat to the status quo. Whites could not use the criminal justice system to suppress blacks if blacks served as the law enforcers. Thus, African-American police officers encountered many problems exercising authority—especially over white citizens. Indeed, the resistance by whites to the exercise of police authority by African Americans engendered much violence during the Reconstruction era. For example, in Texas the Reconstruction government created a state police force, at least one-third of the members of which were African Americans. Governor Edmund J. Davis used the Texas State Police to suppress the recurring violence that plagued the state during elections. During these incidents, the state police fought pitched battles with armed whites and often precipitated violent confrontations by their overzealous actions against white citizens. As a result, white Texans hated the state police, and the force was immediately abolished when the Democrats "redeemed," or regained, political control of the state in 1873. Those African Americans who had served on the force became the victims of white retaliation. In 1910, the author of a "commemorative publication" even bragged (perhaps in exaggeration) that whites were successful in hunting down and killing every African American who had ever served on the hated state police force. According to historian Otis Singletary, whites in Louisiana, Mississippi, and Arkansas reacted the same way to black militia companies organized during Reconstruction to keep order and protect black and white Republicans from mob violence.[17]

The hostile attitude of white Texans toward African-American police officers typified the feelings that existed among whites in other southern cities. In Jacksonville, Florida, for instance, charges of misconduct on the part of African-American police officers forced city officials to fire several of them in order to appease white citizens. Similarly, in 1884 seven African-American police officers in Vicksburg, Mississippi, were forced to resign because white citizens resented being policed by them. White citizens stated that being arrested by "colored policemen" was "humiliating and degrading in the extreme," and they pledged to resist "hereafter the arrest of any white person by a colored policemen." The animosity of whites toward Reconstruction-era African-American police officers was best expressed by Mississippi Whig politician Ethelbert Barksdale, who said, "Law enforcement means domination, and the white man is not used to being dominated by negroes."[18]

White southerners acted on their dislike for black police officers by eliminating most of them from police forces after Redemption. By 1877, most southern states had "redeemed" their governments and had driven blacks and their white Republican allies from elective offices. In turn, African Americans holding minor political offices, such as police officer, were eliminated, either immediately (as in the case of the Texas state police) or gradually through dismissals, resignations (such as the case in Vicksburg cited above), and retirements. By the 1890s, most cities in the South once again had lily-white police forces. (See table 3.)

Even after Redemption, however, African Americans continued to serve on the police forces of several southern cities. For example, in 1878 city officials in Memphis were forced to hire African-Americas police officers because of a devastating outbreak of yellow fever that killed many whites or forced them to leave the city, depleting the white manpower normally available to the police force. In 1887, a post-Reconstruction Republican victory in a city election in Jacksonville, Florida, led to the appointment of twelve black officers to the city's thirty-man police force. Two African Americans, A. R. Jones and Thomas Lancaster, served on Jacksonville's police commission. In 1895, coalition politics between African Americans and the Populists also allowed a few blacks to regain police jobs in Wilmington and New Bern, North Carolina. A small number of black police also continued to serve in Houston, Austin, and Galveston, Texas. By the post-Reconstruction period, however, racial proscriptions were placed on the police powers of African Americans: black police could not arrest whites, and they patrolled only areas and communities inhabited by other African Americans.[19]

Nevertheless, most of these post-Reconstruction black police officers soon lost their jobs. Southern whites found methods to close the loopholes that had allowed blacks to regain or to continue to hold police posts. In Jacksonville, Florida, for example, whites asked the state legislature in Tallahassee to pass a special law in order to eliminate blacks from the police force. As noted above, African Americans had obtained nearly half of the city's police jobs (twelve out of thirty positions) after the Republican victory in 1887. But whites in the city resented the black police presence. They accused black officers of "getting out of their place" and criticized them for abusive behavior, malingering on patrol, and flirting with women while on duty. Unable to vote out of office the six black councilmen (the majority of the city's electorate was black) who supported having blacks on the police force, whites in Jacksonville turned to the state legislature. In 1889, the Democrats in the state legislature introduced House Bill No. 4 to place the selection of the city's government in the hands of the governor, a Democrat. The legislature sent a special committee to investigate the number of black officers on the city's police force and to determine the extent of their authority over whites. Finding that there were too many black police in the city and after observing that they arrested white as well as black citizens, the committee reported back to Tallahassee in May 1889 and urged the legislature to pass House Bill No. 4. After the bill passed, the governor exercised his authority under its provisions and appointed a new city council and police commission which contained both Democrats and Republicans, but no African Americans. All local government offices in Jacksonville were replaced by the new city council. Jacksonville's black police officers did not survive the change in government; the city's police force became all-white.

In 1893, Jacksonville citizens regained local control of their government. Home rule enabled black candidates from the city's Sixth Ward to win election to the city council again. African Americans from that ward served on the city council until 1907, when the ward was gerrymandered and a poll tax adopted to eliminate blacks from city politics. None of these black councilmen were successful in assisting their constituents in regaining positions on the police force.[20]

Whites in Charleston, South Carolina, also used state intervention to eliminate African Americans from that city's police force. Although Wade Hampton and his red shirts had "redeemed" the state in the bloody election of 1876, African Americans retained some public offices. In the 1890s, five were still serving on the Charleston police department—including police lieutenant James Fordham, the highest-ranking black police officer in the country at that time. In 1894, the South Carolina State Assembly passed a Metropolitan Police Law to ensure better enforcement of a prohibition law passed by the Populists two years earlier. Two years after the adoption of the police law, Governor John Gary Evans, a Populist "reformer," invoked it and appointed three new Populist police commissioners in Charleston, who named a new police chief. The new chief then dismissed all of the members of the Charleston police force. Fordham and the other four African Americans on the force were fired along with all of the city police officers who had failed to enforce the state prohibition law. On the surface, it appeared that the African Americans on Charleston's police force were merely victims of the usual politics that plagued nineteenth-century urban police forces. Historian Laylon Jordan maintains, for example, that the Populist "reformers" aimed their purges at not only African Americans but also the Irish Catholics on the force. The effect, however, was to make the Charleston police force all-white. One year later, after the Democrats defeated the reform administration in the next election, all of the white officers who had been fired in 1896 were rehired. But Fordham and the four other fired African-Americans failed to regain their positions on the police force.[21]

New Orleans, the first city where African Americans obtained police jobs, was also one of the last cities where blacks lost access to those jobs. From a high of more than 170 police positions in 1868, the African Americans on the New Orleans police force declined to 60 in 1880, 25 in 1890, and 5 in 1900. Many were dismissed, forced to resign, or barred from the force. Several had reached the age of retirement. By the 1880s, few African Americans were welcome on the city police force. In 1889, for example, after a black suspect had allegedly struck a white sergeant, the sergeant reprimanded two black officers for failing to arrest the suspect and remarked to them that "niggers were not wanted on the force anyhow." In 1909, the last two African-American police officers in New Orleans, Louis J. Terrence and Joseph Tholmer, died in service. Their deaths closed an era for black police in the South.[22]

By 1910, African Americans had literally disappeared from southern police forces. In that year the United States Census Bureau reported only 576 blacks serving as police officers in the United States, most of whom were employed in northern cities. In the South, only four Texas cities—Houston, Austin, Galveston, and San Antonio—and Knoxville, Tennessee, continued to employ African Americans as police officers. There was not a single black officer in the Deep South states of South Carolina, Georgia, Louisiana, Mississippi, and Alabama.[23]

While it was short-lived, the "first coming" of African-American police officers in the South was quite remarkable. Indeed, in cities such as New Orleans, Mobile, and Charleston, African-American officers achieved a level of equality and mobility that they would not achieve again anywhere in the nation until the 1960s! With only a few exceptions, the black police officers who were hired during Reconstruction arrested whites, worked in all areas of the cities where they served, and were instrumental in pacifying some of the postwar violence against black Americans—even though their presence as police officers often provoked that violence.

During the "first coming" of African-American police pioneers in the South, several of them achieved promotions above sergeant. As noted above, Octave Rey was promoted to captain in 1868 and commanded the Fourth District in New Orleans until his dismissal in 1877. James Fordham achieved the rank of lieutenant in Charleston and served for two decades before he was dismissed in 1896. Both men had exemplary careers. Both proved that African Americans could serve as police commanders and make a significant contribution to the law enforcement in their cities in spite of the usual obstacle of racism in nineteenth-century American society. The performances of these two men merited the acknowledgment of the press of their day, and both were commended for their "fidelity" and "service" to their communities. Coincidentally, both men were also mulattoes (of mixed black and white parentage), and they were approximately the same age: in 1880 Rey was forty-one and Fordham forty. Fordham served as a police officer longer than Rey, but Rey was able to use his police career as a stepping stone to the Louisiana state senate. After his dismissal from the Charleston police force in 1896, Fordham retired. Rey and Fordham broke down a barrier in American policing (promotion to command positions) that it would take African Americans in other parts of the country decades to achieve.[24]

The short-lived experience of African Americans as police officers in the South foreshadowed their twentieth-century experience in northern cities such as Chicago and Philadelphia. Just as blacks in the South gained access to police jobs because of their connection to Republican Reconstruction regimes, blacks in northern cities would also have to use political patronage to win access to police jobs. However, blacks in northern cities would not have the police powers initially granted to black police "pioneers" in the South. Nor would they have the same opportunities for advancement through the ranks. Political tokenism would dominate the experience of black police in northern cities such as Chicago and Philadelphia for more than a half-century.

THREE

THE POLITICS OF TOKENISM

As African Americans lost access to police jobs in the South, they gained it in the North. The political patronage system, which was a central part of late-nineteenth-century city politics, played an important role in this integration. On the surface it appeared that blacks could overcome the usual racism that denied them police employment by relying on the political patronage system that provided other American ethnic groups government jobs. Indeed, their participation in northern political machines enabled a few African Americans to win appointment to northern police departments. Just as in the South, however, racism was still the primary factor limiting the number of African-American police officers, and racism also ensured that their status would be little more than tokenism.[1]

In 1872, a Republican mayor appointed the first black police officer in Chicago; this likely was the first such appointment outside the South. The officer, whose name is unknown, served for just three years. In 1875 he was replaced by another African American, who was the appointee of a People's Party mayor. This second officer served for only two years, then he, in turn, was replaced by an African-American appointee of another Republican mayor. This trend of giving African Americans patronage jobs in the police department continued past the turn of the century and, in time, slowly increased the number of blacks on the Chicago police force.[2]

African-American police appointments in Chicago were inextricably linked to machine politics. Each party made use of the practice in an effort to appeal for black votes. As a result of this patronage system, between 1872 and 1930, African Americans received a total of 260 police appointments in Chicago; this figure was higher than for any other city except Philadelphia. (In 1930, the percentage of African Americans reached 2.2 percent of the 6,163 police officers on the Chicago police force. Chicago's black population was about 7 percent.) The most notable as well as the most successful user of the African-American vote was Republican mayor William "Big Bill" Hale Thompson, who during his two administrations (1915–21 and 1927–31) appointed 138 of those 260 African-American police officers.[3]

Chicago politicians achieved some African-American police appointments by subverting the civil service system instituted in the city in 1895. They made temporary appointments to fill vacancies, bypassing the civil service eligible list, and then made the temporary appointments permanent. In this manner politicians such as Thompson continued to tie the black vote in Chicago to the patronage system. Civil service had no impact on machine politics in Chicago, nor did any of the attempts to reform the police department. As late as the 1940s, Chicago politicians made African-American police appointments on the basis of how well African Americans supported the political machines.[4]

A similar pattern emerged in Philadelphia. Indeed, after Mayor Samuel King appointed Charles K. Draper, Alexander G. Davis, Louis W. Carroll, and Richard Norton Caldwell to the Philadelphia police force in 1881, African-American police appointments quickly became linked to the city's patronage system. This pattern lasted until 1952. Moreover, blacks received more appointments in Philadelphia than in Chicago because a Republican political machine dominated the city's politics from 1885 to 1952. No other ethnic group in the city was as loyal to the party. Just as in Chicago, however, African Americans still did not receive their fair share of police jobs. While the percentage of blacks in the city's population grew from 4 percent in 1880 to 11 percent in 1930, their percentage on the police force actually declined. The number of African Americans on the Philadelphia police force increased from 4 in 1881 to 35 in 1884 to 60 by 1890 and 100 by 1905. The number peaked at 260 in 1920, dropped to 219 by 1930, and declined for the next twenty years. By 1950, only 195 African Americans served on a police force of more than 4,500 officers.[5]

There was a pattern of linking black police appointments to political patronage in other cities as well. In 1881, a Democrat Police Board member in Cleveland, Ohio, appointed William H. Tucker, a former slave and a Republican, as that city's first African-American police officer in order to upstage the Republican Police Board members. In 1885, the first African-American city councilman in Columbus, Ohio, the Reverend James Poindexter, supported the appointment of fellow African-American Republican James S. Tyler to the police force. Tyler served for a short time, later accepting another position as deputy sheriff, but he was able to return to the police force in 1893 as police secretary because of his active support of the Republican party in Columbus. In 1890, in Detroit, African-American politicians secured the appointment of Joseph Stowers, the brother of the editor of the *Detroit Plain Dealer,* as the first black police officer after an earlier attempt in 1886 had failed. Stowers served only two months before the police department (for reasons unclear) dropped him. African-American Republicans threatened repeatedly to leave the party until they achieved permanent representation on the force in 1893 with the appointment of L. T. Toliver. In St. Louis, two African Americans, Andrew J. Gordon and Hugh Allen, passed the police exam in 1899 with exceptional scores, but neither received appointments. The reason: both men had failed to join the Democratic party. Two years later, a Democratic mayor appointed Gordon and another African American, Allen Wilkinson, to the police department in order to secure black support for his successful mayoral campaign.[6] (See table 4.)

After these initial appointments, however, the overt political patronage for

African-American police appointments did not continue in these cities as it did in Chicago and Philadelphia. In Columbus, the city adopted civil service in 1900 and an at-large council system in 1912; these two changes substantially reduced the influence that ward councilmen held over police appointments. The reform measures also reduced the number of black police appointments and eliminated African Americans from the city council for fifty years. In Cleveland, too, the introduction of civil service in 1904 reduced, for some thirty years, the number of police jobs available to African Americans. In St. Louis, after the initial black police appointments in 1901, African Americans appear to have received police appointments without the influence of political patronage. In one instance, the police department's official journal announced the appointment of three "negro specials" (the St. Louis Police Department's designation for black police officers), Ferdinand Waller, Mackie D. Williams, and William A. Wallace, and assured white members of the department that the three men had met the normal standards and requirements for appointment.[7]

While political considerations may have declined as the major factor that enabled African Americans to obtain police positions in some cities, whites—inside and outside of American police departments—made race a constant issue from the beginning. In Chicago, police administrators required the first African-American policemen in the 1870s to patrol the streets in plainclothes, not uniforms, in order to make them inconspicuous and to avoid violent white reaction. This action seems justified in light of events in Philadelphia, where in 1884 whites attacked the thirty-five African-American police officers appointed by Mayor King when they first appeared on the street. In Cleveland, in 1889, a Republican-controlled police board failed to appoint three black candidates to the police department even after they had scored higher on the police exam than forty of the fifty whites who were appointed! In Detroit, in 1886, to register their disapproval of a planned African-American appointment, the entire police force threatened to go out on strike; the politicians controlling the department did not make the appointment. In Brooklyn, in 1891, white police officers mutinied when the first African-American officer, Wiley G. Overton, was appointed. Similarly, Irish-American Democrats on the St. Louis Police Department threatened to strike when the mayor named Gordon and Wilkinson to the force. As Chicago had earlier, the St. Louis department assigned both officers to plainclothes duty to make them less conspicuous.[8]

Most of the hostility toward African-American police officers in northern cities passed after the initial appointments. It never reached the levels of repugnance and violence that characterized whites' reaction in the South. Most departments controlled the hostility in a number of ways: assigning African-American police officers to plainclothes, restricting them to beats or assignments in African-American neighborhoods, prohibiting them from arresting whites, and having other officers support them against public violence. White police and white citizens came to accept black policemen in northern cities not only for the above reasons, but also because some of the patrolmen did an outstanding job of policing African-American communities and neighborhoods.[9]

The case of Samuel Battle exemplifies the influence of racism on the appointment of African-American police officers. Battle was the first African American to serve on the New York City Police Department after the consolidation of the five boroughs. After being rejected three times for allegedly having a heart murmur, he secured an outside medical examination and used the influence of a powerful African-American politician in the city to secure his appointment to the force in 1911. Battle's problems began immediately following his appointment. He was assigned to the West Sixty-eighth Street station, where white police officers "hazed" him for more than a year by simply not speaking to him. In addition, he could not sleep in the police barracks with other officers but instead was assigned to a small, cramped room where he had to sleep alone. The black press reported that Battle was subjected to abusive language from both white and African-American suspects who resented being arrested by him. Nevertheless, Battle took his "hazing" stoically and performed his job with ardor and diligence. By the time the department assigned him to the Harlem Station in 1913, he had come to be liked and respected by other officers. In 1919, he won their confidence even more by saving from a Harlem mob a white officer who had shot and killed an African-American citizen. After this difficult beginning, Battle went on to serve as a police officer for thirty-five years and became the New York department's first black police sergeant and lieutenant.[10]

The African Americans who became police officers in the early twentieth century entered American police departments during a period in which the police were experiencing a "first wave of reform" (1890–1930). According to historians Eric Monkkonen and Robert Fogelson, Progressive reformers attempted to remove the police from politics by instituting civil service exams, centralizing police administration, and implementing a military model for policing. They sought thereby to end police corruption, prevent police participation in machine politics, and impede the use of police jobs as a method of social and economic advancement for first-generation immigrants. In short, according to Fogelson, they wanted to "professionalize" the police, improve the standards for selecting police officers, and emphasize the crime-fighting responsibilities of American police forces.[11]

This "first wave of reform" coincided with the entrance of African Americans into city police forces as a result of the machine politics discussed above. As a consequence, according to Fogelson, blacks were one of the first groups negatively affected by the new standards established by reformers for police officers. Allegedly, African Americans were among the "newcomers" who could not pass the new civil service exams, and therefore not many became police officers.[12]

This progressive interpretation ignores the important factor of race in police appointments. As noted above, race was at least as important as politics in the appointment and assignment of African Americans to police work. In this period of American history, it is, in fact, remarkable that African Americans obtained police jobs at all. As historian Rayford W. Logan has written, an overwhelming number of whites regarded African Americans as inferior to themselves—some even believed that blacks were less than human. The popular press expressed and compounded such notions. In addition, the period's numerous anti-black race riots, lynchings of African-American men, and judicial decisions restricting their civil rights attest to a general climate of intense white hostility toward, and contempt for, African Americans.[13]

The police, of course, were not unaffected by the vicious racism permeating American society. In 1912, the *St. Louis Police Journal* published an allegedly humorous, but in fact racist, anecdote to entertain its readers—namely, members of the St. Louis police force. The *Journal* described the experience of an obviously unqualified black candidate for one of the department's "negro special" positions. The candidate passed the physical part of the examination, but answered the oral exam in "Negro dialect" and failed the written test. He then shuffled off trying to find some "quirements" after he was told that he did not meet the department's requirements for police candidates.[14] With such attitudes pervading police departments and American society in general, it is not surprising that the police not only served as the enforcers of the racial status quo, but even participated in the many race riots of the period. In riots in Atlanta, Washington, D.C., East St. Louis, and Chicago, for example, white police officers disarmed, beat, and even shot and killed African Americans attempting to defend themselves from white mobs. In 1919, the anti-black behavior of white police officers in repressing these racial disturbances led the *Christian Recorder,* a black publication, to blame white police officers for the recurrence of racial violence in American society.[15]

In this sort of racial climate in early twentieth-century America, the "first wave of police reform" had no effect on the policies that police departments established for African-American officers, whose experience, despite the emergence of reform in other areas, was still dominated by racism. In most northern cities they were assigned exclusively to black communities, prohibited from arresting white suspects, and denied promotions above the rank of sergeant. Indeed, circumscribing the powers and opportunities of African-American police officers became a national norm.

Even in Chicago, the city in which African Americans made the most progress in terms of the number of promotions that they received, their police experience was indicative of the times and of the failure of police reform to address the color line. In contrast to the situation in other cities, police reform in Chicago actually had little impact on reducing the number of black police officers. African-American police appointments in the city remained linked to the system of political patronage. As historian Mark Haller has observed, African Americans were able to obtain police appointments because they were able to control the vice (gambling, prostitution, and entertainment) and the politics in their communities, especially in the Second and Fourth wards. They achieved this control sooner than did African Americans in any other city. Not only did this enable them to continue to obtain some police appointments, it also allowed them to obtain promotions above the rank of patrolman.[16]

Nevertheless, from 1890 to 1930, the African-American police experience in Chicago was influenced by the color line. The majority of black officers worked in predominantly black communities and neighborhoods. An unwritten policy also required African Americans to work together; interracial teams were *never* assigned to a beat. When the department appointed its first black police sergeants starting in 1897, these men were usually restricted to noncommand assignments. Of the thirteen black sergeants appointed by 1930, only two ever commanded a squad. The other eleven were assigned to foot patrol in pairs or to desk assignments. Black sergeants were, of course, not allowed to command white police officers. In addition, complained the *Chicago Defender,* the department required all African Americans promoted to sergeant and lieutenant to abandon their uniforms and wear plainclothes. Both police and public should not *see* that African Americans held command rank.[17]

The charge of this black newspaper had some merit. The Chicago Police Department attempted not only to hide but even to negate the promotion of African-American officers by placing them in nonessential positions. The case of the department's first black lieutenant, William Childs, is a prime example. Finishing fifth on the departmental lieutenant's exam in 1912, Childs became the first African-American police lieutenant in the history of the Chicago Police Department. A college graduate, Childs was considered to be one of the smartest men on the department. Upon his promotion to lieutenant, he was assigned to the Bureau of Identification. In 1922, when Childs resigned from the Chicago Police Department, the *Defender* reported his bitterness about the treatment that he had received in the department after his promotion. He stated that he was "tired of being buried; tired of being a dummy lieutenant with only a rank and salary; just a clerk." Childs charged that his superiors refused to allow him to command a district, instead relegating him to a desk job during his entire time as a lieutenant. The *Defender* investigated Childs's charges and concluded that he had been treated unfairly. "Italians, Germans, Poles, and every other [white] foreign race [had] humiliated Childs and climbed to glory in the department on the account of their skin color." According to the *Defender,* Childs was a "loyal Republican and a talented member of the [black] Race," but the "[black] Race [had] stood idly by and allowed Childs to be persecuted and humiliated."[18]

Robert Forgy of Philadelphia had a similar experience. Forgy joined that city's police force in 1913, and after twelve years he became the first African American to earn a promotion above patrolman. In 1925 he was appointed a corporal, but he was demoted to patrolman when the department abolished the position in 1928. In 1929, Forgy became the first African American promoted to sergeant in Philadelphia. However, he was not permitted to wear his stripes or uniform and was assigned to plainclothes duty in the department's Homicide Division. He was allowed to appear in his sergeant's uniform only during parades, or when black civic and fraternal organizations, such as the Elks, requested police representation at special functions. Forgy remained the only African American above the rank of patrolman on the police force until 1943, when James Anderson was elevated to sergeant to head a special squad of black detectives. In 1952, Forgy was finally allowed to wear his sergeant's uniform on duty when he became the *desk sergeant* in the 23rd District. By then he was in his thirty-ninth year as a police officer; he died within a year of assuming his first command.[19]

While African Americans on the Chicago and Philadelphia police forces achieved more appointments and promotions than those in other northern cities, they still exemplified the token status of all black police in the North. Their experience proved that the new standards that accompanied police reform did not prevent African Americans from becoming police officers and attaining promotions; the color line did.

The problems that African-American police officers experienced during the "first wave of police reform" remained problems for them in the "second wave of police reform," which according to Fogelson and Samuel Walker was begun in the 1930s by a new group of police reformers—police chiefs such as August Vollmer of Berkeley and Herbert Jenkins of Atlanta. The intent was to improve the image of the police and to further "professionalize" them. The police reformers established new standards for selecting police officers (such as high school diplomas as the minimum educational requirement, intelligence tests for police recruits, and background investigations and polygraphs). Fogelson contends that these revised criteria tended to exclude African Americans from becoming police officers. However, the actual experience of African Americans in police departments indicates that the new standards were negligible, if not superficial, causes of continuing discrimination. Many police departments still hired African Americans only for patronage reasons or barred them altogether through quotas favoring whites.[20]

During the "second wave of reform," several cities in fact continued to appoint black police officers on the basis of the patronage system. Once again, Chicago and Philadelphia present the most glaring examples. With the change in the political alignment of Chicago's African Americans in the 1930s from Republican to Democrat, it was the Democrats who now provided police appointments to African Americans, even appointing the first black police captain, John Scott. Philadelphia also continued the patronage practice, perhaps even to a greater extent than Chicago. Historian James E. Miller, writing in the 1940s, found that African Americans had to be endorsed by ward leaders in order to be appointed as police officers. In addition, the officers had to pay yearly dues to the Republican party in order to protect their positions on the force. During the 1930s, the same pattern emerged in Los Angeles, where African Americans had to rely on the spoils system of Mayor Frank Shaw (1930–1938) to obtain appointments and promotions in the police department. St. Louis fell into this pattern as well. After the St. Louis Police Board (acting upon the recommendation of a Republican governor) appointed ten African Americans to the police force in 1921, blacks received virtually no appointments to the department for the rest of the decade, despite pleas from African-American ward leaders and the *Argus,* one of the city's black newspapers. One white politician even justified the lack of appointments by charging that African-American police officers were inefficient. Reacting to this neglect, and led by black politician Jordan Chambers, African Americans in St. Louis switched their support in 1932 to the Democratic party. Chambers successfully bargained with the party for twenty-five additional police appointments for African Americans during the period 1932 to 1945.[21]

During the "second wave of reform," African Americans found that the so-called merit system operated even more insidiously to bar them from police jobs. Out of seventy black applicants to the St. Louis Police Department in 1921, thirty-seven were rejected for allegedly failing the physical examination. Fourteen years later, the department rejected Thomas E. Brooks, who would become the first African-American police major in St. Louis, because he allegedly had poor eyesight. Brooks had to obtain the services of an outside doctor, as well as the support of ward leader Jordan Chambers, in order to have his initial rejection for a position on the force overruled. African Americans who applied for police jobs in Columbus and Cleveland, Ohio, faced similar problems. In 1934, the Cleveland Police Department rejected more than half of the black applicants for alleged physical ailments. Lynn Coleman, who was rejected for a heart murmur, challenged his physical exam by submitting an outside doctor's statement to disprove the police surgeon's diagnosis. Similarly, Edward Waller, who applied in Columbus in 1941, had to obtain an outside examination to challenge a diagnosis that he had poor eyesight. The New York City Police Department also disqualified a disproportionate number of black police candidates on the physical examination; African Americans in that city learned that they must obtain certification from outside physicians to overrule the "official" exam of the police surgeon.[22]

The merit system of the "second wave of reform" also instituted quotas—hiring ceilings—for black police officers. For example, from 1937 to 1950, the Civil Service Commission in Columbus maintained separate eligible lists for African-American and white police candidates. When an African-American officer died, resigned, or was dismissed, the safety director specifically requested a list of those eligible for the position of "negro patrolman" to fill the vacancy. In Detroit, only 3 percent of the positions on the police force were reserved for African-American applicants. The Detroit Police Department began to approach this quota only in the late 1940s, after many years of holding it at 1 percent. In the 1930s and 1940s, St. Louis also maintained a quota for black police recruits, which never exceeded 11 or 12 percent in those decades. Philadelphia's "merit system" also limited the number of African Americans on the police force, but the quota moved either up or down at the will of city officials. It dropped to 4 percent after 1940 and remained at that figure until 1955.[23]

The "second wave of police reform" did nothing to improve the promotion opportunities for African-American police officers. The new "merit system" only reinforced the old policy of excluding African Americans from command positions. If black police officers did achieve such positions, it was only to command other African-American officers. Chicago had set the tone for the promotion of African-American police officers in the so-called "first wave of police reform," assigning these first black sergeants and lieutenants to noncommand positions and plainclothes details. African-American police officers in Chicago did not achieve actual command positions in the city until 1940, when Captain John Scott assumed command of the Stanton district.[24]

African Americans obtained promotions in other cities later and less frequently. In Columbus, Ohio, Leslie Shaw, the city's first black police sergeant, had to file suit against the city in 1943 in order to obtain his promotion. The St. Louis Police Department promoted Ira Cooper as its first African-American sergeant and lieutenant, in 1923 and 1930, respectively, but in both positions restricted him to commanding a black detective squad. James Wintersmith was the second African American promoted to police sergeant in St. Louis, in 1936; he also commanded the black detective squad. Before 1950, two African Americans served as sergeants in Philadelphia, James Anderson and Robert Forgy. Anderson had the opportunity to serve as a commander, but he also was restricted to commanding a squad of black detectives. In 1934, an African-American police officer in Los Angeles complained in the NAACP's journal, *The Crisis,* that that city's police department had failed to promote any of its black officers since 1925. The complainant also noted that all African-American police promotions had been in the Detective Bureau, where black officers did not receive pay appropriate for the rank. Twelve years later, the black newspaper the *Los Angeles Sentinel* made similar charges. It also exposed the department's policy of not allowing African-American police sergeants and lieutenants to wear uniforms except in parade. Further, the department did not allow African Americans to command any districts, even if those districts were predominantly black.[25] (See table 5.)

The exclusion of African-American police officers from command positions had long coincided with their exclusive assignment to areas and neighborhoods where they would patrol only other black Americans. This policy also resisted reform. Fogelson and Walker have contended that the centralization of police departments eliminated the policy of assigning officers of specific ethnic groups to the areas where their group resided. But, in fact, nothing changed for African-American officers. Black citizens often requested that police departments assign only black police officers to their communities. Usually, police departments did not employ enough African-American officers to allow them to effectively patrol black communities. Those African Americans who were employed by American police departments, however, usually found that their assignments tended to encompass the communities where African-American citizens resided.[26]

In Columbus, black police officers patrolled Flytown and the East Side. In Chicago, African-American police found their beats in the South Side districts. In St. Louis, the locus of "black beats" ranged from the central downtown area to the North Side. African-American police officers in Cleveland patrolled districts east of the Cuyahoga River. The Los Angeles Police Department was probably the only department outside the southern states that set up a special "black watch" for the predominantly black Newton Station district. Los Angeles also followed a policy of moving African-American police patrol areas to follow the shifts in residential patterns of the African-American population. So, for example, the "black beats" in Los Angeles moved in the late 1940s from the Newton District to Watts.[27]

Despite the attempts by reformers to upgrade, professionalize, and reform the police, the color line continued to influence the status of African Americans in northern cities. Black officers were relegated to segregated assignments, quotas, and token roles in urban police departments. To change the role of African-American policemen and to secure better police protection for African-American communities, black leaders, primarily through the black press, challenged race-based police department policies.

This challenge was focused in two key areas: the appointment and promotion of African-American police officers. In virtually every city, African Americans urged the hiring of more black officers. In 1914, for example, the black press in New York City demanded the addition of more African Americans to the police force. It was, of course, simply impossible for two police officers (Samuel Battle and a second African-American appointee) to patrol a community of 65,000 people! One year later, African Americans in Chicago made the same request of the police department in that city. The *Defender* complained that only 8 of 351 candidates who passed a police exam in 1915 were black. Similar demands were echoed in Philadelphia in 1919, Detroit in 1927, Cleveland in 1930, and Columbus in 1935. This call for a minimally adequate number of black police officers was a constant theme among African Americans in northern cities who were concerned about crime and law enforcement in their communities.[28]

African-American leaders in almost every northern city also demanded an upgrade in the status of black officers, specifically in promotions. On numerous occasions, African Americans in Chicago, New York, and Philadelphia challenged the restrictions on promotions for black police officers. They also challenged policies that relegated African-American officers to limited assignments, restricting them to certain beats and race-segregated powers of arrest.[29]

During the "second wave of reform," Chicago was the only northern city that attempted to meet these demands. By 1945, the number of African Americans on the Chicago police force had declined to 122, less than 2 percent of a force of 7,000 officers. In addition, when African Americans moved into a previously all-white housing project on the West Side in 1946, white mobs attacked them and destroyed their property. White officers had "fraternized" with the mobs and failed to protect black citizens adequately. In response to this racial incident, the Chicago Commission on Human Relations, created by Mayor Edward Kelly in July 1943, urged the mayor to increase the number of African-American police officers. The commission sought not only to improve race relations but even to integrate all divisions of the police department. The commission also requested that the police department assign officers to bureaus and districts without regard to race or ethnic background. With Kelly's encouragement, the police department increased the number of African Americans on the force to 238 men by 1950. The department assigned the first African Americans to the traffic, administrative, and selection bureaus, and implemented its first human relations training program for police recruits. A number of African Americans were also assigned to districts beyond the South Side. Nevertheless, an investigation by the commission in 1951 found that the majority of black officers were still assigned to districts in the "heart of the Black Belt."[30]

Chicago's attempts to employ and improve the status of African-American police officers were unique. No other police department appears to have made any efforts in this area prior to the 1960s. Despite fifty years of "police reform," African Americans remained essentially token police officers in northern cities. The number of blacks holding police jobs remained small; according to a survey completed in 1952, they did not hold a proportion of the police jobs in any city at all equal to their percentage of the population. (See table 6.) Even as African-American citizens struggled to increase their numbers and upgrade their status, most police officials were reluctant to alter the status quo.

In their concern for going beyond the merely token status of black officers on American police departments, African Americans in northern cities established the precedent for the black police movement that began in the South in the 1920s and 1930s. Unlike those in northern cities, however, African Americans in the South would find that they had to concede to a limit on the police powers of black officers just to obtain positions for these men.

FOUR

THE SECOND COMING IN THE SOUTH

After Redemption, African-American police officers disappeared from most police departments in the South. The majority were eliminated because they posed a threat to white supremacy. White southerners, unwilling to allow African Americans to hold any position of authority, successfully blocked their access to police jobs for most of the first half of the twentieth century. Up to the 1940s, not a single African American held a police position in the Deep South states of Georgia, Alabama, South Carolina, Mississippi, and Louisiana. Yet in 1930 and 1940, these five states contained a majority of the black population in the United States.[1] African Americans retained police jobs in only a few southern cities—for example, in Houston, Austin, and Galveston, Texas. But even in these cities, they often did not wear uniforms, they could not arrest whites, and they worked exclusively in black neighborhoods. Moreover, it is clear that their status was so low that they were not even regarded as real police officers.[2]

The presence of these quasi–police officers in Texas and in some of the border states, however, gave African Americans in other parts of the South the impetus to demand representation on their own city's or town's police force. Even though they knew that the presence of black police officers would challenge the prevailing norm of white supremacy, they were willing to advance the proposal as a reform to provide better law enforcement in African-American communities. This was especially the case in those cities in the border states where African Americans still retained the right to vote and influence local elections.[3]

In Memphis, Tennessee, in 1919, African-American politician Robert R. Church bargained with the city's Republican machine to obtain black representation on the police force. Church traded black votes for black police jobs and succeeded in getting two African Americans appointed as plainclothes detectives. These two officers were the first in the city since 1905; moreover, they took the jobs of two white police officers. Despite Church's political clout, opposition to the new officers arose immediately, and their tenure on the force was short-lived. One of them did not help matters by shooting a white citizen, thus magnifying the white animosity and opposition that existed toward African-American police officers. After less than six months, the "Negro detective force" was discontinued. Church tried to use his substantial political influence to revive it, but failed. The memory of these abusive officers lingered in Memphis. It was invoked by a Democratic mayor in 1927 to reject a demand from the West Tennessee Civic and Political League, an African-American political organization, for "Negro police." The mayor called the demand "the greatest menace to white supremacy in the city since Reconstruction days." Such white opposition and the negative results of the 1919 experiment forestalled African-American representation on the Memphis police force for twenty years.[4]

African Americans in Louisville, Kentucky, by contrast, were successful in their endeavor to sustain black representation on the police force, but they had to overcome a legacy of police oppression and political neglect by the city's Democratic and Republican parties. Just as in most black communities throughout the nation, the Louisville police had a long history of brutality and violence against the city's African-American population. Indeed, historian George Wright maintains that the Louisville police force was formed in the 1820s specifically to control the black slave population and to enforce an antebellum curfew on free African Americans in the city. According to Wright, the Louisville police force did its job quite well, and it continued to use oppressive tactics after the Civil War to intimidate African Americans and keep them "in their place" in the city. In the postwar period, Democrats dominated the city's politics and used the predominantly Irish Democrat police force to challenge African Americans who tried to vote in elections, in some cases actually driving them away from the polls. In 1885, a committee of African Americans complained to Louisville's mayor about police abuse and asked that blacks be appointed to the police force. The mayor stated that a state law (actually an 1874 city ordinance) prohibited such appointments; besides, he said that he personally did not feel that it was a good idea. Thus, police violence against African Americans and police intimidation of them at the polls continued unabated.[5]

In 1917, the Republicans won the mayor's office in Louisville and ended the dominance of the Democrats in city politics. The Republican victory provided Louisville's African Americans the opportunity they sought to improve their position in the city. As major supporters of the Republican party, African Americans thought that police abuse would end and the party would reward their support with patronage jobs—especially in the police department. In 1918, the leader of the NAACP, Dr. A. C. McIntyre, solicited and received a letter from the mayor of Knoxville, Tennessee, praising the performance of the five African Americans serving on his police force. McIntyre published the letter in an effort to convince Louisville's new Republican administration to add African Americans to that city's police force. His effort was unsuccessful, however, and the party continued to ignore blacks' requests for patronage.[6]

The continuance of politics as usual prompted some African Americans to act to force the Republicans' hand. In 1921, a group of "upstart" blacks formed the Lincoln Independent Party (LIP) to challenge the Republican party. Members of the LIP charged that the Republicans had never recognized the black vote or rewarded African Americans with patronage. They asked other African Americans who normally supported the Republicans to renounce their membership in that party and join the LIP. In the fall election, the LIP ran candidates for mayor and city council seats. The Republican-controlled police force responded to this challenge by allowing members of the black underworld to intimidate members of the LIP through violent attacks and to prevent their supporters from voting. All LIP candidates lost by large margins, as few African Americans switched their allegiance to the new African-American party.[7]

Despite its dismal failure in 1921, the LIP's challenge to the Republican party had a positive result. It forced the Republicans to recognize the black electorate and begin to reward it with patronage appointments. After nearly fifty years of requests, the Republican administration in Louisville finally appointed the city's first four African-American plainclothes police officers in 1923. Five years later, the administration rewarded their African-American supporters by detailing twelve in police uniforms and assigning them to patrol throughout the city (rather than in "black only" neighborhoods, as was the former policy). Louisville's "Negro police detail" became the largest in the South. From that point on, the Republican party continued to reward African Americans not only with patronage in the police department, but also with positions in the fire department and other city jobs.[8]

African Americans in other cities also made demands in this period for representation on the police force, but they were unsuccessful. For example, in 1913, W. B. Driver, the leader of the Birmingham, Alabama, chapter of the National Negro Business League, called on city officials to employ African-American police officers in order to provide Birmingham's black community "a more efficacious" enforcement of the law. Eight years later, African Americans in Charleston, South Carolina, submitted a petition to the mayor and city council requesting the appointment of "a few colored men on the police force" in order to improve "the peace and harmony" in the city. Charleston city officials did not act on the petition; the request fell on deaf ears just as had the request in Birmingham.[9]

In the 1930s and especially in the 1940s, African Americans in the South continued to wage extensive campaigns not only for representation on the police force, but also for better law enforcement in their communities. They lacked the political power that enabled blacks in the North to secure patronage in the police departments, so they argued for the hiring of African-American police officers based on the need of their communities for better law enforcement. An important part of their argument was that black officers were needed to stem the high homicide rate that plagued their communities. African Americans in Baltimore, Dallas, and Atlanta had failed to win representation on their cities' police forces during Reconstruction, so gaining access to police jobs in these three cities proved to be especially difficult.[10]

Ironically, African Americans in Baltimore probably faced the most difficulty. Although Baltimore was in the "upper South" and a "border city," the city's police administration resisted vehemently the demands of African Americans to be represented on the force. In 1898, for example, Police Commissioner Heddinger stated that it would be a "humiliation of Anglo Saxon blood" to appoint "colored policemen" and have them arrest white citizens.[11]

Despite such opposition, Baltimore's African Americans continued to pursue their goal. In 1920, a black delegation attended a Board of Police Commissioners meeting to ask that African-American men be placed on the city's police force. Their request coincided with the application of Frederick Hill, an African-American candidate, for a position on the force. According to the newspaper *Afro-American,* Hill was the first African American in the history of Baltimore to pass the physical examination and to apply for a police appointment. Hill's effort, however, was futile. Three months after he passed the physical, Baltimore police commissioner Charles R. Gaither announced publicly that no African American would ever serve on the city's police force, even if he did pass the police exam and make the eligible list for appointment.[12]

During his tenure as police commissioner, Gaither continued to adhere to this position. His stubbornness on the issue forced the editors of the *Afro-American* to undertake a campaign to change his position. In October 1931, NAACP national executive secretary Walter White came to Baltimore and urged African Americans to form a strong branch of the NAACP in order to agitate for police jobs. He reminded them that the police department spent $4 million annually, but none of the city's 100,000 African-American residents were eligible to share in those funds. The *Afro-American,* adopting the theme presented by White, increased its pressure on Gaither to open up police jobs for African-American candidates. The newspaper legitimately raised the question of the African-American share of the annual police budget, but also presented the argument that African Americans throughout the South were using to support their demands for representation on the police force: Baltimore needed black police officers to control the crime in black communities. In May and June of 1932, the county grand jury and the *Morning Sun* newspaper, respectively, echoed the *Afro-American*'s position and called for African-American police officers for the city's black communities. Commissioner Gaither responded that he had no power to appoint black police officers because all appointees to the department had to pass the police examination. In a statement that was completely contrary to his public position since 1920, he stated: "The colored citizens take the stand that I personally keep colored men off the force. This is not true. I can only appoint from the list submitted to me by the board of examiners. Until they hand me a list containing the name of a colored nominee, I can make no decision in the matter one way or the other."[13] Despite these comments, Gaither remained true to his 1920 position. He retired in 1937 without ever appointing an African American to the Baltimore police force.[14]

Gaither's intractable stand on the issue only motivated African Americans to sustain their pressure. In 1933, they invited Lieutenant Samuel Battle, the first and the highest-ranking African American on the New York City police force, to Baltimore to aid them in their effort. The *Afro-American* invited Police Commissioner Gaither and the governor of Maryland to hear Battle's speech, but neither man attended. Battle's visit to the city aided the *Afro-American* in recruiting 102 African-American men to take the police exam, but none of them scored high enough to become police candidates. Undaunted, the *Afro-American* and other African-American civic organizations—such as the City-Wide Young People's Forum and the Urban League—continued their efforts. In 1935, fifteen African Americans passed the police exam and qualified to become police officers, but none received appointments. In 1936, six black applicants were disqualified for failing to answer several questions on the exam related to police operations. These repeated failures served to frustrate the city's African-American leadership.[15]

In October 1937, members of the Maryland League of Colored Republican Voters, several civic organizations, and fifty-five other persons met to address the recurring failure of African Americans to secure positions on the city's police force. The meeting adopted a resolution to work with city, state, and police officials to train black police candidates. Members of the Morgan State College faculty, Baltimore police officers (several of whom were receptive to the proposal), and an African-American police officer from Washington, D.C., were all drafted to help with the training. One member of the group, Edward Lewis, secretary of the Urban League, also appeared before the county grand jury and implored it to support the appointment of African-American police officers in order to address the specific problem of crime in African-American neighborhoods.[16]

These steps produced immediate results. In December 1937, the new city police commissioner, William P. Lawson, appointed Violet Hill Whyte as the first black member of the Baltimore Police Department. Whyte, a member of the Monument City Urban League Board of Directors, achieved a unique double first. Not only was she the first African American appointed to the police department, but her appointment also marked the first time that a black woman earned a police appointment before black men. Approximately seven months after Violet Whyte's appointment, police commissioner Lawson appointed four African-American men to the department. All four had trained at the "Colored Policeman's Training School" at Morgan State College, and they were among twenty-six black candidates who had passed the police exam. The barriers to police jobs in the city having been broken down, African-American leaders trained two more classes of candidates for the police department. But their efforts would place only five African Americans on the police force by 1943.[17]

The campaign waged by African Americans in Dallas to secure positions on the city's police force lasted much longer than that in Baltimore. Whereas in other southern cities African Americans had first obtained positions on the police force during Reconstruction, blacks in Dallas had been unable to achieve this goal. Nevertheless, as early as 1888 they petitioned the city council to appoint police officers of their race to work in their own neighborhoods. The city council submitted their petition to the city marshal, but he failed to act on it. Six years later, African Americans petitioned again for a police officer of their race to work in their communities. This time the council responded by appointing a special officer, William McDuff, who was assigned to work near an African-American church in the city in order to break up the rowdiness perpetrated by juveniles in the area. McDuff served only two months. He was shot and killed in December 1896 by two of the juveniles that he was attempting to police. The city council did not replace him.[18]

African Americans in Dallas waited two decades before reviving their effort to obtain representation on the police force. In 1919, a Negro Welfare Committee, appointed by the city council to investigate the needs of the city's African-American community, recommended that an African-American police officer be appointed to police black neighborhoods. No action was taken on the committee's recommendation. One year later, however, the committee learned that the city's public safety commissioner, L. D. McGee, had announced that he was considering the appointment of a Mexican-American police officer to work in Mexican-American neighborhoods. The committee recommended that he also appoint an African-American police officer to work in black neighborhoods. In the end, neither of the appointments was made, because the white police in Dallas threatened to strike in protest. In 1927, the Reverend W. L. Dickson, the head of an African-American orphanage, led a delegation to city hall and presented a petition requesting that the city appoint black police officers. Using the arguments that African Americans were making in other parts of the South, Dickson argued not only that African Americans deserved representation in local government, but also that "race police officers" would provide better law enforcement in the black community. Although Mayor Louis Blaylock indicated that he favored such a proposal, the police commissioner disapproved of it and the matter was dropped. Two years later, Dickson returned with a second petition and presented essentially the same arguments that he had made in 1927. Once again, however, his pleas were rejected.[19]

Resolute, African Americans continued to press the issue time and time again. In the 1930s, A. Maceo Smith, the first executive secretary of the Dallas Negro Chamber of Commerce, took on the task of showing city officials why African-American police officers were needed in Dallas. To support his position, Smith decided to present evidence to show how African-American police had performed in other cities. He wrote the police chiefs in San Antonio, Houston, Tulsa, and Oklahoma City to obtain testimonials about the performance of their black officers. He received responses from three police chiefs: all had high praise for their African-American police officers and specifically for their positive impact on crime in the black communities. Smith published these testimonials in the city's African-American and white newspapers in an attempt to persuade city officials to act on the proposal. But the officials were still not convinced.[20]

In 1936, Smith developed a new idea. In conjunction with the Negro Day celebration planned for African-American participation in the Texas Centennial, he invited all of the black police officers in the state of Texas to lead the parade planned for the event. Smith hoped that by displaying the efficiency and esprit de corps of African-American police officers from Houston, Galveston, San Antonio, and Austin, he would show city officials why they needed to appoint black officers in Dallas. He also hoped to embarrass them into acting on the measure since Dallas was the only major city in the state with no blacks on its police force. His plan almost worked. Embarrassed that his police department had no African-American officers to represent the city in the parade, the police chief allowed two black police station orderlies to wear police uniforms and march with the officers from the other cities. But they were returned to their regular jobs after the parade. Smith had failed again to convince stubborn city officials to assign African Americans to the police force.[21]

Undaunted, Smith, Maynard H. Jackson of New Hope Baptist Church, and members of the Negro Chamber of Commerce continued their quest. They had the black officers from Houston, Galveston, San Antonio, and Austin return to the city for the Negro Day parades in 1937 and again in 1938. Moreover, during the 1936 meeting of the officers in Dallas, Smith was instrumental in assisting them to form a statewide chapter of the Texas Negro Peace Officers' Association (TNPOA), the first police association formed by African Americans in the United States. One of the initial objectives of the TNPOA was to assist blacks in Dallas in securing police jobs. Neither their visit in 1937 nor the one in 1938 moved city officials closer to hiring African Americans for the police force. In fact, the 1937 visit was almost canceled because the issue of appointing African-American police officers in the city had sparked racial tension and a threatened strike by white members of the police department.[22]

Racial tension over the appointment of African-American police officers in Dallas developed because Smith and Jackson successfully made it a political issue in the 1937 city council election. After failing in their other endeavors to secure representation on the police force, in the fall of 1936 Smith and Jackson organized the Progressive Voters League (PVL) to sponsor a poll tax payment campaign, to organize the city's black electorate, and to vote as a bloc for candidates running in city government elections. By February 1937, Jackson and Smith, president and vice-president of the PVL, respectively, had succeeded in organizing a bloc of 7,000 African-American voters who were poised to cast possibly deciding votes in the city council election in March. After interviewing prospective candidates from several of the nonpartisan groups running for the city council, the PVL endorsed the candidates of the Forward Dallas Association (FDA) over their chief opponents from the Citizens Charter Association (CCA). In an election in which only 15,000 people voted, the PVL bloc did turn the election in favor of the FDA. In acknowledgment, the FDA promised to build a new African-American high school, employ more African Americans in city jobs, and appoint the city's first black police officers.[23]

On September 10, 1937, the city council voted 5 to 2 to employ African Americans as police officers. The council scheduled a police exam for black candidates on September 23 at Booker T. Washington High School. The *Dallas Express*, the city's largest African-American newspaper, announced these developments on its front page. It appeared that Smith, Jackson, and other African Americans in Dallas had finally achieved one of their objectives of improving the law enforcement in their community by having representation on the city's police force.[24]

However, as soon as the announcement was made that the city council had voted to hire black police officers, opposition began to emerge. George Butcher, a white citizen and former state leader of the Texas Ku Klux Klan, began a petition campaign to force the council to rescind the motion. He also organized a rally of white citizens against the proposal and appeared before the city council on

September 17 to denounce the new policy as ill-advised. Butcher's campaign received a boost on September 15 when the Dallas County Pioneer Association, an organization of some of the city's oldest white citizens, held its annual meeting and submitted a six-page petition opposing the council's decision to hire African-American police officers. As a result of the white opposition to the proposal, another white citizen, George Owen, obtained a court injunction to block the black-only police exam because it allegedly violated the Fourteenth Amendment and discriminated against white citizens.[25]

Facing almost unanimous white opposition to the hiring of African-American police officers, the city council met to reconsider the proposal on September 28. They voted 7 to 2 to rescind their original motion. This decision angered Smith, who charged that the city's black community would continue to be policed by white officers who took payoffs to ignore vice and who ignored crimes committed by African Americans against each other. Since the hiring of black police officers was a campaign promise that FDA council members had made to African Americans for their political support in the March 1937 election, the Dallas newspapers noted that the FDA had to find another way to keep its promise. Hiring African-American police officers was now out of the question, and even the *Express*, the black newspaper that had given the issue the most coverage and editorial support, dropped the topic from its headlines after the white opposition made it an impossibility. In fact, the *Express* did not even raise the issue of hiring African-American police officers again until the next city council race in 1939.[26]

After so many failures in their fifty-year quest to obtain African-American representation on the city's police force, Dallas's African-American leadership temporarily dropped the issue. It would not be raised again until 1943. In that year A. Maceo Smith launched yet another study to obtain information on the performance of African-American police officers in other cities in Texas. His study coincided with the Negro Chamber's launching of a campaign to obtain equal pay for black teachers and to challenge the state's Democratic white primary. Smith completed his second study in 1944 and submitted testimonials from police chiefs in Houston and Austin to Dallas newspapers. His effort was supported by the formation of a "Law and Crime Committee," composed of three whites and two African Americans, that was organized by the city's Council of Social Agencies. The committee studied crime among African Americans and also used Smith's study to support its recommendation to the city council to hire African-American police officers. The committee submitted the results of its study to the press, and from 1945 to 1946, the newspapers ran a number of stories showing the positive impact of African-American police on crime in black communities. The newspapers also ran stories highlighting crime among African Americans in Dallas, with special emphasis on the black-on-black homicide problem. In short, the same process that had emerged in the 1930s campaign reemerged in the 1940s to generate citywide support for the hiring of African-American police officers.[27]

In 1946, after receiving a number of petitions supporting the employment of African Americans as police officers, the city manager, V. R. Smitham, finally recommended to the city council that they be added to the force to work in black neighborhoods to reduce the crime problems in those areas. To support his recommendation, Smitham used Smith's 1944 study, citing the record and performance of African-American police officers in other southern cities. Indeed, a large body of data existed on the performance of black police officers in the South, and Smitham's recommendation came at a time when many cities across the region were moving toward the hiring of black police. (See table 7.) When Lee G. Brotherton and Benjamin Thomas went on duty as the first two official African-American police officers in Dallas in March 1947, Dallas actually became one of the last southern cities to join a movement that was sweeping the South.[28]

Atlanta, like Dallas, was one of the few major cities in the South that did not appoint African Americans as police officers during Reconstruction. African Americans in Atlanta had raised the issue in 1870 when they elected two black city councilmen. The presence of two African Americans on the council usually meant that other African Americans would receive appointments to city jobs. One year later, it appeared that African Americans would obtain appointments to the police force because Mayor Dennis F. Hammond, an independent, appointed a Republican as chair of the council's police committee. But the presence of two black city councilmen and Republican control of the police committee proved to be more than white Democrats on the council could stand. They also believed that the Republican police committee chairman would appoint "African police," and so they acted to remove him from the position. Since Democrats outnumbered the Republicans on the council 6 to 4, they voted to oust the Republican police committee chairman in order to block the possibility of having "African police" imposed upon the white citizens of Atlanta. Moreover, white Democrats in Atlanta were successful in using the specter of "African police" as a political issue to help their party "redeem" the state of Georgia in 1872 and end African-American officeholding in the city.[29]

Although they were thwarted by a trio of "reforms"—Redemption in 1872, the adoption of a poll tax, and the implementation of citywide elections for public offices in the city—African Americans in Atlanta still sought to participate in politics in order to win access to city jobs, including positions on the police force. From 1868 to 1895, African Americans constituted from 10 percent to 39 percent of the registered voters. Black candidates also continued to run for office, if always unsuccessfully. Whites closed ranks to keep African Americans out of office and to curb their demands for jobs in the police and fire departments. In the mayoral election of 1888, African-American voters emerged as the balance of power in a hotly contested election between candidates Walter Brown and John T. Glenn. Black leaders indicated that they would support Brown, but they made some demands: he should appoint African Americans as clerks in the city courthouse and a Negro fire company, support the construction of a school for African-American children, and hire two black police detectives and two black police wagon drivers. When Brown equivocated, his African-American supporters switched their support to Glenn. Once elected, however, Glenn was no more amenable to appointing African-American police officers than Brown. The 1888 election was the last gasp by black Atlantans for political recognition. To end the influence of African Americans on state and local politics, the Democratic party adopted white-only primary measures in 1891 and 1896, and African-American political participation declined significantly thereafter.[30]

Failing to achieve representation on the police force in the nineteenth century, African Americans in Atlanta began a campaign in the twentieth century to obtain police officers of their race in their communities. The Atlanta police, like most police in the South, served as an oppressive force in the black community. In the Atlanta race riot of 1906, for example, the police not only supported the mob that was shooting and killing African Americans and burning them out of their homes, but many officers also participated in the riot by disarming, attacking, and murdering black citizens. In the early years of the twentieth century, two-thirds of the people arrested by the Atlanta police were African Americans, a pattern which indicated a clear mission by the police to oppress the city's black population. As a result of this obvious bias, African Americans called for police officers of their own race in an attempt to obtain more equitable law enforcement.[31]

In 1922, a group of African-American ministers requested that the city appoint members of the race as police officers because African Americans paid taxes just as whites did and deserved representation on the police force. They also pointed out that cities such as Philadelphia, Chicago, and New York employed African-American police and that those officers served with distinction. Moreover, they argued that black police officers would handle crime and gang violence in their neighborhoods more effectively and knowledgeably than white officers. However, this objective was not to be achieved in the 1920s.[32]

Simultaneous with the campaign in Dallas, Atlanta's African Americans renewed their quest in the 1930s and made their best effort to convince city officials that such appointments were needed to attack the crime in African-American neighborhoods. In 1933, a delegation led by C. A. Scott of the *Atlanta Daily World* newspaper and eleven other black leaders visited the home of Mayor James Key and presented a petition for African-American police officers to patrol the city's black neighborhoods. The delegation felt that Key would be amenable to their petition since their votes had helped him to defeat a recall election instituted against him by prohibitionists in the city. Key turned down their request, explaining that neither blacks nor whites in Atlanta were ready for African-American police officers. The delegation presented their petition to the city council anyway. Just as in Dallas, they cited in support of it the fact that African Americans were employed as police officers in cities such as Knoxville, Daytona Beach, San Antonio, Tulsa, and St. Louis. They also argued that blacks made up one-third of the city's population but were denied police protection and an equal opportunity to make a livelihood from public funds. The council accepted their petition but did not act on it.[33]

Jessie Daniel Ames, head of the Atlanta-based Commission on Interracial Cooperation, read of the petition for black police submitted to the council by the city's black leaders in the newspapers. In a letter to the Reverend John Moore, she expressed her support for their request but believed that they should develop "an argument for Negro policemen on the basis of law enforcement and law observance" rather than "on the basis of racial representation," as the leaders had done. Even before Ames's letter to Moore, the CIC had taken action to develop such an argument. Five days earlier, R. B. Eleazer of the CIC had sent questionnaires to fifteen cities in the border states and in the South requesting information about the status and use of black police officers. Attorney A. T. Walden of the NAACP, Eleazer, and Ames developed the questionnaire, which was mailed on October 5, 1933. Ames and the CIC also worked with an interracial Committee of Citizens organized to investigate the employment of black police in Atlanta and to present information at a Police Committee hearing scheduled by the city council for November 2.[34]

Although the CIC and the Committee of Citizens compiled an impressive amount of data to support the appointment of black police in Atlanta, their efforts were unsuccessful. Of the eleven police chiefs who responded to their questionnaire, all but two (those in Baltimore and Muskogee, Oklahoma, two cities that did not employ African Americans as police officers in 1933) responded favorably about the employment of African Americans on their police departments. The information obtained from the questionnaires enabled the CIC and the Committee of Citizens to produce a document entitled "Reasons for Employing Negro Police." It listed five reasons why the city of Atlanta should employ black officers: (1) to reduce Atlanta's high homicide rate; (2) to relieve white police of the burden of policing black areas; (3) to keep order in black communities; (4) to improve the morale of the black community; and (5) because other southern cities were employing them with much success. After having compiled this impressive information, the committee still decided to forgo presenting it to the Atlanta city council. Ames and other committee members learned that at least two members of the council's Police Committee vehemently opposed the appointment of black police and had vowed to fight the proposal "to the death." Ames recommended that the Committee of Citizens table their request and wait until the new year to request that the council consider African Americans for the twenty new police positions that it planned to fill. The Committee of Citizens saved the data that it had gathered and the impressive testimonials from police chiefs from nine cities for later use. But it was to no avail. The city council ignored the committee's request to appoint black police in 1934.[35]

Not to be denied, African Americans in Atlanta proceeded with their campaign to obtain representation on the police force and better law enforcement for their neighborhoods. In 1937, the Atlanta NAACP and the *Daily World* published one of the most important documents of the period. It outlined the important rationale and justifications for the employment of black police in the South. Entitled *Wanted: Negro Police for Negro Districts in Atlanta,* the pamphlet stated that only African-American officers could and would police African-American communities fairly, justly, and impartially. Recounting some of the testimonials that A. Maceo Smith had obtained for the campaign in Dallas and the data gathered by the CIC in 1933, but adding some additional positive support from several chiefs of police departments in Florida that employed African-American officers, the pamphlet noted that all of the evidence supported the employment of black police because of their positive impact on crime and order in black communities. The pamphlet also took the argument a step further. It cited the disproportionate murder rate for African Americans in Atlanta and posited that "race officers" would reduce the rate of black-on-black homicides. This point became the central theme of the fifteen-year campaign led by the *Daily World* to secure "race police officers" in the city of Atlanta.[36]

The editor of the *Daily World*, C. A. Scott, made the integration of the Atlanta police force a personal objective. For fifteen years, he published the crime statistics for the city's African-American neighborhoods and repeatedly asserted that the employment of African-American police would reduce the crime in those areas. In his newspaper he noted the achievements of African-American police officers in other parts of the nation in solving crime and bringing order to their communities, and inferred that the city of Atlanta would obtain similar positive benefits if city officials would only employ members of the race as police officers. Perhaps his boldest assertion was that African-American police were sure to reduce the city's black-on-black homicide rate. Continuing the theme advanced in the 1937 pamphlet, he published the annual tally of black-on-black homicides in Atlanta, compared them year by year from 1936, and editorialized that the numbers would continue to rise until the city provided African-American neighborhoods with "race police officers."[37]

In the meantime, African Americans and some white citizens in Atlanta supported Scott's campaign with petitions and constant demands for the employment of black police officers. In 1943, the Atlanta Council of Church Women, a group of white women, recommended that the mayor and city council make a study of the use of black police in other cities and take under advisement the "employment of trained Negro police for our Negro sections." A year later, after Scott published a story on the appointment of the first African-American police officers in Miami, Florida, black Atlantans asked the city council why no African American could serve on the Atlanta police force. They noted that no city in Georgia had seen fit to appoint any African Americans as police officers, while several cities in Florida had taken the progressive step and were receiving good service from "race officers" as a result. In 1946, more than 300 black veterans of World War II demonstrated in front of city hall demanding the right of appointment to the police force. During the demonstration, a spokesman for the veterans stated that there were more than 105,000 African Americans in Atlanta, but city authorities did not appear to think that even a single one of them deserved to serve on the police force! He also pointed out that black men had served their country against Nazi Germany, but now, back home in peacetime, they could not qualify to serve the city of Atlanta as police officers.[38]

Despite their fifteen-year campaign for representation on the police force, black Atlantans were able to achieve their objective only after they had begun participating more fully in city politics. Just as in Dallas, as early as 1934 African Americans formed a political organization, the Atlanta Colored Voters League (ACVL), to organize the black electorate. The ACVL even ran candidates for political office, but so few African Americans turned out for elections that the candidates had no chance of winning. For example, in a 1934 election in which two African-American candidates ran for office, they received only about 100 votes from a potential black electorate of 15,000! In 1936, noted African-American leader John Wesley Dobbs reorganized the ACVL into the Atlanta Civic and Political League (ACPL). The ACPL adopted a four-point platform, one point of which was "to have Negro firemen and policemen." Over a ten-year period, Dobbs painstakingly built the ACPL and increased the number of African Americans registered to vote. In 1946, his voter registration efforts among African Americans received a boost when the United States Supreme Court struck down the Democratic party's white primary in Georgia. The ACPL increased the number of African Americans registered to vote from just 3,000 in 1940 to more than 21,000 by 1946. In 1944, in anticipation of winning their suit against the Democratic white primary, Dobbs and other black political activists formed the Citizens Democratic Club to organize African Americans to participate in local elections. As in Dallas, they sought to use their newly-won political influence in order to demand improvements for their community, such as the hiring of African-American police officers.[39]

In May 1947, African Americans in Savannah showed black Atlantans the importance of the ballot and political organization in obtaining patronage positions. Savannah became the first Georgia city to appoint African-American police officers when its city officials hired nine on May 17. The event received national attention. These officers were the first hired in a Deep South state (excluding Texas and Florida) in the post-Reconstruction era. The *New York Times* covered the phenomenon and noted that they were hired for two reasons: (1) the end of the white primary allowed African Americans to influence local elections and demand patronage, and (2) to improve law enforcement in African-American communities. African Americans in Atlanta noted how Savannah's African Americans had used politics to achieve the objective that black Atlantans had sought for fifteen years. They promptly organized a Negro Police Committee led by C. A. Scott and Morehouse College president Benjamin E. Mays with the short-term objective of securing representation on the Atlanta police force.[40]

Stung by the fact that another Georgia city had preceded Atlanta in hiring African-American police officers, the Negro Police Committee launched immediate, concerted action. It had supporters of the proposal write letters daily to Atlanta's newspapers, the correspondents extolling the benefits of employing black police. The committee obtained endorsements for the employment of African-American police officers from both black and white civic and religious groups, such as the Atlanta Chamber of Commerce, the Jaycees, the NAACP, the Atlanta Christian Council, and members of the Atlanta Bar Association. The *Daily World* also continued its campaign of highlighting the achievements of African-American police officers in other cities in the South. In July 1947, Benjamin E. Mays appeared before the city council's Police Committee to testify for the appointment of African-American police officers. He also met with Mayor William Hartsfield and outlined four specific reasons why Atlanta should employ black police. Mays argued that such a policy would relieve frustrations among Negroes;

it would generate goodwill among the races; it was the right thing to do; and it was the right thing morally and ethically for Atlanta. According to the *Daily World*, Mays's arguments were "so compelling as to leave nothing to be desired."[41]

The Negro Police Committee's campaign had the desired effect. It forced city officials to act. On October 21, Mayor William Hartsfield announced his support of the proposal to hire black police officers in a speech to an African-American group, the Atlanta Business and Trade Association. Hartsfield's endorsement cleared the way for the city council to consider the proposal. Subsequently, the council responded to the media blitz and the numerous endorsements and petitions that it had received by scheduling a hearing on the matter for November 26, 1947.[42]

The hearing set in motion the same forces that had derailed the attempt to employ black officers in Dallas in 1937. That is, more than one thousand supporters and opponents appeared to testify at the hearing. The opponents of the proposal attempted to carry the day through intimidation and race-baiting. C. A. Scott testified that the employment of African Americans as police officers would reduce the homicide rate in the city's black communities. He cited the record of African-American police officers in other parts of the South to support his contention. Others testifying in support of the proposal included representatives from the *Atlanta Journal* newspaper, the NAACP, the CIO, the Junior Chamber of Commerce, and the First Christian Church. The testimony of supporters was described as dignified and reasonable,[43] but it paled before the racist demagoguery and vitriolic testimony presented by the proposal's opponents, who included the city's former mayor William Sims, State Commissioner of Agriculture Tom Linder, members of the Ku Klux Klan, and an assortment of "race-baiters." They ranted and railed that "niggers" should not serve on the city's police force. They stated that the proposal was "communist-inspired." Commissioner Linder said that white supremacy in Atlanta had to be maintained because "one race must dominate the other," and it had to be "the white race over the Negroes." Former mayor Sims stated that the proposal was a "political move," and he called for an election to allow the voters to decide the issue. Overall, the atmosphere was one of racial intimidation. As the hearing progressed, one speaker after another tried to outdo the preceding speaker in using the term "nigger" and speaking directly to African Americans at the hearing such as C. A. Scott, Martin Luther King, Sr., and Benjamin E. Mays. Only the presence of police chief Herbert Jenkins with a complement of Atlanta police officers prevented the hearing from deteriorating into a small race war.[44]

Unlike in Dallas, however, the racist demagogues did not defeat the proposal. On December 1, the Atlanta City Council adopted a resolution, by a vote of 10 to 7, to employ black police officers. Perhaps the key factor was the stance of police chief Herbert Jenkins, who had investigated the employment of African-American police officers in other parts of the South, finding that the claims for their effectiveness in black neighborhoods were true. As a result, on December 1, 1947, he sent the council a letter endorsing the proposal and outlining four conditions under which he thought that the proposal would work:

1. that they not be allowed to exercise police power over white people;
2. that a Negro police precinct station be established;
3. that a delegation be sent to other southern cities to study their method of operation and regulations;
4. and that they not be given civil service status until their success has been proven.[45]

With Jenkins's endorsement, the employment of black police officers in Atlanta finally became a reality. Although it required a campaign of fifteen years and overcoming a last-minute lawsuit by the opponents of the proposal, African Americans in Atlanta were able to combine civic pressure with their newly won political power to obtain representation on the police force. When Willard Strickland, Willie T. Elkins, Johnnie P. Jones, Robert McKibbens, John Sanders, Jr., Henry H. Hooks, Claude Dixon III, and Ernest Lyons went on duty in April 1948, Atlanta became the second major city in the Deep South to employ African Americans on its police force.[46]

The campaigns that African Americans waged in Baltimore, Dallas, and Atlanta to obtain representation on the police force were repeated throughout the South. Blacks in cities such as Richmond and Norfolk, Virginia; Charleston and Columbia, South Carolina; Memphis and Nashville, Tennessee; Durham and Raleigh, North Carolina; and Montgomery and Mobile, Alabama, worked to achieve the same objective, using the same arguments that African Americans used in Dallas, Baltimore, and Atlanta. (See table 7.) On three occasions, in Norfolk, Virginia, and Mobile and Birmingham, Alabama, African Americans seeking police jobs had to file lawsuits in order to obtain the right to take the civil service examination for police positions. Ironically, African Americans in New Orleans also had to file a lawsuit to gain access to police jobs.[47]

The "second coming" of African-American police officers in New Orleans deserves special mention because of the difficulty that blacks encountered in regaining positions on the police force. As previously noted, the first African-American police officers appointed in the United States were "free men of color" employed in New Orleans. During Reconstruction, more African Americans served on the state-controlled metropolitan police force in New Orleans than in any other American city. New Orleans was also one of the last cities to retain African Americans as police officers after the end of Reconstruction. Despite this heritage, the presence of black police in the city remained a controversial political issue. The Democrats in the city were able to hang the "dark bouquet of negro police" around the neck of the Republicans as late as 1919 and blame them for "putting negroes on the police force."[48]

Just as in other parts of the South, however, African Americans in New Orleans began a twenty-five-year campaign in the 1920s to regain positions on the police force. Periodically, the *Louisiana Weekly,* the city's largest African-American newspaper, and other newspapers published stories extolling the performance of black police officers in other cities and advocating the employment of "race police" in New Orleans to catch criminals among African Americans. Their arguments were the same as those used in Atlanta and Dallas and included the point that African Americans were one-fourth of the population of the city, but could not serve as police officers. Just as in Atlanta and Dallas, the call for the hiring of African-American police officers in the city usually followed outbreaks of excessive crime and black-on-black homicides.[49]

In 1946, the New Orleans Urban League and the NAACP decided to force city officials to act on the issue. With the support of those organizations, several candidates took the police examination with the intent to challenge the city's policy of excluding African Americans from police work. Four black candidates—Herwald Price, Ernest P. Raphael, James L. Russell, and Otis Fisher—passed the exam. The city's civil service commission selected 186 probationary policemen from the list before it expired, but passed over all of the eligible black candidates. One year later, another group of African-American candidates took the police exam. This time only one, Carlton Pecot, passed. Pecot, a World War II veteran and a graduate of Dillard University, earned a score that ranked him tenth on the civil service list of eligible candidates qualified for appointment to the police department. Nevertheless, the New Orleans Police Department refused to appoint him, passed over him repeatedly, and appointed other candidates who had far lower scores on the exam. After Pecot's eligibility for appointment expired on June 1, 1949, Alexander P. Tureaud, the city's veteran NAACP and civil rights lawyer, filed suit against the police department for violating Pecot's rights under the equal protection clause of the Fourteenth Amendment.[50]

Before the court ruled on Pecot's lawsuit, a new district attorney and police superintendent assumed offices in New Orleans. Both Severn Darden, the district attorney, and Joseph L. Scheuring, the police superintendent, expressed their support for the appointment of candidates to the police force who had passed the police examination, regardless of their race. In early 1950, while Pecot's suit was still pending, several citizens' committees—including the Committee on Race Relations chaired by Alfred W. Hobart and the Citizens Committee on Negro Police chaired by Attorney Tureaud—met to expedite the appointment of African Americans to the New Orleans police force. Following a series of meetings that culminated in June 1950, Police Superintendent Scheuring announced the appointment of not only Pecot but also John Raphael. These two men became the first African Americans to serve as police officers in New Orleans in more than forty years.[51]

In the "second coming" of black police in the South, African Americans had to agitate, petition, and argue for nearly half a century to regain representation in law enforcement. Their arguments showed clearly the concern among African Americans for fair, equitable, and just law enforcement. Moreover, they believed quite legitimately that *only* police officers of their race would police their communities fairly and diligently. For African Americans in the South, "race police officers" represented an important stage in the effort not only to reduce the homicides and crimes in the black communities, but also to improve race relations throughout each city.

Winning the first token, African-American police appointments in the 1940s and 1950s, however, was only the beginning of the battle. Now these officers would have to fight to win equality in status with white police officers in order to become *real* police officers. To achieve this objective, they clashed with the foundation of American apartheid—the "separate but equal" doctrine. They would find that the new stage in the struggle required even more effort than had the long battle to earn the initial appointments.

Depiction of the attack on the integrated New Orleans police force, September 14, 1874, by the White League terrorist group. From *Harper's Weekly,* October 3, 1874.

James Mason, 1884–1902.

Hugh B. Draper, 1885–1894.

John Singleton, 1908–1922.

Ernest Scruggs, 1920–1960.

Charles A. Redmon, 1916–1927.

Wilburn Lyons, 1930–1949.

Thomas Nowlin, 1924–1954.

Frank Robinson, 1921–1927.

James Smith, 1919–1933.

Nine African Americans who served as police officers in Knoxville, Tennessee. Knoxville was one of only a handful of southern cities that permitted blacks to serve on the police force after Reconstruction. Most of these officers were appointed after 1910, when a black city alderman in Knoxville used his influence to obtain police jobs for his constituents. Photos courtesy of Beck Cultural Exchange Center, Knoxville, Tennessee.

Nine of the first ten African Americans allowed to wear police uniforms in St. Louis. It was such an important occasion that a postcard was made in September 1921 and sent to black newspapers across the country. New police recruits, from left to right: Artrice Carter, Thomas F. Smith, Philip S. Eldridge, Moses Carter, Elisha Pettis, Lester Kyser, Jerry Dixon, James A. Taylor, and Isaac Bates. Absent: Thomas J. K. Wilson. Courtesy of the James A. Taylor Papers, in the possession of the author.

Lieutenant Ira Cooper, the first sergeant and lieutenant in the St. Louis Police Department. He was hired as a "negro special" in 1906 and became the department's most famous and most noted detective. Photo circa 1930, courtesy of the James A. Taylor Papers, in the possession of the author.

"36 of the World"s Finest Police Officers." This picture appeared on the front page of the *St. Louis American*, November 11, 1943. It showed how successful ward leader Jordan Chambers was in obtaining police jobs for African Americans in St. Louis. Photo courtesy of the James A. Taylor Papers, in the possession of the author.

Sergeant James A. Taylor, St. Louis Police Department, 1946. In 1948, Sergeant Taylor became the first African-American police sergeant to wear a police uniform and command a platoon of black officers, called the "Soul Patrol." Photo courtesy of the James A. Taylor Papers, in the possession of the author.

Inspector Harvey H. Alston, circa 1960, Columbus, Ohio, Police Department. Inspector Alston was one of the first African Americans to win appointment to police captain in the United States. He missed becoming police chief in Columbus by three-tenths of a point on a civil service exam he took in 1954. Photo donated to the author by the late Harvey H. Alston.

FIVE

SEPARATE AND UNEQUAL

When we took the oath, all eight of us had to stand up there and say, "I do solemnly swear as a nigger policeman that I will uphold the segregation laws of the city of Atlanta."

—Claude Dixon, one of the first black police officers appointed in Atlanta, Georgia, in 1948[1]

Black police officers were not required to take an oath any different from that of white officers.

—Herbert Jenkins, former police chief of Atlanta[2]

The paradox of policing in a segregated society confronted black police in the South. After African Americans "integrated" the police forces there for the second time, they found that they were second-class and even quasi—law enforcement officers. As part of the compromise that African-American leaders such as A. Maceo Smith of Dallas and C. A. Scott of Atlanta arranged to obtain police jobs for African Americans, the police powers and opportunities for advancement for black officers were restricted and limited. African-American police officers were usually assigned exclusively to patrol black neighborhoods and communities. They could arrest only black offenders and were prohibited from arresting white offenders by custom and, in some cases, by law. African-American police officers in the South were also ineligible for promotion to ranks above patrolman. The restrictions varied from city to city, but it was clear that black officers were not equal to their white counterparts and were not allowed the privileges and status that the job accorded white men. During the first two decades of the second coming of African Americans in police work in the South, these restrictions limited their opportunities, but they did not keep them from making a place for themselves in the field of law enforcement.

Indeed, by the late 1940s and early 1950s, police chiefs throughout the South were praising the performance of black officers and emphasizing their impact on crime in African-American communities. In Summerton, South Carolina, for example, chief of police Travis Davis reported to the Southern Regional Council that black police had reduced crime in the city's black neighborhoods and decreased the number of "fights and fracases" that had occurred among blacks on Saturday nights. Davis also said that the two black police officers employed by Summerton, Dave Lawson and Ladson "Babe" Stukes, were successful in keeping peace in the town's black community because they "knew more about their people" than white officers and received "better cooperation." Davis's 1946 report was supported by another one year later from Greensboro, North Carolina. Officials in Greensboro had hired the city's first two African-American police officers in 1944 and were so satisfied with the success of the experiment that the city council authorized the addition of two more a year later. In 1953, after most southern cities had employed black police for several years, a survey of police chiefs in Florida, Georgia, Tennessee, Kentucky, Alabama, South Carolina, Virginia, and Texas revealed the ongoing success of the "Negro police experiment." All of the police chiefs in the survey had high praise for the performance of black officers. They lauded them for reducing crime and delinquency among African Americans, improving understanding and cooperation between black citizens and the police, and decreasing police indifference about crime among African Americans.[3]

Police chiefs in several southern cities supported their praise for the performance of African-American police officers with statistics documenting their impact on crime in black communities. In February 1945, six months after Miami's five-man, "negro police detail" went on duty, director of public safety Dan Rosenfeld reported that it had reduced crime in black neighborhoods by 25 percent. Two years later, Miami police chief Frank Mitchell credited the "negro police detail" with saving the city's public hospital some $50,000 a year because it prevented many of the physical injuries and homicides that had plagued the city's black districts. Mitchell also claimed that the detail, which had increased to eighteen men, had reduced black homicides by 60 percent. One year after the introduction of black police in Atlanta, police chief Herbert T. Jenkins cited similar statistics for that city's black officers, reporting that they had reduced crime among blacks by 50 percent. In 1955, one year after the employment of blacks as police officers in the former capital of the Confederacy, Montgomery, Alabama, police chief G. J. Ruppenthal echoed Jenkins's comments when he reported that in their first year of employment, African-American police officers had reduced black-on-black assaults by 15 to 25 percent and the number of black-on-black homicides from nineteen to thirteen. Similar statistical analyses were reported by other police chiefs in the South.[4]

In reality, however, the impact of African-American police officers on crime in black communities appears to have been as much symbolism as actual fact. The presence of black police seems to have increased the pride of African Americans in their communities and given them representation in their local governments for the first time since Reconstruction. There was some decrease in the number of petty crimes committed in black communities because black officers arrested suspects for crimes that white police had previously ignored. Black police also received more cooperation from black citizens than did white officers, which tended to help them solve more crimes than their white counterparts. But the overall impact of African-American police officers on black-on-black crime is hard to determine.

In Atlanta, for example, despite the contention by C. A. Scott of the *Atlanta Daily World* and other proponents of "Negro police for Negro communities" that the employment of black police would reduce the number of black-on-black homicides, it appears to have had a negligible impact. In the five years prior to the employment of black police in 1948, black-on-black murders averaged sixty-nine per year. In the five years after the employment of black police, black-on-black murders averaged eighty per year. Moreover, African Americans, who made up about 40 percent of the city's population, continued to commit a disproportionate number of murders. Nevertheless, Scott still extolled the performance of African-American police officers in reducing homicides. In 1950, for example, he praised them for capturing blacks who murdered other blacks—something white police had never made a serious effort to do.[5]

Overall, the "Negro police experiment" in the South was successful. In fact, both police officials and African-American leaders attempted to guarantee its success by hiring the best black candidates and by monitoring their performance closely. Thus, it is not surprising that the first African Americans appointed in several southern cities had attended college. In Atlanta, for example, four of the first eight appointees—Dixon, Jones, Lyons, and Elkins—had gone to Morehouse College, with Dixon and Elkins eventually graduating. In Dallas, the first two appointees, Lee Brotherton and Benjamin Thomas, were both college graduates. In Greensboro, North Carolina, all six of the first African Americans hired in 1944–45 as police officers had attended college. Moreover, the employment of black police in Greensboro epitomized the care taken and the higher standards used across the South to select the first black officers. When the city council authorized the appointment of African Americans to the city police force, black community leaders were called and consulted on selecting the "best men" for the job. With the assistance of Greensboro's black community leaders, the city manager and police chief then selected the candidates for the city's first African-American police officers. Similar selection procedures were used in Atlanta, Charleston, Miami, Little Rock, Charlotte, North Carolina, and other southern cities in order to select the most capable and qualified members of the black community for police jobs. As a result, the first black police officers in the postwar South tended to be "more qualified" than their white counterparts, or at least better educated.[6]

The performance of African-American police officers was also closely monitored. Usually a white sergeant, lieutenant, or even a captain was selected to command the "negro police detail" in southern cities and to provide black officers close supervision. In Miami, Detective Marion E. Crane commanded the black police detail. In Atlanta, Lieutenant E. B. Brooks handled the supervision of black police officers. In Dallas, Sergeant Edward Preston trained and supervised the "Negro Squad." In New Orleans, Captain William Walker commanded the first black officers on the police force. Similar arrangements existed in other southern cities to ensure close supervision of black police officers and to prevent them from making mistakes—especially in their contacts with white citizens.[7]

This close supervision had a negative side. Those officers who did make mistakes—by committing rules infractions or by arresting whites—were usually dismissed immediately from the police force without the hearings accorded white officers. In Dallas, for example, only ten months after he went on duty, police officer Lee Brotherton was dismissed without a hearing for not turning in stolen property taken from a burglar. Although a citizens' group petitioned to have him reinstated, the city manager upheld his dismissal. Brotherton's experience was repeated in several other southern cities. In 1952, officers Gentry Bledsoe and Otto Willis were dismissed from the Nashville police force and sentenced to a year in jail after they were convicted of illegally entering the homes of several black citizens to force them to pay their bills. In the same year, the Morgantown, North Carolina, town board dismissed Avery Michaux and Forest Fleming from the police force because black residents had filed numerous complaints against them for abusive behavior. In effect, this ended the "Negro police experiment" in Morgantown. By 1959, all five of the African-American police officers that the city of Montgomery, Alabama, had hired in 1954 had left the force either voluntarily or involuntarily. Officers Arthur G. Worthy and Walter L. Jarrett resigned to take better jobs; officers W. C. Miller, Lee E. Jarrett, and C. L. Prather were dismissed for rules infractions such as being late, bad debts, and conduct unbecoming an officer. As a result, the Montgomery police force was again all-white, and the city commission stated that it would not hire any more black officers.[8]

Of course, African-American police officers were under such close scrutiny because their superiors wanted to ensure that they did not commit the most serious offense that a black officer could commit in the South: arresting a white citizen.[9] Two cases illustrate the seriousness of this prohibition. In September 1948, less than six months after Vernell E. Fuller became one of Houston's thirteen new black police officers, he was forced to resign from the department for arresting a white citizen for speeding on his beat. He complained publicly that his sergeant had threatened "all colored officers with immediate dismissal" if they arrested whites. Finding the situation intolerable, Fuller submitted his letter of resignation, which stated:

> This policy means that white people can walk around on your beat and deliberately violate the laws without being apprehended unless a white officer is on the scene. It means that the colored population in time will become indignant of half authorized colored policemen. It means that there are more people who are immune to arrest that the constitution stipulates. And last it means that I cannot pursue my duties as a law enforcement officer knowing that certain limitations are placed upon me.

Fuller was allowed to resign voluntarily; a black officer who committed the same infraction in Washington, D.C., was not as lucky. Although African Americans had served on the metropolitan police force in the city prior to the "second coming" of black police in the South, many of the policies that regulated and restricted their performance were virtually the same as those in the "Deep South" cities. In March 1953, black policeman Norman Allison arrested a white woman for committing a traffic violation. When he presented her at the police station for booking, his captain reprimanded him and told him that he had "no business locking up a white woman." The captain released the woman and suspended Allison from the police force on charges. Allison never returned to duty.[10]

Fortunately for them, not many African-American police officers violated the racial proscriptions that limited their powers. The cases of Fuller and Allison were the exceptions; most black officers in the South understood their "place" and stayed in it. Moreover, the "separate and unequal" policies implemented to facilitate the employment of African-American police in the South usually ensured that these men would not make major mistakes and foment racial discord. This was achieved primarily by restricting black police officers to separate beats, shifts, and facilities.

In Atlanta, black police patrolled during a "black watch" from 6:00 p.m. to 2:00 a.m., in a restricted area centered in the Auburn Avenue black community. Black police in Houston patrolled "black beats" in the city's Third, Fourth, and Fifth wards. A similar combination of a "black beat" and "black watch" formed the police experience of the first African-American policemen in Dallas. These separate beats and watches were accompanied by separate facilities for black officers. In Atlanta, African-American police officers dressed and had roll call at the Butler Street YMCA; they were not allowed to wear their uniforms to and from work. Dallas's black officers met for duty at an office at Roseland Homes, an all-black housing project located just east of their beat in the State-Thomas area. Savannah's black police officers met in a separate "Negro substation" for the first few years that the city employed them. In 1950, the Savannah department moved them to police headquarters and designated a separate area on the second floor for them to assemble before going on duty. Just as in Atlanta, Savannah's black police officers could not wear their uniforms home or appear in them in court. Nashville's African-American officers were allowed to use the regular police station, but they reported to duty one-half hour after the regular roll call. Black police in Montgomery, Alabama, were not as lucky; they had to dress at home and then pick up their equipment at the back door of the police station.[11]

Nowhere in the South, however, was the second-class status of African-American police officers carried to the same extreme as in the city of Miami, Florida. In Miami, law enforcement for African Americans became truly "separate and unequal," and black police officers became an integral part of the city's separate justice system. In 1950, city officials built a black police station and appointed a black judge and bailiff to administer a "black-only" court. Miami's "Negro police station and court" became the only one of its kind in the South.

The "Negro police station and court" epitomized both the best and the worst features of the "separate and unequal" law enforcement accorded African Americans in the South. The status of black police officers in Miami was both enhanced and adversely affected by the resulting dual law enforcement system. On the positive side, during the fourteen-year existence of the "Negro police station and court," the city of Miami employed more black police officers than any other city in the South. On the negative side, the separative policies that the system legitimized established a legacy of inequality that adversely affected the city's African-American police officers long after they were integrated into the regular police force.

Miami's "Negro police station and court" emerged from the same brutal and inequitable law enforcement policies that were endemic to most cities in the South. From the founding of the city in South Florida in 1896, a substantial black population inhabited Miami—ranging from 25 to 40 percent of the population from that date to 1940. Just as in most American cities in the early twentieth century, African Americans were confined to a segregated section of the city called "Colored Town," and white violence and terrorism were used to ensure that they did not encroach on white neighborhoods or threaten the city's white population. Two race riots in 1911 and 1915 in which whites carried out mob actions against Colored Town set a violent tone for race relations in the city. Miami's all-white police force exacerbated this situation. By the 1920s, the police force had established a pattern of violence and abuse against black citizens characterized by police shootings of black citizens and disproportionate arrests of blacks for minor or trumped-up offenses. At the same time, the Miami police winked at and allowed vice crimes such as prostitution and gambling to flourish in Colored Town.[12]

The brutality of the police and white terrorism motivated the citizens of Colored Town as early as 1903 to ask for black police officers and better law enforcement to eliminate the vice in their community. In 1913, both the Civic League of Colored Town and its white counterpart, the Civic League of Miami, urged the police to crack down and arrest violators of vice laws in Colored Town. The police acted on this request for a short period of time, but soon reverted to their previous complicity with the prostitutes, gamblers, and bootleggers. Black citizens made another request for black police officers in 1920, but the police chief rejected the idea. Meanwhile, police violence and white terrorism against blacks continued unabated. In 1924, 1926, and 1928, violence on the part of police officers precipitated three more incidents of racial violence. These incidents and the accompanying lackadaisical law enforcement and police brutality fostered a hostile and violent relationship between blacks and the police in Miami.[13]

The request by African-American citizens for better law enforcement in Colored Town was ignored until blacks in Miami were able to influence city politics. By 1940, the black population of Miami numbered about 40,000. This population growth and the repeal of the poll tax in Florida in 1938 encouraged more African Americans in the city to register to vote. As a result, the number of registered black voters increased from 590 in 1936 to 2,376 in 1938, and to 7,307 in 1944. Despite efforts by the Ku Klux Klan to intimidate blacks and scare them away from the polls, African-American voters helped to determine the outcome of the 1939 city election. By 1944, African Americans had founded a local chapter of the Progressive Voters League to organize the black electorate, and to force white politicians in Miami to be more responsive to blacks' demands for better law enforcement.[14]

Also in 1944, the first five blacks were appointed to the Miami police force. After consultation with black community leaders, city leaders received fifteen names, from which they selected five police candidates. Ralph White, John Milledge, Clyde Lee, "Tops" Kimble, and Moody Hall were trained in secret for six weeks, and were introduced as Miami's first black officers on September 1, 1944.

As in other parts of the South, Miami's black police officers were restricted to patrolling black communities, assigned to a special "black watch" from 6:00 p.m. to 2:00 a.m., and prohibited from arresting white offenders. Initially, the five officers were headquartered at the office of an African-American doctor, Dr. Ira P. Davis, at 1036 Northwest 2nd Avenue in the heart of a major black area. Black police dressed at Dr. Davis's office because they were not allowed to wear their uniforms to and from work. In addition, black officers were separated from white officers by different job titles and uniforms. Black police were called "patrolmen," while white police were "policemen." White officers wore regulation white shirts; black officers wore black shirts. City and police officials wanted to make it clear to the public as well as to black police officers themselves that they were not equal to white officers in authority or prestige.[15]

Despite the separate titles and racially based assignments, African-American police officers soon proved their value by policing Miami's black community very effectively. Within one year, Miami's "negro police detail," lauded as one of the most effective in the South, had made 4,326 arrests which resulted in fines of $56,321. As a result of this success, city officials increased the detail from five officers in 1944 to fifteen in 1945, nineteen in 1946, thirty in 1949, and forty-one by 1950. The city of Miami also granted the "negro police detail" civil service status in 1947 with all of the benefits that such status provided city employees, with the exception of equality with white officers. The success and growth of Miami's "negro police detail" served as a model for other police forces in the South, and Miami police chief Walter Headley willingly extolled its success in a national police publication.[16]

The stage was now set for the city's next innovation in "separate and unequal" law enforcement: the "Negro police station and court." Miami city commissioner H. Leslie Quigg first proposed the building of a separate facility to house black officers in 1948. A year later, the city advertised for bids on a "colored police precinct station" to be built at Northwest 11th Street and 5th Avenue. The $60,000 building was completed and opened for service in May 1950. It housed the Negro police headquarters, detention cells, and space for a branch of the city court. The city appointed attorney Lawson E. Thomas as municipal court judge to preside over the black court. Judge Thomas was assisted by a black prosecutor and a black bailiff.[17]

From its inception, Miami's "Negro police station and court" was hailed throughout the South as an exciting innovation. Miami city officials received praise for the idea from as far away as Jackson, Mississippi, and Dallas, Texas. Police chiefs from other southern cities visited Miami to study the effectiveness of the city's experiment of using black officers exclusively to police black communities. Members of Miami's African-American community also praised and supported the innovation because it provided them not only the opportunity for "self-government," but also a fairer administration of criminal justice. Miami minister John E. Culmer, for example, stated that the all-black court was more capable of judging black lawbreakers because Judge Thomas treated crimes in the black community the same way white judges treated crimes in the white community. The Reverend Culmer said that white judges usually treated black-on-black crime as a joke and were more lenient with black offenders. (No black citizen had received capital punishment for killing another black citizen since 1937!) According to Culmer, the new all-black court replaced the unfairness, contempt, and indifference of the white judicial system with fair trials and respect for law enforcement.[18]

In its first year, the court handled 6,374 cases and collected more than $60,000 in fines and forfeitures. Beyond these statistics, the law enforcement standards established by black police working in the station and the unbiased justice administered by the all-black court improved the respect of African Americans in Miami for the law. In 1955, the number of black police serving the Negro police station had increased to 60 (out of a total of 380 police officers in Miami). No other city in the South even came close to having such a large number of African Americans on its police force. By 1960, there were 71 officers on Miami's "negro police detail," and 4 of them had earned promotions to sergeant. Miami was one of the first southern cities to promote African Americans to the sergeant's position. (See tables 8 and 9.) Thus, the "Negro police station and court" was deemed a success by many just because the city of Miami was willing to hire a substantial number of African Americans to staff it. No other city in the South could match the "opportunities" that the separate police station provided blacks for participation in law enforcement.[19]

Nevertheless, the black police experience in Miami was still beset with the problems that a "separate and unequal," dual justice system embodied. Two of those problems were related to the selection and training of African-American police candidates. After the first five, no other black officers received formal police training for fifteen years. Only two or three vacancies occurred periodically in the "negro police detail"—not enough to start separate training classes at the academy for black recruits. Segregation, of course, prohibited black recruits from attending police training classes with white recruits. Thus, African-American rookies were placed with veteran officers to receive their training "on the streets." Some officers also were hired without the minimum educational requirement, which was a high school diploma. Miami police officials deviated from the standards established in other parts of the South, where black candidates were often "overqualified" for police jobs; they adopted "lower standards" for African-American officers. They seem to have believed that police work in black communities required less-qualified officers than those who worked in the city's white communities.

Police officials also believed that since many African Americans in Miami had not earned high school diplomas, they would not be able to fill vacancies in the "negro police detail" if they required black police to meet the same minimum standards and pass the same qualifying exam as white officers. Thus, by 1955, when black leaders requested that black police meet the same standards as white police, the police department began to encounter problems filling the vacancies on its "negro police detail." The detail reached its authorized strength of eighty-five in 1959, but thereafter the number of black police in the city began to decline, partly because of the integration of black officers into the regular force and the requirement that all officers pass the same entry examination. The decline of black police in Miami continued even after the department implemented an active recruitment campaign in 1968.[20]

African-American police officers in Miami also had to confront the problem of vice in the black community. Early in their experience, black officers learned that they were not supposed to arrest certain individuals in the community linked with gambling—lest they provoke the ire of certain white officers who were linked to the vice in the area and who did not respect the authority of black law enforcement officers. Illegal gambling had long existed in Miami's black community. In 1948, for example, C. O. Huttoe, a white officer, was suspended from the police force for his alleged complicity with the gambling racket there. The *Miami Herald* also reported that Huttoe controlled the employment of blacks on the "negro police detail" by requiring prospective applicants to secure the approval of Ellis "Preacher" Lindsey, a leader of the gambling operation in the black community. After a hearing, the charges against Huttoe were dropped, and he was reinstated on the police force. It appears, however, that the gambling racket continued to exist with police complicity. Twelve years after the Huttoe incident, the *Miami News* reported that a grand jury had found that black police were afraid to arrest gamblers in their district for fear of receiving bad assignments. Mayor Robert High charged that Miami police officers were collecting $10,000 a week, 10 percent of the weekly take from the numbers racket in the city's black community. Mayor High received this information from black patrolmen who feared reprisals from their superiors for reporting the police payoffs. Police chief Walter Headley denied that black police were subject to harassment if they arrested gamblers, and maintained that his officers were doing their best to eradicate vice throughout the city. Moreover, he blamed the NAACP for the charges and stated that the "troublemaking organization" was just trying to get promotions for blacks on the police force. Despite Headley's reassurance and his blaming of the NAACP for the gambling charges, the unequal status of black police in relation to white officers clearly placed the former in an untenable position if they attempted to eradicate the vice allowed to exist in Miami's black community.[21]

The problems inherent in Miami's "separate and unequal" justice system eventually forced the city to upgrade the status of blacks on the police force. Several Miami black community leaders, such as Garth Reeves of the *Miami Times* newspaper and the Reverend Theodore Gibson, provided the impetus for the reforms. When black Miamians began in 1955 to agitate for equal standards and status for the city's African-American police officers, they wanted black officers trained in the same manner as white officers so that the most "poorly trained officers" were not assigned to the section of the city "where good policing was most needed." In the same year, sixty black officers demanded the opportunity to take the competitive examination for promotion to sergeant. The department denied their request, so the officers sued under the auspices of their police association, the Miami Colored Police Benevolent Association. After losing the lawsuit, the department relented and administered a separate exam designed specifically for black candidates seeking promotion to sergeant. Officers Leroy Smith and Louis Duty earned promotions in 1955, and officers Jesse Nash and Lury Bowen in 1957.

Five years after this suit was filed, the department finally allowed a black recruit to attend the Miami police academy. Clarence Dickson, who in 1985 would become Miami's first African-American police chief, completed the training program with a class of white recruits. Dickson's attendance at the academy coincided with the decision by city officials to upgrade the "negro police detail." Separate titles for black and white police officers were dropped, and African-American police officers were granted the right to arrest white offenders "with the assistance of white officers." Despite these reforms, the "Negro police station and court" remained open and staffed by black officers.[22]

The impetus to close the separate facilities came from an outside source. In 1962, the International Association of Chiefs of Police (IACP) Field Services Division conducted a management survey of the Miami police department. In its final report, the IACP survey team noted that the department provided inadequate supervision to its "negro precinct" (the findings were similar for the central police headquarters). The black police precinct had a supervision ratio of only 1 sergeant per 12.5 patrol officers, and the IACP recommended a ratio of 1 supervisor per 6 patrol officers. Concern was also expressed about the inefficiency and costs of maintaining a separate police station for black officers only eleven blocks from the central police station, and at a cost of some $45,000 a year. The IACP survey team made a halfhearted recommendation that the city close the black precinct for more efficient management of the force and to save money. Nevertheless, the team recognized the "sociological implications" of such a move and its potential for "damage to the morale" of the department, and stopped short of strongly recommending the closing. Instead, it stated that closing the precinct would not benefit the department and recommended the continued segregation of black police officers (allegedly because of their lack of police training) in the "negro precinct" until they could be "gradually" consolidated into the overall patrol operation.[23]

Although it was duplicitous, the IACP survey embarrassed Miami city officials. Following the survey, city manager Melvin Reese suggested that the city abolish the Negro precinct. In his budget proposals for 1963, Reese removed the expenditures for the precinct, and the city commission concurred with his suggestion by approving a city budget that did not fund it. In June 1962, Chief Headley took the first step to integrate black police officers into the regular force by assigning some of them to other parts of the city outside the black community. Finally, in July 1963, the city of Miami abolished the black police precinct and "integrated" its seventy-nine officers into the central police station. This ended Miami's unique version of "separate and unequal" law enforcement for African Americans. For the city's black officers, it was only one more stride forward in their quest for equality in the Miami police department.[24]

Miami's decision to abolish its "Negro police station and court" coincided with movements in other parts of the South to upgrade the status of African-American police officers. After nearly twenty years of black police employment in the South, many cities were under pressure from black citizens to end the "separate and unequal" status of blacks in law enforcement. This movement had an ironic twist. While black police advocates in the 1930s and 1940s had pressured southern officials for the appointment of black officers and accepted a second-class status that restricted them to "black beats," denied them the authority to arrest whites, and limited their opportunities for promotion, by the late 1950s this status was being blamed for the continuance of crime among African Americans and for the disrespect that some of them still had for law enforcement. Some African Americans cited "half-authorized," "unequal," and "second-class" black police officers as the new symbol of the segregation and discrimination that impeded black citizenship rights in the South. Many also believed that only when black officers received the full authority to enforce the law and arrest all lawbreakers would they gain respect and foster respect for the law among black citizens.

Even in Houston, Texas, where African Americans had retained police jobs even after Redemption, and where since 1870 at least one black police officer had served on the city force, the status of African-American police officers was no different from that of black police in other cities. That is, black police in Houston were second-class officers assigned to police only blacks, work in black communities, and stay "in their place." In contrast to Miami, where between 1945 and 1955 the number of black police officers had grown rapidly, the number of black police officers in Houston had increased very slowly in eighty years. Only thirty-nine African Americans served on that city's police force by 1960. Moreover, during that long period none had earned promotion above patrolman, and their continuing lower status had become an affront to black Houstonians.[25]

In 1961, Texas Southern University sociologist Henry Bullock blamed part of the homicide problem among black Houstonians on the second-class and segregated status of the city's black police officers. Bullock chaired Mayor Lewis Cutrer's Negro Law Enforcement Committee and reported on the factors that he believed caused the city's disproportionate black-on-black homicide rate. (Houston had 689 homicides in the period 1955–1960, and 70 percent of them were black-on-black.) Bullock maintained that only "fully authorized" black police officers—with the authority to patrol all areas of Houston and arrest all offenders without regard to race—would end the disrespect that black Houstonians had for the city's dual law enforcement system. In his report, he cited the following comment from a black Houstonian as "typical" of the negative attitude that some African Americans had toward black police:

> The Negro policeman is what I call a figure-head—a man wearing a suit. One-half of the policeman so to speak. I have never been hit by a white cop, only a Negro. A Negro is nothing but a snitch. He can't arrest anyone, he holds [you] until the white officer gets there to arrest you. The white policemen don't respect them. I have heard a white policeman call a Negro policeman a "nigger."

According to Bullock, comments such as this one represented an attitude and a belief among Houston's African Americans that black police were just part of a law enforcement system designed to harass and abuse black citizens. Thus, Bullock concluded that, in a sense, the police caused the murder and crime problems in the black community with their selective enforcement of the law and criminal harassment of black citizens. African-American police officers symbolized and epitomized the duality of criminal justice in Houston because they could not arrest whites and had less authority than white police officers.[26]

Since the second-class status of black police officers in Houston was part of the crime problem, Bullock believed that upgrading their status was part of the solution. His 1961 report recommended that not only should Houston's black police officers be fully authorized, but they also should be integrated into all divisions of the police department. According to Bullock, these measures would indicate to members of the black community that black police were "problem-solvers and protectors," just as white officers were in the white community. Bullock concluded that even a symbolic gesture—such as the assignment of an African-American officer as a traffic officer in downtown Houston—would "echo in the various Negro communities like Gabriel's trumpet, and Negroes would answer the call of law enforcement with Christian zeal [because] this would be the symbol of the equality of the Negro policeman under the badge and under the uniform."[27]

The Houston Police Department did not act on Bullock's recommendations. African-American police in Houston remained second-class officers assigned to the city's black neighborhoods. Moreover, even after Bullock's report, the Houston Police Department continued to assign its black officers the worst patrol cars and badge numbers that distinguished them from white officers (all black police officers were assigned badge numbers that contained a 7). Although Mayor Cutrer opened the police station cafeteria to black officers in 1961, the department did not integrate patrol assignments—allowing black officers to serve with white officers—until 1969.[28]

The second-class status of Houston's black police reflected the experiences of African-American officers across the South. In 1959, a survey found that few southern cities had increased the authority of black police officers or made them equal to white officers. The survey, conducted by sociologist Elliott Rudwick under the auspices of the Southern Regional Council and published in 1962, found that the lot of African-American police officers had changed very little since most southern cities began the "experiment" in the 1940s. Most black officers in the South still patrolled black communities and neighborhoods exclusively (83 percent of the cities in the survey relegated black police to segregated districts), and only three cities—Louisville, Durham, and Daytona Beach—had black police officers with ranks above sergeant. The most glaring aspect of the unequal status of African-American police officers was their lack of power to arrest white offenders: Rudwick found that this authority was granted by only one-third of the 130 police departments that responded to his survey. For instance, in the Deep South, African-American police officers could not arrest white offenders in Georgia, Louisiana (except in New Orleans), Mississippi, Alabama, and Arkansas. They were required to hold them until white officers arrived—sixty-five departments (including Houston, Atlanta, Miami, and Nashville) handled the arrests of white offenders in this manner. The remaining departments gave no information (thus the actual percentage may have been even higher), or they stated that the policy varied depending on the circumstance and severity of the crime committed by the white offender.[29]

Ironically, the publication of the findings of Rudwick's survey coincided with an announcement by Atlanta city officials that Chief Herbert Jenkins had recommended the removal of all restrictions on the city's African-American police officers. The council's police committee deliberated and debated the issue for five months from January to May 1962, finally deciding that Atlanta's black officers had "proved their worth" and agreeing to the recommendation. Thus, Atlanta became the first city (with the exception of New Orleans) in the Deep South to grant its black police full authority. Not only could they arrest white offenders, they also became eligible for promotions above the sergeant level. Accordingly, Howard Baugh, who in 1961 became the department's first African-American police sergeant, was promoted to lieutenant and assigned as commander of the 6:00 p.m. uniformed patrol.[30]

Other cities in the South followed suit. One year after black police in Atlanta achieved full authorization, Miami's segregated African-American police detail was upgraded. By the mid-1960s, several southern departments—including Memphis, Dallas, Knoxville, and Mobile—had also taken steps to upgrade their "negro police details." Still, the pattern of relegating black police officers to second-class status continued. In Atlanta, Miami, and Dallas, for example, throughout the 1960s black police officers continued to work on "black beats," to supervise only other black officers, and to be excluded from elite squads and divisions in the police department such as traffic, homicide, and inspection. Merit promotions also eluded them. In short, the policy of upgrading black officers in the South in the 1960s raised them only to the token status that their counterparts in the North had achieved.[31]

By the 1960s, African-American citizens began to challenge the second-class status of black police officers in the South and throughout the nation. The issue became part of the national civil rights movement. African-American citizens not only campaigned to upgrade the status of black police officers, they also attempted to increase their numbers and to have more of them assigned to the nation's black communities.

The campaign was soon joined by black police officers themselves. In cities such as Miami and Houston, where the worst effects of segregation and "separate and unequal" law enforcement were felt, black officers began to file suits to win promotions, back pay, and equality as police officers. Many of them organized associations to help them in their struggle. By the mid-1960s, black police associations became the most important vehicles for improving the status of African-American police officers not only in the South but also throughout the nation.

SIX

THE RISE OF BLACK POLICE UNIONISM

As the "second wave of police reform" got underway, African-American police officers throughout the nation remained in essentially token positions. While the South perpetrated the worst of the racial proscriptions on their police powers, black officers in northern cities also faced a legacy of discrimination in their assignments and in their exclusion from promotion to command positions. The leaders of American police reform—such as Bruce Smith, August Vollmer of Berkeley, and Herbert T. Jenkins of Atlanta—may have addressed problems such as removing the police from politics and upgrading professional standards for police officers, but they did not address the continuing color line in the profession.[1] This was a task that African-American police officers had to undertake themselves by organizing unions.

As members of two subgroups in American society, black police officers often had no choice but to associate and socialize with each other. In fact, older African-American officers were usually required to teach newly appointed black officers "the ropes" of the police profession and instill in them the techniques of negotiating a racially biased, dual law enforcement system. The camaraderie that developed among black police who faced the racial proscriptions of their job led them to organize.[2]

In February 1924, the twenty African-American police officers employed by the St. Louis Police Department applied for membership in the St. Louis Police Relief Association. The Relief Association was the rank-and-file organization that raised money to support pensions and benefits for retired policemen and their widows. At first, the association rejected the applications of the black officers. Then the Executive Committee sent them altered applications that would have required them to relinquish their right to vote and participate in the association's affairs.[3]

After receiving the altered application, Sergeant Ira L. Cooper wrote a reply to the Relief Association on behalf of all the African-American officers on the force. In his letter, Cooper—the department's most famous detective and its first black detective sergeant and lieutenant—rejected the offer of membership on a nonvoting basis and challenged the association's decision by pointing out that an organization of fourteen hundred white men did not need to fear *twenty* African

Americans "rising to a point of supremacy" in it. Apparently, Cooper's letter had its desired effect. The Executive Committee of the Relief Association voted in July 1924 to accept African-American police officers as members without any restriction on their voting rights.[4]

The success achieved in St. Louis was an exceptional case. In nearly all cities, the racial proscriptions that limited the job opportunities of African-American officers also limited their participation in rank-and-file fraternal and benevolent associations. This was especially true in the South, where racial segregation raised an additional barrier to prevent black officers from joining the regular police rank-and-file organizations. It was no coincidence that separate African-American police organizations emerged first in the South.[5]

In 1935, the six African Americans on Houston's police force organized the Texas Negro Peace Officers' Association (TNPOA), the first formal police association organized by black police officers in the United States. Houston's "negro police detail" had laid the groundwork for the association the year before, when its members decided to hold a black-only "police ball" to raise funds for a police officers' retirement and burial fund. The fund benefited all Houston police officers, but black officers had to raise their contribution to it through a separate ball. At the first ball, the Houston "negro police detail" invited African-American police officers from other forces in South Texas. These officers from Beaumont, Galveston, and San Antonio returned for the second ball in 1935 and at that time joined with the Houston "negro police detail" to found the Texas Negro Peace Officers' Association.[6]

In its formative years, the TNPOA served primarily as a social and fraternal organization. African-American police officers in South Texas visited each other for social events such as the police balls and also for the simple camaraderie that the departmental proscriptions precluded them from enjoying. One of the charter members of the TNPOA, retired Galveston police officer Leroy "Buster" Landrum, related that initially the members of the TNPOA were just a group of guys who came together to socialize and share their common bond as police officers. None of them realized at the time that they were laying the groundwork for the African-American police union movement in the United States.[7]

As the TNPOA developed, its objectives expanded to include ways to increase the number of African-American police officers in Texas. This goal became part of the association's mission when members attended the Negro Day celebration in Dallas as part of the 1936 Texas Centennial Exposition. Black civic leaders in the city such as A. Maceo Smith had been petitioning and agitating for years for black police officers to patrol their communities, but to no avail. In October 1936, Smith and leaders of the Dallas Negro Chamber of Commerce invited members of the TNPOA to Dallas to lead the Negro Day parade in order to showcase for the police chief and city government the professionalism and *esprit de corps* of African-American police officers. This was the "coming out party" for the TNPOA. Neither blacks nor whites in Dallas had ever seen black police officers in "full uniform, with badges, and side arms." The editors of the *Dallas Express* called the TNPOA's appearance "one of the most thrilling features of the parade." Nevertheless, the appearance of the TNPOA in Dallas did not help blacks to win permanent positions on the police force. No further action was taken in this regard. In 1937 and 1938, members of the association returned to Dallas for the Negro Day parades with the same objective of promoting the appointment of African Americans to the Dallas police force. On neither occasion, however, did their presence lead to the achievement of their goal.[8]

The TNPOA also worked to improve the status of African-American officers already in police forces in Texas and in the South generally. Members sought to achieve this objective in several ways. First, they held annual conventions featuring the latest topics in police science in order to improve the professionalism of black officers. Second, they moved their conventions around to different Texas cities in order to introduce themselves to police chiefs throughout the state; one reason they did this was so that the chiefs could intervene on their behalf, for African-Americans officers often had embarrassing and demeaning confrontations with white police officers who harassed black policemen when they traveled outside their jurisdictions and carried their firearms. Third, the TNPOA attempted to organize a regional "Negro Police Association," first in Texas and Oklahoma and then throughout the South, to unite all African-American police officers in the cause of raising their status.[9]

Significantly, the TNPOA succeeded only in those objectives that did not challenge the existing status quo of African-American police officers in the 1930s and 1940s. At their annual conventions, TNPOA members succeeded in securing the support of police chiefs throughout the state of Texas for their separate rank-and-file organization. While the contact with Texas police chiefs did serve to protect the association members' limited police powers and to reduce their confrontations with white officers, these advances did not change the racial proscriptions on African-American police. Moreover, TNPOA members failed in their efforts to form a regional or southern Negro police association. Although they had some apparent early success, forming in 1937 the "Texas and Oklahoma Association of Negro Peace Officers," this organization passed out of existence within two years.[10]

The TNPOA became the model for similar organizations that emerged in Florida, Oklahoma, Louisiana, and other parts of the country in the 1940s and 1950s. African-American officers in Miami founded the second of the early black police associations in an effort to solve virtually the same problems that their counterparts had confronted in Houston. After blacks were allowed to join the Miami police force in 1944, they found that the department's Police Benevolent Association would not accept them for membership.[11] As in Houston, African-American officers had to form their own social and benevolent organization. In 1946, they established the Miami Colored Police Benevolent Association (MCPBA). Ralph White, one of Miami's first five black police officers and a charter member of the MCPBA, described how and why the organization formed:

> When Isaac Davis joined [the department], he became interested in uniting black officers—trying to make improvements for black officers. So then we decided to have a meeting to organize. So we did, and he [Davis] was the first president of

> the black PBA. We had quite a bit of opposition. Our supervisors gave us a hard time when they learned that we had met to organize an organization. But the community got behind it, and we were able to continue to grow. The purpose was to help train black policemen and to bring about a better relation between the community and the policeman, and also the department.[12]

The MCPBA immediately became important to African-American police officers in Miami in their fight to end segregation within the police department. Unlike the TNPOA in Texas, the MCPBA did not attempt to work with white police administrators or the white rank-and-file police association as a response to the problem of internal discrimination. The problems of African-American police officers in Miami represented the nadir of the South's dual law enforcement system. African-American police officers had their own separate police station complete with an African-American bailiff and judge presiding over a black-only court; they were designated as "patrolmen" instead of as police officers; they had no opportunity for promotion or advancement; and they received no formal training before being assigned to duty.[13] Such conditions forced the MCPBA's leaders to adopt a confrontational approach from the start. As early as 1950, they challenged the officers' status as "patrolmen"; they sought to become "police officers" like white members of the police force. In 1955, the MCPBA challenged its members' exclusion from promotional opportunities and forced the Miami Police Department to make what at that time was a major concession: separate promotional exams for African-American police officers. The association then filed one of the earliest racial discrimination civil rights suits against a police department.[14]

In addition to its activist political role, the MCPBA served as a social outlet for the African-American members on the Miami police force. Like the TNPOA, the MCPBA sponsored balls, dances, and fundraisers for its members. For Miami's African-American police officers, who in their separate police station were isolated from the force's white officers, the association provided a much-needed social and fraternal respite. Like the TNPOA, the MCPBA also became an important model for later African-American police associations.[15]

In the South, African-American police officers created these early associations in Houston and Miami both to meet their fraternal needs and to protect their limited police powers. In the case of the MCPBA, its members also hoped to challenge and end the stifling racial policies in their police department, policies which limited them to assignments on "negro police details" and to "Negro police beats." The hostile, segregated environment, both public and professional, in which the lower South's two largest African-American police forces worked had forced them to organize. They had few other options.[16]

In the northern cities, the earliest black police organizations formed for reasons similar to those in Miami and Houston. The environment in which such organizations developed, however, was different. Black police had served continuously on the police forces in most major cities in the North since the beginning of the twentieth century. While they were essentially, and politically, "token" officers, their tenure in their respective departments had allowed them to begin the process of challenging and eliminating many of the more rigid racial barriers that restricted the police powers of African-American police officers in the South. For instance, by the 1940s, black officers in most northern cities could and did arrest white offenders without the assistance of white police officers. They also had achieved some token promotional opportunities. Therefore, African-American police organizations in the North were not solely a response to the racism that black police officers confronted in their departments.[17]

In 1943, African-American police officers in New York City began efforts to organize the Guardians Association. Robert Mangum, a member of the police recruit class of 1942 and one of the founders of the Guardians, began recruiting African-American police officers in Harlem's 28th Precinct to start an organization that would "recognize the views and ideals of black policemen in New York City."[18] In the beginning, several factors inhibited the growth of the organization. First, African-American ranking officers in the police department refused to support it. Second, supervisors in the police department opposed the group so strongly that its members had to meet secretly at the Harlem YMCA. Third, World War II interrupted the initial organization of the Guardians; its leaders did not attempt to reorganize until after the war. Finally, after the association became public, some African-American politicians and police officials urged African-American police to abandon it, to stop "self-segregating" themselves, and to try to integrate organizations such as the department's Patrolmen's Benevolent Association.[19]

Despite all this opposition, the Guardians received its charter of organization from the city of New York in 1949. The group used the support of Harlem congressman Adam Clayton Powell to pressure the city for recognition. Members also argued, successfully, that other ethnic groups in the New City Police Department had fraternal organizations representing their interests and concerns.[20]

The Guardians Association soon became the representative organization for African Americans in the New York City Police Department. It did not have the same influence as some of the other ethnic groups in the department, but its members worked incessantly to obtain equal treatment for African Americans. The members of New York City's Guardians attempted to imitate the "hooking" system of the Irish and the "rabbi" network of the Jewish members of the police department, used by these two ethnic groups as a means of obtaining strategic supervisory positions in order to appoint or promote other members of their respective groups. Thus, when an Irish member of the police force had or knew of an opening, he would appoint or recommend another Irish officer for the position. In this manner, Irish (and Jewish) officers enhanced and solidified the position of their groups in the department.[21] The Irish and Jewish police officers had the numbers, and the presence of second- and third-generation police supervisors, to make these networks work effectively for them. The members of the Guardians, who were primarily first-generation police officers, attempted to establish such a future network by working to bring more African Americans into the police department. The Guardians established the "Dutch Uncle" program, in which a member adopted a young potential police recruit and encouraged him to pursue a police career. For the members of the Guardians, this meant spending time with young people in the community and involving themselves in community affairs in order to attract more young people to police work.[22]

Community involvement became the forte of the Guardians. In addition to their efforts to recruit more African-American police officers, they supported community protests against unfair law enforcement, acted as a clearinghouse for complaints against the police, and played a major role in trying to resolve the issues that led to the 1964 race riot in Harlem. Members also served as marshals and security for the 1963 March on Washington. In the scope of its work, the Guardians Association was one of the earliest African-American police associations to base its activities and concerns in the community rather than within the police department.[23]

The minor controversies over the organization of the Guardians Association and the MCPBA did not compare with the hostility that African-American police officers in Cleveland, Ohio, encountered when they established the Shield Club. In 1946, African-American police officer Lynn Coleman and his partner attempted to defend black and white members of the Congress of Racial Equality (CORE) who were integrating a public dance hall in an area in West Cleveland called Euclid Beach. Private guards hired by the dance hall beat and harassed CORE members and then turned on the two officers, shooting Coleman and severely beating his partner. Coleman was placed in a hospital in an all-white area of Cleveland. While there, he refused to surrender his gun to other Cleveland police officers because of his fear of reprisals from other officers as well as white citizens in the area. Finally, a white police captain forcibly disarmed Coleman (while Coleman was in his hospital bed) and called him a number of racial slurs. Coleman demanded and received a police guard outside his room until he was discharged. In a subsequent hearing, the Cleveland Police Department suspended Coleman from the police force for three months without pay on the charge of "conduct unbecoming an officer." The department did not prosecute his assailants.[24]

This incident in 1946, referred to as the Euclid Beach Incident, rallied the support of other African-American police officers for Coleman; they felt so strongly that they organized the Shield Club, both to support Coleman and to present their grievances to the Cleveland Police Department. Cleveland police officials did not respond to the grievances, nor did the department recognize the organization as the bargaining agent for African-American officers. The Shield Club violated the department's policy against police associations, and subsequently other members faced harassment from their supervisors for their participation in its formation.[25]

The Cleveland Police Department's insensitivity actually aided the growth of the Shield Club. The department's policy of nonrecognition, and its refusal to ameliorate the token status of its African-American officers, ensured the survival of the club, even after the furor over Euclid Beach ended. A martyr figure, Coleman became the central symbol in the movement to organize African-American police officers in Cleveland. The Shield Club subsequently became active in community service much as had the Guardians of New York. The organization sponsored trips to ball games for underprivileged youth and conducted food drives for needy families. It also intensified its efforts to recruit more African-American police officers. By the 1960s, with the election of Carl Stokes as the first black mayor of Cleveland, and because of a confrontation with the Cleveland chapter of the Fraternal Order of Police, the organization would find itself embroiled in controversy again.[26]

Early African-American police organizations—for example, the MCPBA, the Guardians, and the Shield Club—attempted to address the specific needs of African-American police officers. While the other rank-and-file organizations, such as the Fraternal Order of Police (FOP) and Patrolmen's Benevolent Association (PBA), were concerned with better working conditions, shorter hours, and better pay, black police organizations also confronted and tried to reform the heritage of discrimination against black officers, to end the quota system limiting the number of black police, and to provide more and real promotional opportunities for them.

In the 1940s and 1950s, the African-American police movements won minor victories. With the support of other organizations and groups in the black community (such as the NAACP and the black press), the organizations succeeded in removing some of the barriers in their departments which had limited their numbers and promotional opportunities. Partially as a result of the pressure from African-American police and their supporters, several major urban police departments took steps to integrate African Americans and to assign them to command positions. In 1955 in Miami, the MCPBA won the right for black police officers to take promotional exams. In 1959 in New York City, George Redding became the first black deputy police inspector. In Philadelphia, the end of the Republican machine's stranglehold over city politics in 1952 resulted in the implementation of a fairer police entry examination and the employment and promotion of more African-American officers.[27]

Not until the 1960s did the position of African-American police nationwide begin to improve substantially. Many departments inaugurated programs to recruit black officers in order to improve the image of the police department with black citizens and with white liberals. Most departments began to eliminate overt discrimination against African-American police officers. For example, the Miami Police Department closed its Negro police station in 1963, and the Atlanta department disbanded its "black police beat" in 1969. The departments in Detroit and Houston began to assign all police officers as partners without regard to race in 1959 and 1969, respectively. Police superintendent O. W. Wilson of Chicago and police director Dominic A. Spina of Newark also implemented important reforms to upgrade the status of black officers in their departments. During his eight years in Chicago (1960–1967), Wilson increased the number of African Americans on the police force by more than 50 percent, from approximately 700 to 1,200, and appointed fifty black sergeants and three black police captains. On a smaller scale than in Chicago, Spina in Newark in 1962 promoted ten African Americans to the rank of police sergeant. This reform was made in order to integrate blacks into all areas of his department. Spina also began the policy of pairing black and white officers ("salt and pepper teams") in patrol cars. Finally, police officials in Jackson, Mississippi, and in Birmingham, Alabama, made the

1960s truly a decade of progress for blacks in law enforcement by appointing the first African-American police officers in those two cities in 1963 and 1966, respectively. Concurrent with their stubbornness on black civil rights, city leaders and police administrators in those two cities had blocked the employment of black police for twenty years.[28]

An important reform was the assignment of African-American police officers as district or precinct commanders. The appointment of black captains represented a significant step toward eradicating the color line in police assignments. (See table 10.) In the early decades of the twentieth century, political bosses had controlled police captain appointments, reserving them for favored ethnic groups in the political machine. Captains controlled not only their districts but also the crime and graft (payoffs) occurring in the ward that encompassed their district or precinct (police district or precinct lines often paralleled ward lines). Before 1950, African Americans had participated in machine politics in every major American city, but they had achieved a police captaincy in only one: Chicago.[29]

By the 1950s and 1960s, when African-American officers began to assume police commands, such appointments no longer represented the same potential for political corruption and graft that they once had. Nevertheless, the appointment of African Americans as police captains represents a concession to blacks' control of the law enforcement in their own communities. In 1954, when James Reaves became the first black captain in Philadelphia, he commanded the 16th Precinct—one of the largest predominantly black precincts in the city. Similarly, when Eldridge Waith and Lloyd Sealy became the first black captains in New York City to command precincts in 1965, they were assigned to Harlem's 28th and 32nd precincts. Edward Williams became the first black captain in Newark in 1967; he also commanded a predominantly black precinct, the 4th. These appointments indicated that African Americans were overcoming the second-class or "token" status that had previously characterized their positions in American police departments.[30]

The status of African-American police officers changed because the status of all African Americans began to change in the 1950s and 1960s. Through the civil rights movement, blacks ended legal segregation in public accommodations, voting, education, employment, and housing. They achieved many of these gains through the courts, but nonviolent direct action also proved to be a viable tactic. In their numerous sit-ins, marches, wade-ins, and demonstrations, African Americans often confronted the police. In most cases, the police handled civil rights demonstrations without the use of force or loss of life. In others, however, they became essentially riot participants instead of forces to maintain order. In the 1960s riots, in particular, police action precipitated much of the resulting violence.[31]

African-American police officers found themselves caught in the middle of the 1960s civil rights movement. Their duty as police officers required them to perform the task of riot control. Riot duty often placed black police in the position of restraining or arresting other African Americans who were demonstrating for rights that would benefit the officers themselves. African-American police officers had to support other police officers in violent riot situations; this often meant violent, physical action against other African Americans. At the same time, black citizens called upon black police officers to protect them from some of the actions of their overzealous colleagues.[32]

In several situations during the turbulent civil rights era, African-American police had to choose sides. They either had to support the police department and other police officers against black citizens, or defend black citizens against police brutality and unbridled police power. In most cases, they chose the latter course.

In 1966, New York City established a civilian review board for the impartial review of citizens' complaints against the police. The board came under immediate attack from the Patrolmen's Benevolent Association. Believing that it would consist of citizens who were antagonistic to the police and who would make recommendations that would cause some officers to lose their jobs because of the possible use of excessive force when they apprehended a suspect, the PBA conducted a petition campaign to place a referendum on the civilian review board on the November ballot. At the same time, the association paid for an extensive advertising campaign which subtly implied that the review board would prevent the police from taking the necessary action to keep New York from being overrun by the so-called black and Puerto Rican "peril." In contrast to the PBA, the Guardians (the African-American police association) supported the idea of a civilian review board and criticized the PBA for using a racist advertising campaign in its effort to defeat the board. The PBA responded by charging that the members of the Guardians had placed "color ahead of their duty as police officers." In the November election, New York City voters supported the PBA and defeated the civilian review board referendum by an overwhelming majority.[33]

In Cleveland in 1968, a very serious controversy occurred that split African-American and white police officers. In the Glenville area of Cleveland, a shoot-out between police and "black militants" resulted in the deaths and wounding of several white police officers. In the tension-filled aftermath of the shoot-out, Mayor Carl Stokes felt forced to take an action that no other mayor had ever tried. In order to cool racial animosity, he removed all white police officers from the area and replaced them with one hundred African-American officers. Stokes's decision brought immediate reaction from many whites in Cleveland. The press and the business community, as well as other law enforcement agencies (such as the commander of the Ohio National Guard), criticized the mayor vehemently for "interfering with the police function" and "undermining police authority." Charges were made that he had "given in to black militants." White police officers in Cleveland considered African-American officers to be traitors to the profession for not refusing to work in the area in the "black-only" patrol. Nevertheless, Stokes defended his action as the only way to end violence in the area short of an armed assault by riot police. His plan worked: the African-American police patrolling the area did end the violence without taking a single life.[34]

These incidents in New York City and Cleveland clearly drew the racial line between black and white police officers. The line had always existed; the events of the 1960s only magnified it. Many African-American police officers became as radicalized as other groups in the United States, and they began to organize more aggressively to challenge the racial policies that most American police departments had failed to change. A new breed of African-American police officer emerged: one who spoke out against racism in the police department (thus breaking the traditional code of silence among police on such issues) and who adopted the methods, strategies, and tactics of the activists and so-called "black militants" in the African-American community.

Perhaps no organization represented the new breed of black police officers and their new militancy better than the Afro-American Patrolmen's League of Chicago. Organized in 1967 by five officers—Curtis Cowsen, Willie Ware, Frank Lee, Edward Palmer, and Renault Robinson—the AAPL broke with all of the traditions of previous police organizations.[35] It identified its roots and foundation in the African-American community; openly criticized the Chicago Police Department, other police organizations, and American society; and identified African-American police officers as the possible "missing link in the black struggle against oppression." The AAPL's organizational position statement clearly and powerfully identified its purpose:

> We are going to elevate the black policeman in the black community to the same image-status enjoyed by the white policeman in the white community; that is as a protector of citizenry and not as a brutal oppressor. We find it impossible to operate within the framework of existing police associations. For example, we disagree categorically with the position of the Fraternal Order of Police supporting "Stop and Frisk," and their position supporting the order to "shoot to kill" or maim looters during civil disorders. We will no longer permit ourselves to be relegated to the role of brutal pawns in a chess game affecting the communities we serve. We are husbands, fathers, brothers, neighbors, and members of the black community. Donning the blue uniform has not changed this. On the contrary, it has sharpened our perception of our responsibilities as black males in a society seemingly unresponsive to the needs of black people. We see our role as the role of a protector of this community and this is the role we intend to fulfill.[36]

The AAPL's first president, Renault Robinson, was a firm spokesman for the organization's stand against racism in American policing. In April 1971, Robinson appeared on the nationally syndicated "Phil Donahue Show" with several other African Americans to discuss the "problems of black America." Of all the guests on the show, Robinson generated the most animosity and condemnation from Donahue as well as from the other guests because of his insistence that African Americans could solve their own problems through Black Nationalism. In the month following the broadcast, Robinson received many letters from citizens across the country. Some applauded his stand, but most condemned the hatred that he appeared to display.[37]

Robinson not only received publicity for the militant stand of the AAPL, he also became the chief object of the Chicago Police Department's campaign to disrupt the league and persecute its members. Robinson and other members of the AAPL were repeatedly suspended from duty on frivolous charges, such as not wearing a hat. With no reason given, they were transferred from district to district by their supervisors. The department even assigned Robinson to patrol an alley behind the police station![38] More insidious, a former African-American police officer (not a member of the AAPL) who had been convicted and was serving a prison term for murder charged that the Chicago Police Department and the FBI had framed him in their effort to "get" Robinson. The officer, whose last name was also Robinson, alleged that the individuals who framed him had erroneously thought that he was Renault Robinson when they implicated him for several murders in the city in 1970.[39]

The Chicago Police Department failed in its efforts to "get" Renault Robinson and other members of the AAPL. In fact, as one author termed it, Robinson and the AAPL "beat clout city." That is, Robinson beat the "clout" or power wielded by Chicago's political machine—a power that usually forced blacks to accede to the wishes of the white politicians who controlled the machine. In 1971, Robinson and the AAPL filed suit against the city of Chicago and the police department; they succeeded in freezing federal revenue sharing and Law Enforcement Assistance Administration funds allocated to Chicago. Robinson's suit charged the city and the police department with discrimination against African-American police officers and requested personal damages for himself and other members of the AAPL. In 1977, Robinson won a judgment of $125,000 from the city of Chicago.[40]

There is some irony in the fact that the most militant and successful black police association developed in Chicago. Chicago was the first major northern city to hire African Americans as police officers. The first black police sergeants, lieutenants, and captains outside of the Reconstruction South were employed there. Two notable reform movements—one led by the Human Relations Commission in the 1940s and a second under police superintendent O. W. Wilson in the 1960s—had worked to improve the status of black police officers in the city. Yet, African Americans still remained "tokens" on the Chicago police force; racism still influenced their assignments, and they were promoted to command positions at the whim of Chicago's politicians. In fact, after 1967 and the retirement of O. W. Wilson, the department returned to "business as usual" in relegating black police to second-class status, and the department continued to be plagued by corruption. If African-American police officers still faced racial discrimination in Chicago—where they had been employed longer than in any other city—and needed an AAPL to challenge racist policies, so too did black police in other cities.[41]

This was especially true in Philadelphia, where, as in Chicago, politics and racism had combined historically both to limit the access of African Americans to police jobs and to determine their status on the police force. In 1956, black police officers formed the Guardians Civic League of Philadelphia (GCL). Just as in Chicago, New York City, and Cleveland, the GCL initially faced opposition from the city's politicians as well as from the department's supervisory personnel. The organization survived primarily because in its early years it was more social than political. The GCL's focus changed when Alphonso Deal, a black police officer who was also a leader of the city's NAACP, became president and decided to resurrect it as an organization to address the occupational concerns of black officers. Under Deal, the GCL sought to solve the complaints of African-American police officers about discriminatory assignments, lack of promotions, and the fact that black officers charged with offenses received more severe punishments than whites. Deal found that the Philadelphia FOP would not address these issues; nor would the FOP form a special committee to handle racial problems in the department.

Eventually, Deal and the GCL alienated white members of the FOP and Mayor Frank Rizzo because of their stance against racial discrimination in the department and police abuse of black citizens. In 1978, Deal criticized the Philadelphia police force's brutal handling of the MOVE organization, a predominantly black "back-to-nature cult" that had alienated even many blacks because of its eccentric philosophy. Mayor Rizzo promised to "get a piece of him" if Deal did not retire from the police force. The FOP supported the mayor's threat by suspending Deal from the organization for two years and fining him $1,000 for "conduct unbecoming a member." By that time, Deal and the GCL had the successful example of Renault Robinson of Chicago as a model of how to fight harassment from city and police officials. Deal and the GCL struck back, winning suits against the FOP and the city of Philadelphia that exonerated Deal from the FOP's suspension and forced the city of Philadelphia to agree to a consent decree to hire and promote African-American police officers on an equitable basis with whites.[42]

In 1968, San Francisco's black officers and one white officer formed the Officers for Justice (OFJ) Peace Officers' Association in order to protest twenty years of departmental policies that limited employment and promotional opportunities for African Americans on the police force. Though their grievances were similar to those expressed by African-American officers in Chicago and Philadelphia, the experience of black police in San Francisco was more similar to that of their colleagues in the South. The San Francisco Police Department did not employ its first permanent black officer until 1948. Because of the lack of a large black population in the Bay Area prior to 1940 (in that year approximately five thousand African Americans lived in San Francisco, forming less than 1 percent of the voting population),[43] blacks wielded little political clout.

The African-American experience on the San Francisco police force was indicative of the lack of black political power in the city. First, few African Americans were hired as police officers; only five served on the police force in 1950, and by 1970 there were eighty-five (5 percent) on a force of eighteen hundred men. Second, African-American police were assigned to the worst details ("shit duty"). In 1963, the city's first permanent black officer, Richard Finis, resigned in disgust, charging that he had received unfair assignments and had been relegated to "Siberia" because the department had tried to hide him away from public view. Most blacks who joined the force after Finis were assigned exclusively to patrol in the predominantly black Hunter's Point area. Third, by 1970 only nine black officers had ever achieved promotion in the department, and these had come very recently: in 1964 Rotea Gilford was appointed as the first black inspector, and in 1968 Willie Frazier became the first black sergeant. Other black officers found achieving promotions very difficult because the department's promotion system favored those officers with the most seniority. Finally, both black and white officers charged the department with ignoring long-standing blatant racist practices. Some white officers used racial slurs without fear of reprimand. Richard Hongisto, a white founder of the OFJ, stated that during his ten years as a San Francisco police officer (1960–1970), it was common to hear his colleagues refer to African Americans as "niggers." In 1977, Hongisto would testify in the OFJ's lawsuit against the department that he had heard literally thousands of racial slurs used by his fellow officers. Other officers beat and brutalized black citizens with impunity. In 1966, the city's first major racial disturbance in Hunter's Point was provoked by a police shooting of a sixteen-year-old black youth and by the subsequent mistreatment, manhandling, and verbal abuse that the San Francisco police meted out to black citizens to control it. During the disturbance, white police even beat some black officers who were on duty in plainclothes.[44]

Similar to the AAPL in Chicago, the Officers for Justice was organized to address the problem of racism in the San Francisco Police Department. Many African-American officers had belonged to the department's rank-and-file organization, the Police Officers' Association (POA). In 1968, however, black officers complained that the POA would not address the issue of racism in the department; nor would it address the grievances of black officers about promotions and assignments. As early as 1965, Richard Hongisto and several black officers had attempted to organize an alternative to the POA, but failed. In 1968, African-American officer Henry Williams, Hongisto, and other black police officers in San Francisco began meeting to create such an organization. They also met with San Francisco mayor Joseph Alioto and several members of the San Francisco police commission to inform them of their plans. Alioto and the members of the police commission discouraged them. (Alioto called the organization a "segregated unit.") Under Williams's leadership, however, these officers persevered in their efforts, and in October 1968 they submitted a petition to the police commission for the recognition of the Officers for Justice. Through the efforts of the commission's first African-American member, Dr. Washington Garner, the OFJ was approved.[45]

After winning departmental recognition, members of the OFJ encountered the same harassment and struggle for equality that confronted members of the AAPL and the GCL. The black officers who formed the organization were labeled "militants" by their colleagues. Several members had the word "nigger" scratched on the doors of their lockers. Hongisto's office desk was removed and was never replaced. The OFJ's leaders attempted to negotiate with the leadership of the POA to revise the department's promotion system, but the latter group walked out of a meeting and refused to discuss the matter. In 1972, the OFJ co-sponsored a minority recruitment plan with the department; the POA criticized and condemned it. In 1973, the members of the OFJ filed a lawsuit against the police department and won a judgment mandating the hiring of minority officers on a quota basis (three minorities for every two whites hired until minorities reached 30 percent of the force). The OFJ won a second suit in 1977 and obtained a consent decree ordering the department to promote minority officers to the rank of sergeant, regardless of their position on the civil service eligible list. These court decisions brought even more resistance and harassment from members of the POA who opposed the appointment and promotion of black and Hispanic officers solely on the basis of race.[46]

The successful examples of the AAPL, the GCL, and the OFJ spread to other cities. The African-American police movement revived some of the older police associations and created new ones. (See table 11.) Common to all of the organizations was the objective of improving the status of African-American police officers and reforming the racial policies of American police departments. Examples of the new militancy among African-American police emerged in almost every major American city. For example, in Cleveland in 1967–68, the election of Carl Stokes and the Glenville riot incident boosted the membership of the Shield Club. That organization challenged the department's hiring policies for African-American police recruits and also filed a lawsuit against the Cleveland FOP for using the membership dues of black police officers to support the 1968 presidential campaign of George Wallace.[47] In New York City, following the review board issue, the Guardians had more conflict with the PBA. The PBA had publicly opposed the department's efforts to recruit more minority police officers; the Guardians responded by actively and publicly supporting such policies.[48] In Los Angeles, in September 1968, African-American police officers organized the Oscar Joel Bryant Association (OJB) in honor of a fellow officer killed in the line of duty. The OJB managed to avoid the open racial conflict that confronted black police officers in other parts of the country, but it did announce that it aimed to "close the gap between the police and the black community."[49] In the South, Miami's MCPBA filed one of the earliest lawsuits charging a police department with racial discrimination in hiring and promotion. Members of the MCPBA requested compensation for the department's failure to provide them police training and for the many years that the department had relegated them to a separate facility. In 1971, the MCPBA charged that Miami police officials had persecuted African-American police officers who spoke out against improper arrests by white police officers.[50] Similarly, in Atlanta, after African-American police officers there had organized a chapter of the Afro-American Patrolmen's League in 1969, they became embroiled in conflict with the Atlanta Police Department. Several Atlanta AAPL members charged the department with long-term policies of discrimination against African-American police officers; Atlanta police chief John Inman responded by suspending and demoting the men.[51]

Such individual and collective charges and grievances, filed against American police departments by black police officers through their organizations, not only became key issues in law enforcement, they also received a national forum. Since the problems that African-American police sought to redress had always existed, the national attention to them represented the success of the new breed of African-American police in publicizing their perception of the failure of reform in American police departments. This success also exemplified the emerging clout of African Americans in local politics and their bid to control the police in the cities where they had electoral majorities. Black police officers were voicing the grievances of the black community as they launched their attack on the continuing problems of police brutality, discrimination in hiring and assignment, and lack of promotional opportunities. These activists proposed a "third wave of reform" to address the failure of earlier movements to eliminate the long-established color line in American policing.[52]

African-American police officers and organizations proposed a new standard of professionalism for all police officers. Some of their proposals concurred with those of previous reformers, but most did not. They felt that a police officer's duty was to serve the community; he or she was first and foremost a public servant accountable to the people of the community, not to politicians, police administrators, or police unions. African-American police officers also believed that the police should involve the public in law enforcement through neighborhood watches and regular meetings between police and public. The ultimate goal was to have a community-based police force that existed to serve the people, not simply to deter crime; it should be a public-service agency thoroughly involved in all aspects of the community.

African-American police organizations also proposed new standards for training and advancement in police work. To serve his or her community, an officer had to have thorough training not only in police work but also in community and race relations. Ideally, each recruit should possess a college degree. With such qualifications and training, an officer would be able to work in any area or neighborhood and enforce the law impartially. Police departments would obtain better candidates by having a selection process with validated, job-related exams and a promotion procedure that was nondiscriminatory. African-American police also believed that, while merit promotions should continue to exist, new opportunities for lateral entry into police jobs would provide the department with candidates who had better skills in specific areas of police work. An important proposed reform involved financial compensation for officers who had been previously denied promotions and job assignments under the old, racially biased "merit" system.[53]

African-American police organizations throughout the United States based their rationale for organizing on the need both to make the police more "professional" and to reform long-standing, nationwide racial police policies. The resulting formation of a national police association represented the culmination of the effort begun by the Texas Negro Peace Officers' Association in the 1930s. In August 1972, the St. Louis Black Police Association hosted the "First National Conference of Black Policemen." African-American police officers from eight cities met to organize a "national black policemen's fraternal association." Norman Seay, a member of the St. Louis chapter of CORE's police monitoring committee and the coordinator of the conference, listed the goals of the organization:

1. To improve the relationship between the black community and the police department.
2. To improve the professional status of black policemen, individually and collectively.
3. To encourage more black citizens to actively apply for employment with law enforcement agencies.
4. To assist in reducing the causes of crime.
5. To encourage the further development of law enforcement as a profession.

Seay also justified such an organization by citing the fact that African Americans had formed similar groups among black doctors, lawyers, and postal workers. According to Seay, instead of being discriminatory or self-segregating, these groups promoted brotherhood and respect for the profession.[54]

The National Black Police Association (NBPA) emerged from the St. Louis conference. From the initial eight cities, the NBPA grew to represent African-American police organizations in thirty-five major cities and twenty-two states. Beginning in 1972, the NBPA held annual conferences that served as forums for issues that affected African-American police officers. Unlike the law enforcement topics that dominated the annual conventions of the early TNPOA, the agendas at NBPA conventions tended to focus on civil rights and other current political issues. The conventions also discussed new ideas such as team policing and new policies regulating use of deadly force against suspects.[55]

The National Black Police Association was the culmination of forty years of work by African-American police organizations. It represented the triumph of black police unionism, since it differed significantly from the primarily fraternal efforts of the earlier police associations such as the TNPOA. The NBPA was a powerful new presence. It represented fifty-four city and county police associations that had emerged as pressure groups and police unions to challenge the failure of reform in American police departments. The difference in objectives and in success between the TNPOA and NBPA was indicative of how the status of African-American police officers had changed since the 1930s, from that of "tokens" to being regarded as full members of the police establishment. The next step was to gain access to police administration.

SEVEN

BLACK POLICE ADMINISTRATORS

I would not expect to serve a predominantly white community with a predominantly black police force. And I cannot understand why people want me to serve a predominantly black community with a predominantly white police force. A white community wouldn't tolerate it and it's unfortunate that a black community is forced to tolerate it.

—A. Reginald Eaves, Atlanta's first black public safety commissioner

When Newark had an Irish mayor, we had an Irish [police director]; when we had an Italian mayor, we had an Italian director. Now we have a black mayor and all of a sudden the racists jump out of the closets.

—Councilman Sharpe James of Newark, New Jersey

It's our turn.

—1983 mayoral campaign slogan for Harold Washington of Chicago[1]

Winning access to police administrative positions proved to be an even more difficult task for African Americans than winning equal opportunity as law enforcement officers. Prior to the 1950s, only two African Americans in the entire country, Octave Rey of New Orleans and John Scott of Chicago, were promoted to the level of captain. Rey and Scott ascended to command positions in the two cities where African Americans had made the most progress as law enforcement officers. Redemption and the return of the Democrats to political power in Louisiana ended Rey's short tenure (1868–1877) in New Orleans. Scott (1940–1946), by contrast, had the political support in Chicago that enabled him to serve until he retired. Moreover, Harry B. Deas succeeded Scott as South Side Chicago's black police captain, and the strength of African-American political power in that city enabled blacks to retain a police captaincy continuously thereafter. Not until the 1950s and 1960s would African Americans gain access to top police administration jobs in any other cities.

Two scholars have proposed theories to explain this exclusion. Larry E. Moss has argued that command opportunities were limited for African Americans because of the fear among whites of the "black peril"—that is, American police agencies must always remain under white control, lest the "black criminal hordes" overrun white America. Mack Jones, on the other hand, cites the overall fear among whites that blacks would exact vengeance if they ever gained control of political power. Making blacks, historically "the objects of policing," into policemen contradicted one of the reasons for the establishment of law enforcement agencies. To give African Americans command of those agencies would be an even greater, more dangerous contradiction. It would require black political power as well as controversial political machinations to overcome one of the last bastions of white supremacy.[2]

In 1937, Harvey Alston joined the Columbus, Ohio, police department and began a career that he thought would lead him to the top administrative position on the force. Leslie Shaw became the first black police sergeant in Columbus in 1943 after filing a lawsuit to force the department to open that rank to African-American officers. In 1946, Alston succeeded Shaw as the department's second black police sergeant. He then earned promotions to lieutenant in 1948 and to captain in 1952, becoming the first African American outside of Chicago and New Orleans to attain the rank of police captain. Alston's police knowledge was exceptional. He had scored in the top five on every promotional exam that he had ever taken, and he had finished first on the sergeant's exam—preventing the department from passing him over or failing to promote him when his name was reached on the promotion list. As a result, Alston was on the threshold of becoming the first African-American police chief in a major American city.[3]

But Alston's advancement was soon thwarted. In 1954, he took the police chief's examination and finished second to the eventual chief, George Scholer, by three-tenths of a point. The closeness between the two men' scores led several black community leaders to request an investigation to determine if Alston had been denied the top score on the exam because he was black. At Alston's request, however, the call for an investigation was dropped. Alston stated that he knew that his score on the police chief's exam was fair, and he saw no need to pursue the issue. He eventually became the department's first African-American inspector, second in command to the chief.[4]

Some black Americans, however, did become police chiefs. Prior to the 1970s, this typically occurred only in cities and towns with small black populations, and where African Americans were not a threat to the status quo of white supremacy. For example, in 1958 Payton I. Flournoy became chief in Palmyra, New Jersey, a little-known suburb of Philadelphia with a population of 7,000. In 1962, Theodore Wilburn became police chief in Portsmouth, Ohio, a small city in the southern part of the state with a population of 34,000. Both men ascended to command in these cities because they first served as "acting chiefs," replacing white police chiefs who were unable to fulfill their duties. Flournoy replaced a chief who was suffering from a brain illness, and Wilburn replaced one who had been suspended because of a police scandal. Both men, in other words, just happened to be in the right place at the right time to demonstrate that an African American was capable of administering a police department, and that crime and disorder would not increase because an African American was in command.[5]

In two other small cities, African Americans rose to command under controversial circumstances. In 1959, Mayor Paul Egan of Aurora, Illinois, appointed Baptist minister Robert Wesby as police chief in order to insult and provoke members of the city council. Egan used Wesby as a pawn to defy the council members who had refused to approve his other appointments. His plan backfired; the city council approved Wesby as the city's police chief. In 1965, African American Jesse Meadows, a self-avowed "Negro segregationist" in Crawfordville, Georgia, became that town's law enforcement pawn. The city council appointed Meadows police chief—although he was sixty-six-years old and had no formal education—because he had publicly stated that he supported segregation and would carry out the task of arresting and controlling civil rights activists who were demonstrating in Crawfordville to challenge the town's policy of segregation. Meadows served only one week. Pressure on his family as well as the national publicity that he received as a defender of segregation forced him to resign from the position.[6]

The controversy over the appointment of Wesby and Meadows as police chiefs paled before the furor that arose in several major American cities when African Americans became mayors and attempted to control the police. The emergence of black political power in the 1960s and 1970s not only made it possible for African Americans to win police jobs throughout the nation,[7] it also led to the appointment of black police administrators in several major cities. (See table 12.)

Cleveland, Ohio, was the first to achieve the milestone of having a black police administrator. In 1967, Carl Stokes became mayor of Cleveland.[8] African Americans were not a majority of the city's population, so his election as the first black mayor was unique. (With only a few exceptions, the election of black mayors—and most African-American political candidates—in American cities required black electoral majorities.) He was elected by a coalition of the city's black and white voters. Nevertheless, Stokes considered his election a mandate "to reform the police department, to have them do their jobs, protect the public, enforce the law, and be responsive to the needs of the people." He also wanted to increase the number of blacks on the Cleveland Police Department, from which they had historically been excluded. Stokes went through four white police chiefs in his efforts to reform the department. In 1970, however, he attempted to resolve the situation by appointing the city's first black public safety director, Benjamin O. Davis, Jr. Unfortunately, this appointment proved to be one of Stokes's biggest mistakes.[9]

When Stokes began to woo Davis for the position as public safety director, he believed that he had chosen the ideal person for the job. Lieutenant General Davis was the son of Benjamin O. Davis, Sr., the United States Army's first African-American four-star general, and he was a graduate of West Point. Davis was the first black general in the United States Air Force, and during World War II he had commanded the historic 99th Pursuit Squadron, the first African-American fighter plane squadron. Stokes felt that Davis's patriotic military background would allay the fears of his white constituents that Davis might be "soft on crime" and that he did not have the administrative experience to command a big-city police department. The fact that Davis was an African American also seemed ideal: not only would he serve as a clear example of the Stokes administration's effort to provide African Americans access to top city jobs, but he would also allay fears among African Americans that the police department would continue to use excessive force against black citizens.[10]

Davis, however, proved to be as much a problem for the Stokes administration as would any conservative public safety director serving a liberal mayor. He sided with the police department against the administration on issues such as the use of lethal dum-dum bullets by Cleveland police officers, the relocation of the police department to a proposed justice center complex being built by the city, and the use of force against demonstrators and Black Nationalists who Davis claimed were breaking the law. He also took the position that the "enemies of law enforcement" were responsible for the city's ongoing racial problems. He even blamed Black Nationalists for inciting violence at a previously all-white school (Collingwood High School) then undergoing desegregation—when it was whites who had attacked black students for attempting to attend their school. On one occasion, Mayor Stokes had to order Davis to go to Collingwood High to supervise the protection of black students trying to attend classes. But Davis was reluctant to use police authority to support the integration of Collingwood; conversely, the city's black leaders and the *Call and Post* newspaper criticized him for his approval of massive police tactical squads to harass and arrest civil rights demonstrators and Black Nationalists. Davis was clearly on the side of defending "law and order" and maintaining the status quo in Cleveland.[11]

Given the untenable position that Davis had taken with the Stokes administration, it was no surprise that his tenure as public safety director lasted less than six months. In July 1970 he submitted his letter of resignation to Mayor Stokes, citing his differences with the mayor over how to handle the threat posed to American society by "black militants" and the "enemies of law enforcement." Davis accused Stokes of supporting and siding with these groups against the police department. When prodded by Stokes to identify the "enemies of law enforcement" who were making his job so difficult, Davis as expected named as one of them Black Nationalist leader Harllel Jones. But Davis did not stop with Jones. He also named several black ministers, the Cleveland Council of Churches, and the *Call and Post* newspaper. Earlier in his administration, Davis had suggested to Stokes that he retaliate against these groups who were criticizing him and the police. Stokes had rebuked Davis for even suggesting that he should silence dissenters. To Davis, Stokes's failure to suppress dissenters and to cut them off from his administration made him a supporter of the "enemies of law enforcement," rather than a defender of "law and order" and "integration." Distraught over Davis's charges of his alleged complicity with the "enemies of law enforcement," Stokes published Davis's "enemies list." This action—which was a shrewd political move to counter charges that the Stokes administration had alienated the services of one of the nation's "greatest generals"—showed Davis's defenders that "the General" was a black right-wing conservative who did not believe that dissenters should have the basic American rights of freedom of speech and freedom of assembly. The uproar that followed the publication of the list even led to a protest in front of Davis's apartment complex.[12]

Stokes replaced Davis with a white public safety director—his third in three years. The appointment of Cleveland's first black public safety director had ended in failure. Stokes was distressed beyond words because the appointment was supposed to have been a progressive move to show that an African-American mayor could be just as tough on criminals and maintain civic order just as effectively as had all the white mayors before him. Despite the publication of Davis's "enemies list," the Stokes administration was still blamed by the Cleveland media and business establishment for allowing "black militants" to end the tenure of one of the nation's leading military men as the top law enforcement officer in Cleveland. The media also criticized Stokes for "interfering" with the city's police department. The resignation of Davis, Stokes's handling of the Glenville riot, and a cheating scandal involving the police promotional examination (which resulted from Stokes's attempt to hire and promote more black officers) forced Mayor Stokes to resign himself to maintaining the status quo in the police department. Whites were simply not prepared for black control of the police function in Cleveland.[13]

When voters in Newark, New Jersey, elected Kenneth Gibson as the second African-American big-city mayor in 1970, he had Carl Stokes's failures with the Cleveland Police Department as an example of what he should *not* do in his dealings with the Newark police force. As the city's first black mayor, Gibson seemed to have learned from Stokes's experience that he should not appoint a black police chief and upset the majority-white police force or Newark's white citizens. Three years earlier, Newark's predominantly white police force had expressed its resentment toward the appointment of the department's first black police captain, Edward Williams, because they felt that he received his appointment only because of his race. In fact, Williams was promoted to captain after a major civil disturbance in Newark in July 1967. A fourteen-year veteran and a lieutenant who had risen through the ranks, Williams was more than qualified for his promotion. Nevertheless, many white Newark police officers demonstrated outside the police station against his appointment and used their police radios to disparage the city's first "nigger police captain." Knowing that such sentiments existed in the department as well as in Newark's white ethnic communities, Gibson appointed John Redden, a white police administrator who was a protégé of New York City police commissioner Patrick V. Murphy (1970–1973), as the city's police director. Although African-American leaders such as Black Nationalist poet Imamu Amiri Baraka criticized Gibson's choice of a white police director, the majority of both the black and white communities in Newark approved of his selection of Redden. Besides, when Gibson took office in 1970, it was clear that the majority-white city council would not support an African-American police director.[14]

Despite his safe choice of a white police director, Gibson's honeymoon as Newark's first black mayor lasted only two years. Just as in Cleveland, the actions of a Black Nationalist group forced Gibson to choose sides. In this case, poet Imamu Amiri Baraka's group, Kawaida Temple, attempted to build an all-black housing project (Kawaida Towers) in a previously all-white neighborhood in Newark's North Ward. White citizens in the neighborhood opposed the project because of its size (sixteen floors and 216 units) and its sponsors. In fall 1972, whites in the North Ward demonstrated against the housing project and physically prevented construction workers from completing it. Gibson not only ordered the police to protect the workers against physical violence, he also expressed his support for the project. Although they were ordered to protect the construction workers, many Newark police officers were sympathetic to the citizens of the North Ward. Some of them felt that they were caught in the middle of a political battle they could not win.

No one expressed the opposition of the police to their role in the Kawaida Towers conflict more vehemently than Police Director Redden. In November 1972, Redden attacked the city council and the Gibson administration for placing the department in a no-win situation. He stated that his officers were being attacked from all sides by the citizens who opposed the project, the Black Nationalist sponsors of the project, and their supporters (members of Students for a Democratic Society). Essentially, Redden did not believe that the police should provide protection for the project because of its "political" nature. To express his displeasure with Gibson's position on the project, on December 1, 1972, Redden resigned as Newark's police director.[15]

Redden's resignation provided Gibson the opportunity to appoint Newark's first black police director, Lieutenant Edward Kerr, on December 10, 1972. Kerr, a fourteen-year veteran on the Newark police force, was characterized as a "by-the-book" police administrator. Before his promotion, he was Newark's highest-ranking black officer, and nothing in his career seemed to distinguish him for the job as the city's first African-American police director. (Of course, the same could be said about quite a few whites who have been appointed police chiefs in American cities.)[16] This led Gibson's (and Kerr's) opponents on the city council to criticize Kerr as unqualified and to condemn his appointment as "racially motivated." The white members of Newark's city council, who outnumbered the black members six to three, expressed their displeasure with Kerr by voting against his confirmation four times. Kerr served six months as "interim" police director because the council would not confirm him. Finally, on July 11, 1973, Kerr won confirmation by a vote of five to three. Two white council members—one who switched his vote because he felt that Kerr had earned the job, and a second who was acting as an interim replacement for her husband—voted with the three black councilmen to confirm him.[17]

Kerr served only one year as police director. Gibson's critics later charged that the mayor was only "testing the waters" for a permanent African-American police director who would carry out his wishes in the police department. Kerr did seem to serve that purpose. Nevertheless, he carried out the law enforcement task that

Redden had refused to do: he enforced the court order that prevented white demonstrators in Newark's North Ward from stopping the Kawaida Towers project, and the controversial project was completed. Despite his success in this effort, he was criticized by some of his black critics, namely Imamu Amiri Baraka, for being "too close" to the Newark Police Department's white chain of command and for being "frightened that white folks will disapprove of him." Based on Kerr's performance, however, neither of these criticisms seems to have any foundation.[18]

In June 1974, Gibson won a second term as Newark's mayor. He used his reelection as an opportunity to announce that he was replacing Edward Kerr as police director with Lieutenant Hubert Williams, another African American. Gibson praised the work of Kerr, but stated that he was appointing Williams in order to link the police department more closely to the High Impact Crime Project that Williams had been administering under a $20 million federal grant. Williams was eminently qualified to become Newark's new police director. In fact, he had one of the most extensive academic backgrounds in the department's history. Thirty-four-years old, he had earned a law degree from Rutgers Law School and a master's in public administration from the City University of New York. In 1971, he had also participated as a fellow at Harvard Law School's Center for Criminal Justice. A native of Georgia and a twelve-year veteran of Newark's police force, Williams was Gibson's ideal candidate for police director. Although there was some grumbling among the rank-and-file on the force about Williams's academic background, he was readily approved by the city council.[19]

Hubert Williams not only served longer (1974–1985) than any previous police director in Newark, he also enacted innovations and personnel policies to make the department more responsive to and representative of Newark's citizens. Upon assuming command, Williams demoted and transferred several entrenched deputy chiefs and captains in the department. He implemented a 911 system to increase police response to citizens' calls for service, and placed police decoys on city streets to deter muggers. Among the innovations that Williams introduced in Newark were police sweeps of high-crime areas, roadblocks to deter drunken drivers, a truancy task force to discourage teenage crime, and police storefront offices that established police officers in Newark not only as law enforcement officers but also as community service workers. Williams also admitted that he used "color-conscious" policies in promoting and assigning officers; he believed that in a city where the composition of most neighborhoods was more than 50 percent African American, it was good policy and good management to assign detectives and administrators who reflected the composition of those neighborhoods.[20] Otherwise, he disciplined and treated all officers fairly. Indeed, many black officers in Newark complained that Williams was too fair and did not reward black officers for the past discrimination that they had faced in the department. In 1983 and 1985, two outside studies evaluated the performance of Newark's Police Department after eight and ten years of Williams's leadership, respectively. Both studies found that the department was flexible, innovative, and well-managed in spite of reductions in manpower and funding. The department also had reduced crime levels in several categories.[21]

Williams's achievements in Newark proved that an African-American police administrator could manage a modern police department and be as tough on crime as any white administrator. He reduced the fears among white officers that a black police administrator would use the same blatantly race-based policies (favoring blacks instead of whites) in assignments and promotions that his predecessors had used. He also showed Newark's white citizens that he would not neglect law enforcement and allow crime to flourish in white communities as some of his predecessors had done in regard to the crime in black communities. Williams brought an evenhanded and fair approach to police administration in Newark. In fact, his successful performance led to his appointment as the first African-American president of the Police Foundation.[22]

While Williams was proving in Newark that a black man could run a big-city police department effectively, Maynard Jackson of Atlanta was trying to gain control of that city's police department. In 1974, Jackson became the nation's third big-city African-American mayor. Like Stokes, he attempted to use his election as a mandate to reform Atlanta's police department. Prior to Jackson's winning the office of mayor, black police officers in the Atlanta AAPL had filed a lawsuit charging that the police department discriminated against African Americans in promotions and assignments. One of Jackson's first actions after taking office was to fire police chief John Inman, who had retaliated against the members of the Afro-American Patrolmen's League for their suit by demoting and reassigning them. Inman had also resisted a court order to hire more black police officers and kept surveillance files on Atlanta's black city councilmen and other black elected officials. Jackson's firing of Inman was a declaration of war, and Inman fought back with the support of the Atlanta media, the business community, and the courts. He obtained a court injunction prohibiting Jackson from removing him from his post. He also barricaded himself in the chief's office, and three hundred white Atlanta police officers vowed to "go to any extreme" to keep him as police chief. Like Stokes before him, Jackson found gaining control of the police department to be a difficult and highly controversial task.[23]

However, whereas Stokes was a black mayor in a city that was still mostly white, Jackson was mayor in a city that was 60 percent black. He also had a recently approved new city charter that gave the mayor more control over city departments—especially the police department. Black political power and the new charter proved to be the decisive factors in his gaining control of the city's police administration. Despite the support of the city's black majority for Jackson's removal of Inman as police chief, Jackson lost his first battle with Inman in court. In May 1974 a Fulton County court judge upheld Inman's right to remain as police chief because he had an eight-year contract from former mayor Sam Massell, a contract which did not expire until 1980. Three months later, however, the Georgia Supreme Court upheld the new city charter, which gave Jackson and the city council power to reorganize the police department over Inman's objections.[24]

Although Jackson could not remove Inman from the position of police chief, he could use the power given him by the new city charter to undercut Inman's authority in the police department. With the support of the city council, he created the position of public safety commissioner as a "super chief" of all of the city's public safety departments—police, fire, and civil defense. The chief of police job was renamed "director of police services," and five "deputy directors" were named under him to administer various functions of the department—operations, inspection, investigations, administration, and auxiliary services. In effect, the reorganization stripped Inman of his power from above and below. He became nothing but a figurehead because the real power to administer police services was in the hands of the new public safety commissioner.[25]

Jackson's next task was to name a public safety commissioner who would effectively carry out his new police reforms. In August 1974 he appointed A. Reginald Eaves, a personal friend and a former classmate at Morehouse College who had served as Boston's penal commissioner. Of course, Eaves was also an African American: he represented the first opportunity for black Atlantans to control the city's police force. The Atlanta media, the business community, and white members of the police force criticized Jackson for appointing an "outsider" and a man with no police administration experience as public safety commissioner. The media and the business community accused Jackson of "cronyism" for appointing a former classmate. The Atlanta business community even threatened to move its operations outside the city in protest, calling Jackson's appointment of Eaves "black racism." It was clear that many did not believe that Eaves (or any African American) could do the job of controlling the city's spiraling crime rate. But Jackson defended his choice, stating that Eaves was the right man for the job because of his experience and training in administration. Despite some resistance from city council president Wyche Fowler, the council approved the appointment by a vote of twelve to six. Three white councilmen voted with the nine blacks on the council for confirmation.[26]

As Atlanta's first African-American top law enforcement officer, Eaves proved to be more than capable of dealing with all aspects of the job. He took the obligatory tough stand on crime and reduced the number of major crimes in Atlanta during the first year of his administration. He was credited with reducing homicides in the city from 248 in 1974 to 185 in 1975. Overall, major crimes—armed robberies, burglaries, and other violent crimes—in Atlanta dropped by more than 8 percent. Part of the decrease can be attributed to Eaves's implementation of the city's first team policing program. Team policing was an innovative program in which police officers formed ties with community residents and worked with them to develop methods to prevent and solve crimes. The new concept was adopted by police departments around the country in the 1970s to deter crime and to improve relations between the police and black community residents. For Eaves, the use of team policing was a means of changing the negative relationship that historically had existed between black Atlantans and the Atlanta police, and of fighting crime more effectively.

As the first African American to direct law enforcement in a major southern city, Eaves attracted considerable media attention. He became quite astute in manipulating the media to emphasize his tough stand against crime. Nevertheless, he received better publicity nationally than he did from the local press. He was never able to please the local media, which played up every mistake he made. According to Atlanta's media, crime was escalating in the city because Eaves and Jackson were preoccupied with establishing their own power base by rewarding their black supporters with city jobs and contracts.[27]

One of Eaves's (and Jackson's) chief objectives was to change the composition of the Atlanta police force in order to make it more representative of the city's population.[28] Upon assuming the job of public safety commissioner, Eaves began to carry out Jackson's wishes with regard to integrating the department and promoting black officers so that African Americans were in the top echelons of the department and making the policy decisions that affected the lives of black citizens. During his first month in office, Eaves demoted six assistant chiefs and more than one hundred other supervisory personnel, installing his own team to replace them. Thirty African Americans received promotions under his reorganization plan. He also increased black police recruitment in the department. When Eaves became public safety commissioner, only 23 percent of the department (355 of 1,545 officers) was African-American. By the time that he resigned, the department was 35 percent black. Indeed, the integration of the Atlanta police department became one of Eaves's—and by extension Jackson's—greatest accomplishments. By 1981, when Jackson finished his first two terms in office, the department was second only to Washington, D.C., in having the percentage of blacks on the police force proportionate to the percentage of blacks in the city's population. (See tables 13 and 14.) This achievement seemed to indicate what black control of police administration could mean for American cities: more black police officers with a corresponding improvement in police relations with black citizens.[29]

The integration of the Atlanta police force did not go unchallenged. As Eaves hired and promoted more African-American officers, white officers charged him with "reverse discrimination." The Atlanta FOP and PBA took over the racial discrimination suit that the AAPL had filed against Chief Inman in 1973, claiming that the department's black administrators were discriminating against whites. In 1976, the two organizations succeeded in obtaining an injunction which blocked all hiring and promotions in the Atlanta Police Department.

The FOP's and PBA's intervention in the racial discrimination suit was ironic. Three years earlier, when police chief John Inman controlled the police department, both organizations had defended the status quo which allowed the Atlanta police chief to make all promotions at his discretion. (Police Chief Herbert Jenkins called this discretion "command prerogatives.") That system was unfair and hindered the promotion of black *and* white officers who were not in the inner circle of the department. When Eaves assumed command, he implemented the department's first promotional exam system, under which all officers actually had an equal chance for advancement—not just those who were favored by the police chief. The new system consisted of a written exam (weighted 50 percent), an evaluation of an officer's record (20 percent) and performance (20 percent), and an oral interview (10 percent). The white members of the FOP and PBA charged that it placed too much weight on the oral interviews and that black commanding officers made up the majority of the interview panels.

Even if the new promotional system was not designed to favor African-American officers, it was clear that they benefited the most from it. In 1975, for example, Eaves appointed nine police captains, seven of whom were black. He also appointed twenty-eight sergeants, and twenty-one of them were black. Moreover, by 1976, five of the police department's ten majors were African Americans; only two of eight under Chief John Inman had been black. The FOP and PBA also charged that 75 percent of the officers promoted by Eaves were black; in fact, 63 percent of the officers promoted by Eaves were black.

Despite two years of promotions that favored African Americans, the Atlanta Police Department was still predominantly white. Whites still dominated every rank below major: 652 of 908 patrolmen, 22 of 31 captains, 48 of 57 lieutenants, 136 of 205 detectives, and 99 of 164 sergeants were white. Nevertheless, Judge Charles Moye of the United States District Court accepted the arguments of the FOP and PBA that Eaves and other police officials in Atlanta were discriminating against white officers. After Judge Moye blocked all appointments and promotions in the department for three years, in 1979 he forced the city of Atlanta to agree to hire and promote black and white officers on a fifty-fifty basis, and to compensate those applicants who had been denied jobs under the department's past discriminatory policies.[30]

Eaves's tenure as Atlanta public safety commissioner lasted only four years, and it was filled with political turmoil. In addition to being regarded by the Atlanta media and business community as "unqualified," he made many enemies for his handling of police promotions and his criticisms of the media's reporting of crime in Atlanta. Even some black officers who were passed over by Eaves for promotions emerged as among his most ardent critics. In addition, Eaves did not help his own cause by making two mistakes: hiring a convicted felon as his personal secretary, and using his influence to obtain a city job for his nephew. These incidents almost led to his resignation in March 1975. It took a concerted effort by some of Atlanta's black leaders to keep him in office and to convince Maynard Jackson to continue to support him as public safety commissioner. In 1978, however, he was forced to resign after a police exam cheating scandal implicated members of his administration for allegedly providing advance copies of the promotional examination to a select group of black officers (mainly members of Atlanta's AAPL). Once again, just as in Cleveland, the media charged that Jackson and Eaves had attempted to "break the rules" in order to recruit and promote more African Americans for jobs in the Atlanta Police Department. Neither Eaves nor Jackson personally had any knowledge of the cheating on the police examinations, but both were blamed by the Atlanta media for allegedly encouraging their aides and supporters to do whatever was necessary to integrate the department. The incident seemed to confirm that black mayors and police administrators would "lower standards" and even violate the law to "Africanize" the police—at the expense of police protection for white citizens. After Eaves resigned, he later became a Fulton County commissioner.[31]

One positive result of the Atlanta police cheating scandal was that Lee P. Brown became the city's second African-American public safety commissioner.

The job was Brown's first big-city administration post, and it continued one of the most illustrious police administration careers ever of any American (not just African-American) law enforcement officer—matching and superseding those of O. W. Wilson and Patrick J. Murphy.[32] Brown had begun his police career in 1960 with the San Jose, California, Police Department, where he served as a police officer for eight years. During that time he earned a Ph.D. in criminology from Berkeley. From 1968 to 1975, he held university positions at Portland State University and Howard University; he directed Howard's Institute for Urban Affairs and Research. In 1975 he became sheriff and director of public safety in Multnomah County, which encompassed Portland, Oregon. In 1978 he accepted the position of director of the Law Enforcement Assistance Administration (LEAA) with the United States Justice Department. But after less than six months, he left the LEAA to accept Atlanta mayor Maynard Jackson's offer to succeed A. Reginald Eaves as that city's public safety commissioner.[33]

Brown's assumption of the position in Atlanta coincided with that city's child murders case. Brown helped to coordinate the joint police-FBI investigation team that solved two of the serial murders of twenty-eight black children and young men. After the first body was discovered in 1979, Brown led a two-year investigation that ended with the arrest and conviction of Wayne Williams for two of the murders. The case, which attracted national attention, added to Brown's already high profile as a police administrator. In addition, he did a credible job in Atlanta of succeeding Eaves and continuing the process of reforming and integrating the police force. His success in capturing and convicting a suspect in the child murders, and his reputation for stabilizing the volatile race relations in the Atlanta Police Department, made him an attractive candidate for other police administration jobs around the country. In 1982, these factors led Mayor Kathy Whitmire to coax him away to Houston.[34]

Just by taking the job as police chief in Houston, Brown achieved several firsts. He became the first African American appointed police chief by a white mayor in a predominantly white city. He became the Houston Police Department's first African-American chief, and he was the first outsider to become chief in Houston in forty years. He was also the first African American to hold a rank above sergeant in the history of the Houston Police Department.

Nevertheless, his uniqueness did not win him any favor with the city's predominantly white police force. White officers in Houston called Brown's appointment a "slap in the face," and several members of the Houston Police Officers' Association (HPOA) went to Atlanta in an attempt to find information to discredit him. The HPOA produced a critical fifteen-page report on Brown's tenure in Atlanta in an unsuccessful effort to block his confirmation. To support the opposition of the department's rank and file as well as to protest Brown's selection, the city's Ku Klux Klan chapter also marched. Despite the dissent from the police department over his appointment, Houston's city council confirmed him by a strong vote of eleven to three. One member of the council voted for Brown in spite of having received two death threats.

The resistance to Brown on the part of Houston's rank and file was indicative of why Mayor Whitmire had selected him. Houston's police department had established a national reputation for its brutality against black and Hispanic citizens. Under previous chiefs, its officers had exhibited a "cowboy" attitude of "shoot first and ask questions later." In 1978, for example, the United States Department of Justice had to prosecute two Houston officers for "violating the civil rights" of a Mexican-American citizen. The two officers brutally beat José Campos Torres and then threw him in Buffalo Bayou, where he drowned. (They received suspended sentences on a misdemeanor charge in local courts.) Like Atlanta's police force before Mayor Jackson gained control of it, the Houston police kept surveillance files on the city's black politicians such as Congresswoman Barbara Jordan and filled the files with derogatory and defamatory references.

The Houston department also had a long history of discriminating against and limiting the promotional opportunities of African-American officers. Blacks on the force remained second-class officers assigned exclusively to Houston's black communities. In the 110 years that blacks had served on the force, only one had ever achieved promotion above sergeant—Sergeant Jerry R. Jones was promoted to lieutenant fourteen days before Brown assumed command of the department on April 19, 1982.

In addition to the obvious problems in the police department, Houston itself had a history of violence. Homicides had always been a problem in the city; in 1979, 670 homicides were recorded there. In 1981, Houston led the nation in the number of homicides, with another record of 701. This atmosphere of violence threatened the lives of the city's police officers and made them more willing to use deadly force to protect themselves. In the year that Brown assumed command of the department, nine officers died violently. Such were the problems that Brown encountered when he became the department's first African-American police chief.[35]

Just as he had done in Atlanta, Brown once again proved that he was more than equal to the task of reforming the police department, with its sordid history of violence and citizen abuse. After studying the department for a year and consulting with his administrative staff, in 1983 he issued a forty-one-page booklet entitled *Plan of Action,* in which he set forth his blueprint for reform. His goals included improving the department's operations, respecting the city's neighborhoods and their diversity, and ensuring that the department delivered "its services in a manner that preserves and advances democratic values." The cornerstone of Brown's program was the Directed Area Responsibility Team (DART) patrol plan, a community policing plan based on decentralized management and emphasizing community involvement. Formulation of the idea for the DART plan had begun under Brown's predecessor, Deputy Chief J. P. Bales. In 1983, Brown implemented it as the operational format for directed, community-oriented policing. The plan, which consisted of having patrol officers and civilian community service officers work with community residents, was developed concurrently with the establishment of "community command stations" and police storefront offices in Houston's neighborhoods. All were innovative ways to reduce crime, to make the police more responsive to the people they served, and to project the image of the police as "public servants" rather than as "oppressors."

Brown's innovations enjoyed some success. The police storefronts earned him a national award for leadership, and they became a model for police departments around the country. He was able to increase the number of officers on the force and put more of them on the streets. Violent crimes also dropped more than 10 percent during his first two years as chief. He improved discipline among the rank and file by taking a tough stand against the abuse of citizens. Although he refused to support a citizens' police review board, he took strong action against officers who abused citizens: he fired them from the force. Brown also implemented departmental rules governing the discharge of firearms by police officers to reduce police shootings of suspects. Of course, as some white officers charged, just by being a "black police chief" he was able to improve the department's image and relations with Houston's African-American citizens and reduce the acrimonious charges of police brutality and abuse that had plagued the department.

As he had done in Atlanta, Brown also implemented an affirmative action plan to hire and promote more minorities on the Houston police force. In 1982, when he was appointed chief, 8.5 percent of the force was African American and 8.2 percent was Hispanic. Within two years he had increased the number of blacks from 273 to 401 and the number of Hispanics from 266 to 350. By 1987, the percentage of blacks and Hispanics on the Houston police force had increased to 13.5 percent and 10.9 percent, respectively. He also promoted African-American and Hispanic officers to command positions. For example, Brown appointed the department's first black police captain, and he appointed three other African Americans as lieutenants. The first two Hispanic captains in the department were also appointed under Brown. He would later state that he was able to increase the opportunities for blacks and Hispanics in the Houston department by removing the barriers that had previously hindered their mobility. Although there were some minor charges from the HPOA that Brown provided black officers more opportunities than whites, he did not incite the bitter charges of "reverse discrimination" and provoke the racial discrimination lawsuits from white officers that occurred in other cities when minority officers received long-overdue promotions.[36]

By 1989, Lee Brown had successfully reformed the Houston Police Department. It was still not a model department, however; during his last year as the city's police chief, several controversial police shootings occurred that marred his tenure. Nevertheless, his work in Houston enhanced his reputation as a reformer, innovator, and troubleshooter. He became a popular lecturer and consultant in the police profession, especially on the topics of community policing and reducing police abuse of citizens. Two images of Brown emerged from his Houston experience: his critics among the Houston rank and file began to call him "Out-of-Town Brown" because of his frequent trips on the lecture and consulting circuit, and to charge that he was insensitive to the needs of the officer on the street. Most of his supporters and colleagues, on the other hand, probably agreed with Patrick V. Murphy's assessment of him in 1989 as "the best police chief in the country."[37]

In December 1989, Brown's sterling reputation earned him the job as police commissioner of New York City. His selection over three other candidates (including an in-house incumbent) marked his advancement to the pinnacle of his profession.

He was chief administrative officer of the nation's largest police department and the holder of a plum that had been reserved for years for Irish-American police administrators. Brown was not the first African American to serve as police commissioner of the New York City Police Department. In 1983, Mayor Edward Koch had appointed former New York corrections commissioner Benjamin Ward to the post. Ward served six turbulent years before resigning because of health reasons (asthma) in fall 1989. Brown was not only replacing Ward, he was also assuming the city's top law enforcement position under the city's first black mayor, David Dinkins. For the first time in the history of New York City, African Americans held two of the city's top political and administrative positions.[38]

Upon becoming New York City's second African-American police commissioner, Brown inherited all of the problems that had confronted Benjamin Ward. Under Ward, the city's crime rate had increased every year in every major category except rape and burglary. Ward had attempted to implement a Community Patrol Officer program in order to put more officers back in neighborhoods, but crimes related to drug abuse had forced him to deploy resources and personnel in that direction. He had also faced a hostile, majority-white police force that was upset over affirmative action programs to hire and promote minority officers, and that seemed to resent disciplinary control from civilian administrators. Ward's abrasive management style had also been part of the problem. He had made derogatory public statements about Hispanics and women. He was combative and fought with the PBA over the department's affirmative action promotions. Yet, as a twenty-two-year veteran of "New York's finest" himself, he stripped the city's Civilian Complaint Review Board of the power to *recommend* punishments for officers for abusing citizens. He took that action at a time when many New York City citizens were upset over the number of police abuse cases.[39]

Unlike Ward, Brown promised New Yorkers a "partnership of trust" and pledged to make the New York City police force a part of the community. One of his first official acts was to appoint a committee, chaired by former commissioner Patrick V. Murphy, to design a firearms policy for New York City police officers. Drawing upon his experiences in Atlanta and Houston, he also planned to implement his community policing and foot patrol ideas in the city's police department. In April 1990, he took the first steps in this direction when he ordered 1,775 members of the force who were serving as detectives and non-uniform personnel to work at least one shift per week in uniform, preferably on foot patrol. Three months later, he implemented Operation Take Back, a plan that placed extra foot patrols in seven high-crime precincts supported by narcotics officers, detectives, and patrol cars. This program was designed to "take back" the streets from the criminals and reduce the fear of crime among the public. Both plans had an immediate impact. The city's crime rate, which had increased steadily during the first half of 1990, began to drop after July.[40]

Despite these early efforts to address the city's crime problems, Brown's critics charged that his style of management and his deliberate approach to planning in the police department were inappropriate for New York City. Both the press and some rank-and-file officers expressed the opinion that Brown was not spontaneous enough in dealing with the city's crime problems, and that he did not have a forceful enough personality to serve as the city's top law enforcement officer. According to his critics, Brown's plan to implement his community policing ideas in New York would not work because "New York was not Texas." His critics in and outside the department also thought that he was too naive and idealistic. For example, in 1991 Brown wrote the department's first "Code of Values" for police officers. He had it posted in each precinct and incorporated as part of the training program for new recruits at the police academy. In a newspaper article following the publication of the code, several officers called it unrealistic and stated their belief that such a Code would not work for officers in New York City.[41]

Before Brown could prove his critics wrong, in August 1992 he abruptly resigned, citing his need to spend more time with his ailing wife as the reason. His resignation meant that his plans to implement community policing in the nation's largest police department were placed on hold. Thus, compared to his performances in Atlanta and Houston, Brown left a mixed legacy in New York City. After two and a half years as police commissioner, he had succeeded in reducing crime an average of 10 percent in all categories. He appointed the second-highest-ranking African-American female officer in the department's history, deputy police commissioner Elsie Scott, who was in charge of the department's training programs. He had also increased fourfold the number of officers assigned to foot patrol (from 750 to 3,000). Still, he had implemented his community policing program in only one precinct, and he had not trained enough officers to implement it fully. He also had not substantially increased the number of minority officers on the force. Shortly after Brown's departure, a study completed by University of Nebraska at Omaha researcher Samuel Walker found that New York City had the lowest percentage of blacks on its police force (11.4 percent) of any major city in the country. The percentage of blacks remained the same in 1992 as it had been in 1983, even though the force had increased by 4,000 officers during that ten-year period![42]

The fact that African Americans had made few gains on the New York City police force under Brown's administration was indicative of the tough task that he had faced in his effort to reform the nation's largest police force. Given time, perhaps he would have succeeded in working the same magic in New York City that he had worked in Atlanta and Houston. The events following his resignation, however, indicated that even the nation's "best police chief" would have continued to meet resistance in implementing his plans. For instance, less than one month after Brown's resignation, 1,000 police officers demonstrated outside of city hall to protest Mayor Dinkins's plans for a new Civilian Complaint Review Board (which Brown had opposed), his appointment of a commission to investigate police corruption, and his refusal to allow police to carry semi-automatic weapons. The demonstration turned ugly as the officers blocked traffic and made derisive comments about Dinkins as the "nigger mayor." The incident showed, at the least, that some members of the New York City police force were not ready for reform; nor were some of them ready for the leadership of a black mayor *and* a black police commissioner. Fortunately for Brown, when this incident occurred he had already left the city and accepted a teaching position at Texas Southern University in Houston.[43]

Before Lee Brown began his illustrious career as the top law enforcement officer in Atlanta, Houston, and New York City, three other African Americans had become police administrators in major American cities. In 1973, Theodore McNeal became the first black president of the St. Louis Board of Police Commissioners. In 1976, Mayor Coleman Young of Detroit appointed William Hart as that city's first black police chief. Two years later, veteran African-American police officer Burtell Jefferson assumed command of the police force in Washington, D.C. The appointments of these three men brought the total number of cities that employed their first black police executive in the 1970s to seven. (See table 12.) Just as in Cleveland, Atlanta, Newark, and Houston, all three of these appointments engendered and fostered controversy, hostility, and charges of "reverse discrimination" from white officers.

Upon his appointment in 1973, McNeal became only the fourth African American in U.S. history to lead a board of police commissioners. He was the second to serve as a police commission president in the twentieth century.[44] McNeal was a retired Missouri state senator and organizer for the Brotherhood of Sleeping Car Porters. While he was in the Missouri legislature, he had criticized the St. Louis Metropolitan Police Department for its failure to hire and promote blacks. In 1972, Governor Kit Bond, a Republican, decided to challenge McNeal to improve the department's hiring policies for black officers by offering him an appointment as the president of the Board of Police Commissioners. McNeal accepted on the condition that the governor not interfere in the decisions made by the board.[45]

As the first black president of St. Louis's Board of Police Commissioners, McNeal had a unique opportunity. Unlike most big-city departments, the SLPD's board was under state control—appointed by the governor for four-year terms and not responsible to the mayor or the city's aldermen. Only two other cities, Kansas City and Baltimore, had state-controlled police boards. The governor of Missouri had appointed the city's police commissioners since the Civil War, and there had been only a brief interlude (1899) when the local politicians had control of the administration of the police department. This allowed the police commissioners to act independently of local politics in their supervision of the department. Few police commissioners would carry out policies that were objectionable to local politicians. Nevertheless, they could hire, fire, and promote police officers without fear of political retaliation. For McNeal, the absence of local control provided him the opportunity to do what black mayors were trying to do in Newark, Atlanta, and Detroit: integrate the police department.[46]

In the four years that McNeal served as the city's top civilian law enforcement administrator, he attempted to hire and promote as many "qualified" black applicants as he could find. Before he became president of the police board, 355 African Americans served on the police force, accounting for about 15 percent of the force. (About 42 percent of St. Louis's population was black.) McNeal was not totally successful with his plan to integrate the department; he increased the number of black officers only to 18 percent (389 of 2,099 officers). He achieved his greatest success, however, by implementing a policy to promote African

Americans to command ranks. In 1972, no African American served as lieutenant colonel or captain in the department; there were only one black major, seven lieutenants, and thirty sergeants. By the end of McNeal's tenure as president of the police board in 1977, Adkins Warren had become the first black lieutenant colonel in the department; two African Americans held the rank of major, five were captains, ten were lieutenants and forty-one were sergeants. Thanks to McNeal's leadership, the St. Louis police force had a larger proportion of black officers above the rank of sergeant than any other police force in the country. But when compared to the actual numbers appointed in Atlanta under A. Reginald Eaves during the same period (1974–1978), the number of African Americans promoted by McNeal's police board was actually rather modest.[47]

Despite the promotional gains made by African Americans in the department as a result of McNeal's leadership, he still faced considerable opposition in his effort to upgrade their status on the police force. He later recalled that he had secured a consensus of all four members of the police board to make his changes in the department; he did not promote African-American officers arbitrarily without the support of other board members. Nevertheless, opponents of the promotions in the department accused McNeal of "lowering standards" and using race as a criterion for police promotions. In 1974, the mayor of St. Louis expressed his opposition to McNeal's promotions by announcing that he would seek legislation to return the police department to local control. In 1975, the St. Louis Police Officers Association publicly condemned the promotion of black officers as "reverse discrimination," detrimental to department morale. One year later, the POA unsuccessfully petitioned for an injunction to block promotions made by the police board. McNeal's hirings and promotions in the department also did not please the other side of the political spectrum in St. Louis. Norman Seay, chairman of CORE's police monitoring committee, criticized McNeal for not hiring and promoting *enough* black officers and for maintaining the department's quota for blacks on the force![48]

McNeal's retirement from the police board in 1977, after his four-year term was over, ended the hostility and opposition that his promotions in the police department had caused. Earlier, he had threatened to resign in 1974 when the mayor of St. Louis sought to undermine his authority by appealing to the state legislature to return control of the city police to local officials. He changed his mind, however, when the St. Louis branch of the NAACP and the St. Louis Ethical Police Society (the black police association) announced that they would fight the mayor's effort to gain control of police administration. Both organizations also announced their support of McNeal's policies in the police department. With this support, he continued to make his mark as the city's first African-American president of the Board of Police Commissioners. In addition to promoting more black officers than any other police board, he also successfully implemented a team policing program in one of the city's northern precincts. McNeal's term as president was the last opportunity for an African American to control police administration in St. Louis until 1991, when Clarence Harmon became the city's first black police chief.[49]

McNeal's tenure as the president of the St. Louis Board of Police Commissioners coincided with Coleman Young's first term as mayor of Detroit. Like Stokes in Cleveland and Jackson in Atlanta, Young took his election in 1973 as a mandate to reform the police department and make it more responsive to the needs of Detroit's black majority. After his inauguration, he disbanded the department's controversial STRESS unit (Stop the Robberies, Ensure Safe Streets), a police decoy unit which had established a reputation for shooting black citizens. In 1973, several black politicians in Detroit called the STRESS unit the "genocide unit" because it had killed seventeen African-American citizens. The majority-white police force also had a history of disrespecting and discriminating against black police officers. When Young began his administration in 1974, only 19 percent of the police force was African-American. The first black administrative officer in the department was not appointed until after the 1967 civil disturbance. Indeed, police abuse of the city's black population was cited as one of the prime factors causing that violent racial disturbance.[50]

Given the sordid history of racial discrimination in the police department, Young made integration of the police force one of his top priorities. Like Stokes and Gibson, he attempted to allay the fears of his white constituents that he, as a black mayor, was going to run a totally black government in Detroit. He promised that his administration would be 50 percent black and 50 percent white. Thus, he retained Phillip Tannian, a white former FBI agent appointed by Detroit's previous mayor, as his police chief. He also appointed Douglas Fraser of the United Auto Workers union as chair of the city's newly created Board of Police Commissioners. To ensure that African Americans were represented in police administration, however, he created the position of executive deputy chief of police and appointed Frank Blount, an African-American officer, to fill it. He then implemented an affirmative action plan under which the police department promoted a black officer for every white officer that was promoted. In effect, Young established a quota system for promoting officers in the police department. To achieve his goal of integrating the department by 1977, he also planned to hire 1,000 new African-American officers.[51]

Young's plan encountered several problems. Just as in other cities, white police officers resisted the affirmative action plan to promote black and white officers on a quota basis. In 1977, the Detroit Police Officers Association (DPOA) filed a lawsuit to block the plan and to force the city to promote officers strictly on the basis of "merit" and seniority, rather than by quota. The DPOA lawsuit was only a minor problem. In 1975, a devastating fiscal crisis forced the city of Detroit to lay off several thousand city employees, including more than eight hundred police officers. Since the layoffs affected newly hired blacks and women on the police force first, these two groups filed a lawsuit in federal district court to retain their jobs. They argued that the layoffs defeated the purpose of the city's affirmative action plan. The court agreed, ordering the city of Detroit to lay off white officers with more seniority first. The ruling only exacerbated racial tensions. In protest, white police officers demonstrated outside the federal court building and beat a black officer who attempted to intervene in the demonstration. Young also could not continue his integration plan in the police department because all hirings in the city were frozen.[52]

In the midst of these problems, Young was forced to appoint the city's first African-American police chief. Young had appointed Frank Blount as executive deputy chief with the understanding that he would eventually become chief. Blount's presence created an untenable situation for Police Chief Tannian because Blount acted as if he were already the police chief; members of the department often did not know *who* was in charge. Blount soon removed himself from contention as chief; he was named in a federal investigation of narcotics trafficking in the department, although he was never indicted. Chief Tannian allowed the federal investigation to continue for six months without informing Young. Young eventually read about it in the Detroit newspapers. Disturbed by Tannian's disloyalty, Young decided to remove him as police chief. In September 1976, Young named William Hart as the Detroit's first black police chief.[53]

Hart not only became Detroit's longest-serving police chief, he became the longest-serving African-American police chief in American history. (See table 15.) At the time of his appointment, Hart was a twenty-four-year force veteran who held a Doctor of Philosophy degree in psychology from Wayne State University. Described as "low key," Hart rose through the ranks of the Detroit police force and achieved his first major promotion in 1974, when Young appointed him deputy chief. He became one of Young's most loyal appointees.

While Young battled the city's fiscal crisis and the DPOA's "reverse discrimination" lawsuit, Hart concentrated on improving police services. He proved to be an innovative administrator. Shortly after becoming chief, he implemented a Crime Prevention Section in the department and increased the number of officers assigned to the community relations unit. As part of his efforts to improve relations between the Detroit police and the community, Hart established fifty-two mini-stations—one-room police offices scattered throughout the city of Detroit. The objective was to stimulate and improve citizen participation with the police and to involve citizens in crime prevention. In 1982, his program won him a national award from the Crime Prevention Coalition.

The impact of Hart's innovations on crime in the city was mixed. One study reported that between 1978 and 1983, reported crimes rose 26 percent, arrests fell 19 percent, and cases cleared by arrest went down 21 percent. Homicides, which had given Detroit the infamous title of "murder capital of the world" in 1974, dropped from a peak of 801 in 1974 to 502 in 1981. A second study reported that the mini-stations and crime prevention program had a negligible impact on crime in the city, but noted that the programs improved the department's community relations and reassured the public that something was being done about crime. Hart's innovations had a less tangible result: they combined with Young's affirmative action program to change the image of the Detroit police force as an "occupying army of outsiders."[54]

Despite Hart's achievements, however, a scandal ended his tenure as Detroit's first African-American police chief. In February 1991, the FBI indicted Hart and deputy chief Kenneth Weiner for embezzling $2.6 million from a police undercover operations fund. Hart denied the charge and sought to retain his job by taking a paid leave of absence to fight the charges against him. But the evidence against him was so overwhelming that Young replaced him with Stanley Knox, the city's second black police chief. Hart was convicted of the embezzlement charge in May 1992 and sentenced to ten years in prison.[55]

The last African-American police chief appointed in the 1970s was Burtell Jefferson of Washington, D.C. Mayor Walter Washington, the city's first black mayor, appointed Jefferson twelve years after African Americans in the District of Columbia had achieved "home rule." In one of the nation's first black-majority cities, however, the issue of appointing a black police chief had emerged as early as the 1974 mayoral election campaign, when mayoral candidate Clifford Alexander attempted to win votes by promising to appoint a black chief to alleviate some of the hostility between the District's black residents and the majority-white police force. Mayor Washington did not make such a promise, but like his counterparts in Cleveland, Atlanta, Newark, and Detroit, he knew that his black constituents wanted more control of the police. He finally appointed Jefferson as the District's first black police chief near the end of his term as mayor.[56]

After one year in command, Burtell Jefferson confronted the same problem that his counterparts in Atlanta and Detroit were facing. The Metropolitan Police Officers Association (MPOA), an organization of two hundred officers with ranks above lieutenant, accused him of using a racial quota to promote officers in the District's police department. The MPOA charged that every time Jefferson promoted a white officer, he also promoted a black officer. According to the MPOA, the discretionary system for promoting captains, inspectors, deputy chiefs, and assistant chiefs had suddenly become unfair (the system had been used by the chiefs of the Metropolitan police force for more than fifty years!). The MPOA charged that officers received no performance evaluations or ratings, and as a result, career police officers never knew where they stood. Ultimately, the members of the MPOA who were filing the complaint felt that Jefferson's promotions were especially detrimental to white members of the force because they made up a majority of the officers eligible for promotion.

The MPOA never had the opportunity to file its complaint against Jefferson's promotion policy formally in court. African-American members of the association who had not attended the meeting in which the complaint against Jefferson was announced requested more discussion of the matter before the MPOA proceeded to court. Whereas in Detroit and Atlanta white officers completely dominated departmental organizations, there were enough black members of the MPOA to challenge the filing of a lawsuit against Jefferson. Under Mayor Washington's administration, the District of Columbia police force had begun to integrate and had promoted black officers to its command ranks. In 1979, almost 45 percent of the District's police force was black. After forcing a vote to table the complaint against Jefferson until the June meeting of the MPOA, the African-American members of the MPOA succeeded in winning a vote (43–37) to rescind the complaint against Jefferson.[57]

Despite overcoming a challenge to his authority over promotions in the department, Jefferson's tenure as police chief in the District of Columbia was short, lasting less than three and a half years. His "by-the-book" style of police management clashed with the more activist style of his new boss as of 1979: newly elected District of Columbia mayor Marion Barry. Only five months into his term as mayor, Barry had angered Jefferson by interfering in the department to set policy, by meeting and negotiating with the police union without Jefferson's input, and by involving himself in promotions in the police department. Eventually, Barry and Jefferson resolved their disagreement over who should run the department: Barry reaffirmed Jefferson's leadership by publicly announcing that Jefferson was "my police chief," while Jefferson held a press conference to announce that he served at the mayor's pleasure and would continue as chief as long as the mayor retained him. After this incident, Jefferson served two more years, then resigned. Mayor Barry appointed Maurice Turner as the District's second African-American police chief.[58]

By the 1980s, black police chiefs were no longer a novelty in American cities. Although control of the police would continue to be a political issue for both blacks and whites, the fear and negative reactions that had confronted the appointment of the first black police administrators in the 1970s had somewhat dissipated.[59] As a result, by 1982 African Americans served as police chiefs in fifty American cities. Only ten, however, served in major cities. (See tables 12 and 15.) By the end of the 1980s, the number of African-American police chiefs had increased to 130, and they served in six of the nation's largest cities (Baltimore, New York, Detroit, Chicago, Philadelphia, and Houston). This unprecedented phenomenon in American history represented a 180-degree change from the second-class status that African Americans had traditionally held in American law enforcement.[60]

As noted above, there were several reasons for the emergence of African Americans as the nation's top law enforcement officers. Obviously, the emergence of black electoral majorities in cities such as Atlanta, Newark, and Washington, D.C., accounted for the quest for black control of the police function in those cities. The election of African-American mayors in American cities was usually followed by the appointment of African-American police administrators. Nevertheless, this explains only part of the phenomenon. By the 1980s, white mayors in cities such as New York City and Houston also had appointed African-American police chiefs. Other white mayors followed suit, and African Americans became police chiefs in Dayton, Ohio; Charleston, South Carolina; and Pittsburgh, Pennsylvania. This trend indicated that the mayors in these cities were looking beyond race and attempting to find the best person for the job.

To many mayors, both black and white, African Americans were increasingly perceived as the best persons for the job of police chief. African Americans became the new innovators in the police profession. That is, as the profession searched for new answers to the spiraling crime problem in American cities and the often hostile relationship between the police and black citizens, African-American police chiefs provided some of the new answers. Specifically, as we have seen, black police chiefs implemented programs such as team policing, police storefront offices, and community policing. Like the black police associations analyzed in chapter 6, black chiefs deliberately solicited support for their policies and innovations from the communities they served, and defined law enforcement as a "community service." Moreover, an African-American police chief could implement the tough and controversial law enforcement policies—such as neighborhood "stop and frisk" sweeps and patrol saturation in high-crime areas—without the charges of racism, police abuse, and harassment that they would provoke from the black community if implemented by a white police chief. Of course, the African-American leaders who were likely to make such charges would argue that the underlying motivations for such police tactics were different coming from a black police chief than from a white one. This was an important difference; African Americans could not charge a black police chief with racism just because he or she targeted certain areas in the black community for intensive law enforcement.[61]

Perhaps the most important reason for the emergence of African Americans as top law enforcement officers was timing. African Americans had served as police officers in American cities for more than a century (excluding the "pioneers" in New Orleans) and had almost always been "second-class" police officers, "tokens," "negro specials," "colored police brigades," and "colored police for colored people." Unlike other ethnic groups in American society, they had found their opportunities for advancement in the police profession blocked by racism. Thus, their ascendancy to police administration in the 1970s and 1980s was actually long overdue, and further indication of how the primacy of race in American society had long limited the talents of African Americans. In an earlier period, African Americans such as Hubert Williams, Lee Brown, and Reuben Greenberg of Charleston would have never had a chance to command big-city police departments, in spite of their obvious qualifications. The black police chiefs who emerged in the 1980s represented the culmination of three generations of African-American law enforcement officers who, in spite of the odds, had made significant contributions to American law enforcement.

EIGHT

THREE GENERATIONS

African Americans had to define their position as law enforcement officers in a racist society that usually regarded them as "blacks in police uniforms," rather than as police officers who happened to be black. Their unique role in the profession has taken more than one hundred years to develop, encompassing three generations. These three generations are nominally categorized as the "crime fighters" (black officers who served from the Reconstruction period to the 1940s), the "reformers" (those who served in the 1950s and 1960s), and the "professionals" (those who have served from the 1960s to the present). Each generation increased the effectiveness and authority of African-American police officers, and each made its own unique contribution to the history of African Americans in U.S. law enforcement.

The "crime fighters" straddled two eras in American law enforcement history. Some of them began their careers during the late nineteenth century, when most police officers were untrained and some were brutal and corrupt. Others served in the early twentieth century, when Progressive reformers sought to introduce the "military model" to American policing. Like many of their white counterparts, these officers maintained order by using physical force. While most did not have the luxury and latitude to be as corrupt as some of their white colleagues, they were often just as brutal.[1]

Racism was a very important factor in how black "crime fighters" performed their jobs, severely limiting the police experience of most African Americans in this generation. African-American police officers in the Reconstruction South often had full authority to enforce the law with both blacks and whites. The racial violence of the period mandated that they should have such authority. But like their counterparts in the postbellum North, they were also appointed for political reasons and usually to police other African Americans. In fact, after the Reconstruction period all black police officers served almost exclusively in black communities and were charged with keeping other blacks in line. To carry out their charge, the first generation of African-American police officers was given carte blanche to use physical force against black citizens. Several African-American officers earned notorious reputations in this regard.

The use of physical force against lawbreakers required strength and ability. Thus, physical prowess often superseded any other qualifications that blacks may have had for the job. African Americans who could handle a gun and physically restrain lawbreakers were hired in the Reconstruction South out of necessity—in order to deal with the recurring political violence that plagued most communities where blacks were in conflict with whites. The first black officers appointed in several cities were imposing figures as well. In 1886, Robert William Stewart became the first African American appointed to the Los Angeles police force. He was over six feet tall and a perfect physical specimen. Pictures of Stewart depicted him and his white colleagues with their shirts off and in a pose symbolizing their readiness to do battle with the criminals on the streets. Like Stewart, Hugh Allen, the first African American considered for a police job in St. Louis, was described in terms of his physical capabilities; it is less well known that he was also intelligent, achieving one of the highest scores ever on the St. Louis police exam. Even Samuel Battle, New York City's first black officer, had his height of six feet, three inches and his weight of 235 pounds noted in the newspapers repeatedly in order to confirm the notion that he had the "right" attributes for the job.[2]

Despite the charge that black "crime fighters" were sometimes too quick to use physical force to control the criminals among their own people, some of them applied that force in a legitimate manner. For example, in 1919 the *Houston Informer* lauded Houston police officer W. E. "Ned" Jones for "cleaning up" the "toughs," lawbreakers, and disorderly people in Houston's Third Ward. He was commended for handling a crime situation that had threatened the law-abiding citizens of the area. Similarly, Howard C. Gilbert and George Garrison, two black officers who joined the Columbus Police Department in 1904 and 1920, respectively, were lauded for their crime-fighting efforts in the city's Flytown area. Gilbert, a veteran of both the Spanish-American War and World War I, was described as six feet, four inches tall, 260 pounds, and athletic in stature. The legend of his work in "cleaning up" Flytown was heralded as far away as Knoxville, Tennessee. Following Gilbert as the patrol officer in Flytown was George Garrison, who was nicknamed "Black Gold." He also earned a reputation as a "two-fisted head breaker" for his work in the area.[3]

Probably the most significant African-American police officer of this generation was Ira L. Cooper of St. Louis. Appointed in 1906 as one of the department's "negro specials," Cooper was its first college graduate and its most famous detective and crime fighter. During his career he overcame the racial restrictions imposed upon him by the St. Louis department to solve several important crimes. In 1917, for example, he exposed a $35,000 bank embezzlement scheme concocted by a black porter. (White police detectives had failed to solve the year-old case because none of them believed that a black man had the intelligence to commit such a crime.) In 1930, Cooper solved the Jacob Hoffman kidnapping and broke up a kidnapping ring that was operating in the city. He also had the toughness that characterized black police officers of the "crime fighter" generation; in 1911 he singlehandedly faced down a mob and prevented a lynching by threatening to shoot anyone who approached him and his prisoner. Unlike many of his black contemporaries in other cities, Cooper was rewarded for his intelligence and ability. He became the department's first African-American sergeant and lieutenant and commanded a squad of black detectives. His reputation as a crime fighter and detective earned him listings in *Who's Who in Colored America*. When Cooper died in 1939, he was eulogized as "St. Louis' greatest police officer," and one city official remarked that "but for his color he would have been made chief of the department."[4]

Few black police officers in Cooper's day could match his achievements. In fact, while African-American officers such as Cooper represented the positive side, there was also a negative side to the "crime fighter" generation. Some of the officers were overly zealous in their effort to suppress crime and disorder among their own people. Black officers of this generation had unofficial sanction—from the department that they served as well as from some law-abiding African Americans—to do whatever was necessary to keep black criminals in line. This encouraged brutal tactics and methods on the part of some of them.

Sylvester "Two-Gun Pete" Washington of Chicago was one of the best-known police officers of the "crime fighter" generation. Washington was what the police department and the white public had in mind when they referred to a "good colored cop," because he "kept the niggers in line." Washington served as a police officer on Chicago's South Side for more than a quarter of a century, from 1934 to 1960. During that time he shot and killed more than a dozen black men. In a magazine article published in 1950, he also reported that he had made more than twenty thousand arrests in a sixteen-year period. Washington justified the number of black men that he had killed and the number of arrests by pointing out that he worked in one of Chicago's worst districts, an area known as the "Bucket of Blood." According to Washington, seven police officers had been killed in this district, and he was determined not to be the eighth. Experience had taught him to carry two .357 magnum handguns—earlier when he had carried only one gun, he had run out of bullets in a shoot-out with criminals, nearly losing his life. A reporter for the *Chicago Defender* newspaper gave Washington the nickname of "Two-Gun Pete" in 1936, and as a result of his reputation as a "shoot first and ask questions later" police officer, the name stuck with him throughout his career on the Chicago police force.[5]

From 1928 to 1946, the New York City Police Department employed a legendary officer similar to Washington. Benjamin "Big Ben" Wallace fit the physical characteristics of the "crime fighter" generation: he was six feet, five inches tall and weighed 280 pounds. During the course of his career, he developed a notorious reputation in Harlem's 28th Precinct for shooting and killing black criminals. By 1943 he had killed five and wounded several others. Wallace's tactics prompted former New York City police officer Herbert Klein, a white officer who served as a rookie in Harlem just before Wallace's demise, to observe that black police could brutalize, shoot, and kill African Americans with impunity and still not earn the charges of police brutality that a white officer would provoke for simply doing his job. Klein failed to note, however, that Wallace's reputation for shooting black criminals also placed his own life in peril. Eventually, in 1946, one of the criminals pursued by Wallace shot and killed him—but not before Wallace pumped five bullets into him and sent him to his death. The New York City Police Department gave Wallace a funeral with full honors for dying in the line of duty.[6]

Washington and Wallace served in the transitional period between the first and second generations of African-American police officers. They were "throwbacks" and misfits in an era when black officers, in some sense, were becoming better trained and being hired to serve as "reformers" in the African-American community. The appointment of African-American women as police officers symbolized the transition from the "crime fighter" generation to the "reformer" generation.

In 1916, the Los Angeles Police Department was the first big-city police force to hire an African-American policewoman, following a year-long campaign by the city's black citizens. Georgia A. Robinson, a social worker, an "ardent suffragist," and a "race" woman, was appointed for a specific reason: to work with young black women in Los Angeles and to deter them from immoral and criminal behavior. In other words, Robinson was not hired to patrol a beat and enforce the law; she was to serve as a social worker to handle cases involving black women. As Sam Walker has observed, the early twentieth-century crime prevention movement was characterized by the employment of women as social welfare workers in American police departments.[7]

Robinson's appointment was an innovation for the Los Angeles Police Department. By hiring her, the LAPD attempted to provide a service to African-American citizens. The department was also attempting to solve a law enforcement problem by not arresting young black women and burdening them with a police record. Instead, Robinson referred them to other social agencies in the black community, and attempted to keep wayward young women off the streets. For African Americans in Los Angeles, the hiring of a black policewoman meant that the LAPD was extending its crime prevention efforts to include them and was not entirely accepting the notion prevalent among early twentieth-century white Americans that African-American men and women were naturally predisposed to crime. Thus, Robinson's employment and her job assignment were definitely a reform idea.

Other big-city police departments followed Los Angeles's example. In 1918, the Chicago Police Department hired Grace Wilson as its first African-American policewoman. The Pittsburgh police force followed suit in 1919, hiring Sara McClanahan. In the same year, Cora I. Parchment became New York City's first black female officer. Black policewomen were also hired in Indianapolis, Detroit, and Columbus and Toledo, Ohio. In the 1940s and 1950s, black policewomen were hired on several southern police departments. In 1950, six black women became traffic guards and school patrol officers in Atlanta. Margie Duty became the first black policewoman in Houston in 1953. Knoxville, Tennessee, hired its first black policewoman in 1955.[8] (See table 16.)

Like their white counterparts, black policewomen worked primarily with women and juveniles. None were assigned to patrol duty in this period. Instead, they worked at dance halls, as "guardians of juvenile morals," and some still served in the traditional role of police matrons for black women prisoners. Occasionally, black policewomen had other duties. In 1929, for example, Pittsburgh policewoman Sheard Hawkins traveled to Rockford, Tennessee, to capture a black woman who had fled there after murdering her husband in Pittsburgh. When Jean Clayton joined the Cleveland police force in 1951 as a member of the Women's Bureau, she worked with the Detective Bureau as a member of the Pandering Unit. It was a unique job; she assisted prostitutes in filing charges against males for procuring. In addition to working in a job that departed from previous police policy regarding vice crimes in Cleveland, Clayton joined the Shield Club and worked to make the police department more responsive to the needs of its black citizens. In general, black policewomen epitomized the "reformer" generation because of their assignment as social welfare workers serving the African-American community.[9]

The hiring of African-American policewomen coincided with other reforms developed by black officers. In 1925, police officer Leslie Shaw of Columbus, Ohio, organized the Friendly Service Bureau as a part of the police department. Co-sponsored by the Columbus Urban League, the Friendly Service Bureau was a crime prevention program aimed at African Americans who had migrated to the Ohio capital from the South. Its methodology was simple: to deter black migrants from committing crimes in Columbus, the bureau met them upon their arrival in the city, helped them to find housing and jobs, and taught them the "dos and don'ts" of city life in Columbus. Shaw's program was unique; it attempted to dispel the notion among most whites and some of Shaw's superiors that blacks were natural criminals.

Georgia Robinson, Leslie Shaw, and the policewomen appointed before the 1950s were the first of the second generation of African-American police officers. Robinson and Shaw were reformers who believed that African Americans were not natural criminals and could be saved from the American criminal justice system. This was a progressive idea for early twentieth-century American society, because most people believed that blacks were predisposed to crime. Shaw lectured throughout the country in an attempt to reform the attitudes of law enforcers about the alleged criminality of African Americans. His Friendly Service Bureau became a model for other police departments attempting to prevent crimes among blacks.[10]

The appointment of African-American police officers in the South also exemplified the emergence of blacks as "reformers" in American law enforcement. In the 1940s and 1950s, black officers were hired in southern cities specifically to patrol black communities, to prevent crime, and to improve race relations. Some of these officers were college graduates and were considered to be the "best of the Negro race." Many of them accepted the idea that they were employed specifically to control the crime, vice, and chaos that had historically plagued many black neighborhoods. Unlike the officers of the "crime fighter" generation that preceded them, these African Americans rejected the police abuse, brutality, and heavy-handed methods that traditionally had been used in the nation's black communities. The "reformer" generation sought to improve the quality of law enforcement accorded African Americans.

In 1950, Marshall Jenkins, a Houston police officer and president of the local chapter of the Texas Negro Peace Officers' Association, presented a lecture to Houston's Fifth Ward Civic Club and the Knights of Peter Claver fraternal organization. In explaining the new relationship between black policemen and citizens of the black community, he said that "the old time untrained Negro officer is being replaced by intelligent well trained men." He observed that "the old Negro officers were placed on the force with no training and used force and violence to take the place of training, but today's [1950] officers are carefully selected and highly trained, not only in handling prisoners, but in methods of treating the public." Jenkins also said that black police wanted to provide the African-American community the best policing possible. Ironically, Jenkins gave his speech less than one year after Sylvester "Two-Gun Pete" Washington of Chicago had published his article justifying his killing of eleven black criminals and his violent methods of suppressing crime in Chicago's South Side black community. Jenkins's speech was an indication that African-American police officers were ready to complete the transition from the "crime fighter" generation to the "reformer" generation.[11]

African-American police officers redefined their role in the 1950s and 1960s, largely through black police associations such as the Guardians and the Afro-American Patrolmen's League. The leaders of those organizations, police officers such as Renault Robinson of Chicago, A. V. Young of Houston, Al Deal of Philadelphia, and Henry Williams of San Francisco, emerged as the new breed of black police officers. Unlike other American police reformers, they advocated the end of long-standing racial policies that hindered the advancement of black officers and that shortchanged the police protection provided the nation's African-American communities. One of the most significant questions that the "reformer" generation raised was, How could the American police establishment claim to advocate "professionalism" when many of its leaders and members still supported racist police practices against black citizens as well as against black police officers? This was a question (and a dilemma) that the American police establishment had failed to address since the beginning of formal, uniformed police forces in the nineteenth century.[12]

The "professional" generation of black police officers began to force the police establishment to address this dilemma. Rank-and-file black officers, through their associations, and black police administrators in cities such as Newark, Houston, and Detroit proposed a "new professionalism" for the American police establishment. Although the new professionalism was aimed specifically at ending racist practices, it also included the revival of earlier ideas about police training and community relations, and some new ideas such as policies for police use of deadly force and the conception of police officers as "public servants" subject to community regulation and citizen review.

Black police administrators such as Hubert Williams, Lee Brown, William Hart, and A. Reginald Eaves implemented many reform policies that the police establishment had traditionally opposed. These policies were aimed at regulating police use of deadly force, creating team and community policing programs, implementing affirmative action programs for the employment and promotion of women and minority officers, and developing innovative programs to reduce the hostility between the police and the communities that they served. To institutionalize the policies that they advocated, in 1976 black police administrators formed their own organization, the National Order of Black Law Enforcement Executives (NOBLE). Like the IACP, which was the embodiment of professionalism among white police executives ninety-seven years earlier, NOBLE became the symbol of the new professionalism advocated by black police executives. It lobbied state and national government bodies for legislation to address the problem of black-on-black crime and for policies to reform police practices. Like the NBPA, NOBLE held annual conferences at which its members discussed such issues as police use of deadly force, community policing, and new methods of crime prevention. As a result of the presence of African-American police chiefs in half of the nation's largest cities in the 1980s, NOBLE became as important as the IACP. Its members and leaders, police administrators such as Lee Brown and Hubert Williams, made NOBLE the nation's most progressive police organization.[13]

Black police administrators were not the only officers advocating the new professionalism in American policing. Advocates have also come from the rank and file. The black officers of the contemporary professional generation are the best trained of the three generations that have served in American law enforcement. The "reformer" generation that preceded them eliminated some of the racial barriers that had limited the opportunities of African Americans entering law enforcement, enabling those who make up the current generation to take advantage of these new opportunities.

While attending San Francisco State College in the late 1960s, Wilbert K. Battle decided to pursue a career in law enforcement. He enrolled in the San Francisco Police Department's new cadet program and participated for three years until he was twenty-one and eligible to attend the police academy. Unlike many of the officers who preceded him, who often entered the field because it was one of the best jobs available to blacks at the time, Battle consciously chose police work as his life-long profession. He soon learned, however, that racism still plagued the SFPD.

Upon beginning his police career officially in 1971, Battle was given poor assignments and labeled as a "militant" by his superiors when he requested better treatment. He had several altercations with his supervisors when he complained about the use of derogatory terms for blacks by his fellow officers. He also disagreed with the abusive treatment that some of his colleagues used against black suspects during arrests. As a result of the hostility and harassment that he faced for challenging racist practices in the SFPD, by 1973 he was ready to quit the police force.

Battle did not quit, however. Instead, he became a member of the department's black police association, the Officers for Justice. He later credited the veteran officers in the OFJ for saving his career by teaching him the "survival techniques" needed to negotiate racist practices in the SFPD. Nevertheless, Battle was not satisfied with just coping with racism in the department; he wanted to change these practices and force his colleagues to behave more professionally. The OFJ became the vehicle through which he began to advocate a new standard of professionalism for San Francisco police officers. In 1977, at the age of twenty-seven, he became the youngest president of the OFJ. He used the office as a platform not only to speak out against the racist practices that he had witnessed in the police department, but also to advocate more professional standards for police officers. He was assigned to the department's Community Relations unit and continued to be one of department's leading advocates for police professionalism.

In 1979, Battle became the youngest national chairman of the National Black Police Association. During his one-year tenure, he helped that organization to continue its growth as the leading association advocating the advancement of black police officers. The chairmanship of the NBPA gave him a national forum for his ideas on police professionalism. He continued to call for an end to police abuse of citizens, for the implementation of policies to regulate police use of deadly force, and for better police training in community relations. After leaving the chairmanship of the NBPA, he became coordinator of an anti-crime program with the San Francisco Housing Authority. His successful leadership of this program further established him as an able police professional, and in 1988 he was even mentioned as a possible candidate for police chief of the SFPD when that position became vacant.[14]

Two years before Wilbert Battle became the national chairman of the National Black Police Association, women members of the organization introduced an important issue at the annual conference in New Orleans. They wanted the NBPA to use the name National Black *Police* Association rather than National Black *Policemen's* Association. They asked male members to recognize that police work was no longer an exclusively male occupation. Officers such as Peggy Triplett of New York City, Jean Clayton of Cleveland, and Mary Jarrett of Detroit led this fight. They pointed out that the organization vacillated between the use of the gender-neutral name and the sexist name. At the session where the women raised this issue, Triplett showed several items, including an organization tee shirt and the organization's official stationery, which used the sexist "Policemen's Association." The women won their case; national chairman Gustave Thomas of New Orleans and national information officer Renault Robinson of Chicago (who had printed and used the offensive stationery) vowed to correct the sexist oversights.[15]

The women members of the NBPA had gained some ground in the struggle of African-American women of the professional generation to be recognized as full police officers. As noted above, black policewomen in the reform era had the same duties as white policewomen: they worked primarily with women and juvenile offenders. Although some, such as Jean Clayton of Cleveland and Vivian Strange of Los Angeles, worked undercover in vice units, policewomen were more social workers than police officers. Rarely were they assigned to patrol duty or to supervision. Even when the first black women achieved promotions, they remained in the assigned roles reserved for policewomen. In 1950, for example, Vivian Strange became the first black woman promoted to police sergeant. She was assigned as a community relations officer. Similarly, in 1955, when Violet Hill

Whyte became Baltimore's first black woman police sergeant, her duties did not change significantly. Although she was assigned to supervise other policewomen, she continued her same duties as community liaison officer in Baltimore's Northwestern police station. While the 1950s and 1960s were the decades when African-American men began to change their role in the police establishment, there were still limited roles for policewomen—especially African-American policewomen.[16]

At the beginning of the professional generation, the status and role of policewomen began to change. In the 1970s, several police departments began to eliminate gender-specific duties and to assign women to patrol duty on the same basis as men. Two interrelated factors led to the use of women as patrol officers. The first was the 1972 amendment to the Civil Rights Act of 1964 which extended the act's coverage to public employees and prohibited job discrimination on the basis of sex. The second was an investigation conducted by the Police Foundation in the early 1970s on the performance of women patrol officers. In general, the studies found that women officers carried out their duties effectively. The only variance from the performance of male officers was that they made fewer arrests and gave fewer traffic citations. The studies also found that women police officers were less likely than their male counterparts to engage in unbecoming conduct.[17]

With the support of anti-discrimination laws and corroboration of their effectiveness as patrol officers, women began to join police forces across the country in increasing numbers. In the mid-1970s, for example, the number of women police officers in New York City doubled, from about 300 to 650. More than half of those officers (359) were African Americans. Women also made significant gains in other big-city police departments, particularly those with African-American police administrators. As a result of affirmative action hiring programs in Newark, Detroit, Atlanta, Washington, D.C., and Houston, women doubled their percentage in the police ranks nationally from about 4 percent in 1975 to 9 percent in 1990.[18]

African-American women benefited the most from the increased hiring of women as police officers. In Detroit, for example, by 1980 women held 12 percent of the police jobs; 63 percent of those jobs were held by black women. Smaller but substantial increases occurred in other cities where blacks controlled police administration. Thus, by 1990 more than 35 percent of the women police officers employed in the United States were African Americans. Black women also constituted 30 percent of all African-American police officers—a significant statistic in light of the fact that only 15 percent of all police were African Americans. Thus, in just twenty years, black women police officers had made substantial gains in the profession, and they became the best example of the professional generation of African-American police officers.[19]

Several black women have demonstrated that gender is no barrier to professional policing. In 1981, Jackie Davis joined the New Orleans Police Department at the age of twenty-four. Davis was a former homeless person who had turned her life around, taken the police exam, and secured a job as a police officer. She was assigned to the rape squad in 1985 and achieved a perfect arrest record on all of the cases assigned to her. This led to her assignment to the homicide squad, and she became the first woman ever to work in the NOPD's homicide division. Her assignment did not meet with the approval of her male colleagues, who attempted to intimidate her by leaving dog feces on her desk, removing her name from the duty roster, and placing a picture of a gorilla in her mailbox. She responded to these acts by proving to her colleagues that she was more than qualified to serve in the division. In her first year she solved all fourteen of the homicide cases assigned to her. In her first five years in the division, she solved eighty cases out of the eighty-two that she was assigned, a 97 percent success rate. Her achievements as a homicide detective won her acclaim from the mayor as well as from New Orleans's Black Organization of Police. Her more enlightened colleagues in the NOPD accepted her exceptional ability and remarked that no one in the history of the department had ever had such a success rate in solving homicides.[20]

Other African-American women rose to administrative positions in the profession. In 1982, Beverly Harvard, a graduate of Morris Brown College and a ten-year veteran of the Atlanta Police Department, became that city's first female deputy police chief. She headed the Career Development and Criminal Investigations Division. By 1991 she had become second in command in the Atlanta department and supervised its day-to-day operations. In 1984, police commissioner Benjamin Ward appointed Billie Holliday as New York City's first black woman deputy police commissioner. Holliday held a master's degree from the New School for Social Research in New York. Although her appointment as deputy commissioner was a lateral entry, she previously had served as a commissioner on the New York State Parole Board. She was in charge of community relations for the NYPD and developed two important programs: one required sensitivity training for new police recruits; the other was a community outreach program to identify and address problems before they required police intervention. Following Harvard and Holliday into police administration in the 1980s was Joyce F. Leland, who in 1985 became the first female deputy chief of the District of Columbia's metropolitan police force. Leland, a graduate of Howard University, had served on the police force for twenty years. She was assigned as commander of the Seventh Police District, one of the Capital City's toughest districts.[21]

Perhaps the most significant appointment of a woman police administrator representing the professional generation was that of Dr. Elsie Scott. In 1991, New York City police commissioner Lee Brown appointed Scott as deputy police commissioner for education and training. Scott's appointment was significant for several reasons. First, she was a black woman who had been raised in the South and had witnessed the shooting of her father by "nightriders" (the shooter was, in fact, a city policeman by day). Second, she brought to the job a strong educational background in criminal justice, having earned a bachelor's degree at Southern University, a master's from Atlanta University, and a doctorate from the University of Iowa. Third, she had also done a considerable amount of research in the field of criminal justice. Thus, her preparation for the job matched and even superseded the educational and training backgrounds of earlier police reformers turned police administrators.[22] Scott had taught criminal justice at three universities and also had served as the executive director of the National Order of Black Law Enforcement Executives. In short, she epitomized the professional generation of black police officers who were attempting to improve policing in American society and to make the police more responsive to the people that they served.[23]

Lee Brown appointed Scott as head of police training for one reason: to train the officers of the New York City Police Department in his gospel of community policing. Her background and training made her the best person for this awesome task. She began by overhauling the department's police training curriculum. Her objective was to prepare officers to be community-oriented "problem solvers," rather than to merely react from one emergency call to the next. She established one-day training sessions for supervisory personnel in the concept of community policing as a way of gradually implementing it in the department. In her first year, three thousand officers received five hours of such training. Before she could take the training to the next level, however, Lee Brown resigned as police commissioner and the program was placed on hold.[24]

The professional generation has proven that African Americans are the new innovators in police work. The black women and men who have risen to the top of the American police profession represent the culmination of more than one hundred years of the black experience in American law enforcement. That experience was filled with setbacks, racism, and violence, as well as much progress. The experience of African Americans in U.S. law enforcement has closely paralleled their experience in American society overall. The institution that was historically developed, in part, to suppress and regulate the behavior of Africans in America has now become the measure of African-American acceptance and progress in modern American society.

APPENDIX A

R. B. Eleazer's Letter and Questionnaire to Police Chiefs Employing African-American Police Officers

Oct. 5, 1933

Chief of Police
Louisville, Kentucky

Dear Sir:

As a means of lessening the tension between the police department of Atlanta and the large Negro element of the population, it has been suggested that the appointment of a few Negro police to patrol their own areas might be distinctly helpful. Before sponsoring such a step, however, the group of citizens who are considering it feel the need of definite information as to the results of this policy in other Southern cities.

On behalf of the committee, I am therefore writing to request of you the information asked on the enclosed blank, and also any further light of fact or opinion which you may care to throw upon the situation. This information will be of very great value to the Committee and will be deeply appreciated. We trust you can supply it without inconvenience.

A meeting of the committee will be held next week and we hope to have your reply in hand before that time. Assuring you of our hearty appreciation of the expected help, I am

Yours very truly,
R. B. Eleazer

QUESTIONNAIRE

How long has your city employed Negro police?

Why were they first appointed, if for some specific reason?

How many are employed?

In what sections do they serve, and what are their duties?

Have you found them efficient, or otherwise?

What has been the effect upon Negro crime?

What upon the attitude of colored people toward the law?

What is their relation to white offenders?

What is the public attitude toward their employment?

Further information or observations:

Signed____________________________

Office____________________________

SOURCE: Committee on Interracial Cooperation Papers, Special Collections, Woodruff Library, Atlanta University Center, Atlanta, Georgia.

APPENDIX B: TABLES

TABLE 1
Year of Organization of Formal Police Force in Selected Cities

City	*Year*
Boston	1838
New York City	1845
Philadelphia	1845
New Orleans	1852
Cincinnati	1852
Chicago	1855
St. Louis	1855
Newark	1857
Baltimore	1857
Detroit	1865

Source: Williams and Murphy, "The Evolving Strategy of Policing," 3.

TABLE 2
Year of First Reconstruction African-American Police Appointments in Selected Cities

City	*Year*
New Orleans	1867
Selma	1867
Mobile	1867
Montgomery	1868
Raleigh	1868
Washington, D.C.	1869
Houston	1870
Austin	1872
Chattanooga	1872
Jacksonville	1873
Memphis	1878

Sources: (New Orleans) *New Orleans Tribune,* May 31, 1867; (Mobile) *New Orleans Tribune,* July 3, 1867; (Selma) Kolchin, *First Freedom,* 158; (Montgomery) Fitzgerald, *The Union League Movement in the Deep South,* 192; (Washington) Alfers, *Law and Order in the Capital City,* 35; (Houston) *Houston Telegraph,* December 13, 1870; (Austin) White, *Pictorial History of Black Policemen in Austin,* 2; (Memphis) Rousey, "Yellow Fever and Black Policemen in Memphis," 357; (Chattanooga, Raleigh, and Jacksonville) Rabinowitz, "Conflict between Blacks and the Police," 65–66.

TABLE 3
African-American Police Percentage in Selected Southern Cities during Reconstruction

	1870		*1880*	
City	*% of Police*	*% of Population*	*% of Police*	*% of Population*
New Orleans	28	26	7	27
Charleston	42	54	19	55
Mobile	37	44	0	42
Memphis	0	39	23	44
Montgomery	50	49	0	59
Vicksburg	50	55	15	49
Norfolk	3	46	0	46
Portsmouth	29	35	0	34

Source: Rousey, "The New Orleans Police," 329.

Table 4

Year of First African-American Police Appointments in Selected Cities

City	*Year*
Chicago	1872
Pittsburgh	1875
Indianapolis	1876
Boston	1878
Cleveland	1881
Philadelphia	1881
Columbus, Ohio	1885
Los Angeles	1886
Cincinnati	1886
Detroit	1890
Brooklyn, New York (before consolidation)	1891
St. Louis	1901
New York City (after consolidation)	1911

Sources: (Chicago) Gosnell, *Negro Politicians,* 247; (Pittsburgh) *Pittsburgh Times,* July 25, 1909; (Indianapolis) *Cleveland Gazette,* January 28, 1888; (Boston) *The National Advocate,* October 3, 1914; (Philadelphia) Reaves, *Black Cops,* 11, and Sprogle, *The Philadelphia Police,* 173; (Cleveland) *Cleveland Leader,* June 4, 1881; (Columbus) *Cleveland Gazette,* January 9, 1886; (Los Angeles) Broome, *LAPD's Black History,* 43; (Cincinnati) *Cleveland Gazette,* June 26, 1886; (Detroit) Katzman, *Before the Ghetto,* 120; (Brooklyn) Alexander, *Blue Coats, Black Skin,* 16; (St. Louis) *St. Louis Globe-Democrat,* March 29, 1901; (New York City) Alexander, *Blue Coats, Black Skin,* 20.

Table 5

Year of First African-American Promotion to Sergeant in Selected Cities

City	*Year*
Boston	1895 (1937)*
Chicago	1897
Los Angeles	1917 (1943)
Detroit	1918
St. Louis	1923 (1948)
New York City	1923 (1926)
Philadelphia	1929 (1943)
Columbus, Ohio	1943 (1946)
Cincinnati	1949
Cleveland	1949

Sources: (Boston) *National Advocate,* October 3, 1914; "Boston Gets First Colored Police Sergeant," press release, August 1937, ANP Clipping File; (Chicago) Gosnell, *Negro Politicians,* 263–264; (Los Angeles) Broome, *LAPD's Black History,* 48 and 98; (Detroit) *Pittsburgh Courier,* June 18, 1932; (St. Louis) "Detective Ira Cooper Promoted To Detective Sergeant," 9, and *Pittsburgh Courier,* December 18, 1948; (New York) *New York Age,* May 26, 1923, and *New York Times,* May 22, 1926; (Philadelphia), Reaves, *Black Cops,* 147; (Columbus, Ohio) Dulaney, "Blacks as Policemen in Columbus, Ohio, 1895–1945," 14–15; (Cincinnati) "Cincinnati Has First Negro Police Sergeant," press release, September 7, 1949, ANP Clipping File; (Cleveland) Davis, *Black Americans in Cleveland,* 369–370.

*The dates in parentheses indicate when African-American "*police* sergeants" or sergeants with "command responsibilities" were appointed. Usually African Americans were appointed as "detective sergeants" and were not allowed to supervise other officers or to command districts.

Table 6
African-American Police Representation in Selected Cities, 1952

City	*Total No. of Police*	*% African-American Population*	*% African-American Police*
Chicago	7,023	13.6	3.9
Cincinnati	818	15.5	7.5
Cleveland	1,812	16.2	4.3
Detroit	4,232	16.2	0.8
Los Angeles	4,207	8.7	2.9
New York City	19,478	9.5	3.1
Pittsburgh	1,311	12.2	4.7
Philadelphia	4,224	15.1	3.5
St. Louis	1,912	17.9	5.0
San Francisco	1,579	5.6	0.3

Source: Kephart, "The Integration of Negroes into the Urban Police Force," 326 and 329.

Table 7
Year of First Post-Reconstruction African-American Police Appointment in Selected Southern Cities

City	*Year*	*City*	*Year*
Louisville, Kentucky	1923	Macon, Georgia	1948
Baltimore, Maryland	1937	Memphis, Tennessee	1948
Charlotte, North Carolina	1941	Nashville, Tennessee	1948
Raleigh, North Carolina	1942	Chattanooga, Tennessee	1948
Little Rock, Arkansas	1942	Columbia, South Carolina	1949
Durham, North Carolina	1944	Charleston, South Carolina	1950
Miami, Florida	1944	New Orleans, Louisiana	1950
Norfolk, Virginia	1945	Fort Worth, Texas	1953
Richmond, Virginia	1946	Mobile, Alabama	1954
Dallas, Texas	1947	Montgomery, Alabama	1954
Savannah, Georgia	1947	Jackson, Mississippi	1963
Atlanta, Georgia	1948		

Sources: (Louisville) *Louisville News*, July 14, 1923; (Baltimore) *Baltimore Afro-American*, December 11, 1937; (Charlotte) *Charlotte Observer*, June 19 and July 10, 1941; (Little Rock) *Memphis Commercial Appeal*, August 20, 1942; (Raleigh) *Norfolk Journal and Guide*, December 5, 1942; (Norfolk) *Richmond Times-Dispatch*, November 8, 1945, and *Kansas City Call*, November 23, 1945; (Durham) *Durham Herald*, July 2, 1944; (Miami) *Atlanta Daily World*, September 3 and 8, 1944; (Richmond) *Richmond Times-Dispatch*, May 1 and June 4, 1946; (Dallas) *Dallas Morning News*, March 25, 1947; (Savannah) *Savannah News*, May 1, 1947, and *New York Times*, June 26, 1947; (Memphis) *Memphis Commercial Appeal*, September 10 and 11, 1948, and *Atlanta Daily World*, October 28, 1948; (Nashville) *Pittsburgh Courier*, April 24, 1948, and *Chicago Defender*, May 29, 1948; (Chattanooga) *Chattanooga Daily World*, June 4, 1948; (Macon) *Atlanta Constitution*, June 8, 1948; (Columbia, South Carolina) *Columbia Lighthouse and Informer*, December 19, 1948, and *Chicago Defender*, March 12, 1949; (Charleston) *Charleston News and Courier*, August 29, 1950, and *Chicago Defender*, September 9, 1950; (New Orleans) *Louisiana Weekly*, June 24, 1950; (Fort Worth) *Houston Informer*, January 10, 1953; (Mobile) *Birmingham World*, February 12, 1954; (Montgomery) *Montgomery Advertiser*, May 1 and 9, 1954; (Jackson) *Jackson Clarion-Ledger*, June 21, 1963.

Table 8

Number of African-American Police Officers in Selected Southern Cities, 1949–1959

City	*1949*	*1954*	*1959*
Miami	30	58	85
Houston	17	26	35
Dallas	4	4	6
Louisville	34	32	37
Atlanta	6	16	31
Greensboro, North Carolina	5	9	8
Montgomery	0	5	0
Mobile	0	2	12
Memphis	12	15	10
Richmond	7	21	21
Charleston	0	9	12
New Orleans	0	12	42

Sources: *Memphis World*, February 25, 1949; "Negro Policemen in Southern Cities," 1; Rudwick, "Negro Police Employment in the Urban South," 102; Rudwick, *The Unequal Badge*, 6 and 8; *New York Times*, July 27, 1959.

TABLE 9
Year of First African-American Police Sergeant Appointment in Selected Southern Cities

City	*Year*
Louisville	1944
Baltimore	1947
Memphis	1950
Richmond (Det. Sgt.)	1952
Miami	1955
Charlotte	1956
Atlanta	1961
Galveston	1961
San Antonio	1966
Dallas	1966
Austin	1969
Charleston	1971
Houston	1974

Sources: (Louisville) *Louisville Courier-Journal,* April 15, 1944; *Atlanta Daily World,* April 18, 1944; (Baltimore) "Police Administration and Courts," *Race Relations,* March 1947, 235; (Memphis) "Two Memphis Cops Win Promotion," press release, October 2, 1950, ANP Clipping File; (Richmond) "Richmond Gets First Negro Detective Sergeant," press release, January 28, 1952, ANP Clipping File; (Miami) *Miami Times,* July 18, 1969; (Charlotte) *Norfolk Journal and Guide,* May 19, 1956; (Atlanta) *Atlanta Daily World,* April 2, 1961; (Galveston) *Dallas Express,* February 4, 1961; (San Antonio) *San Antonio Express,* August 24, 1966; (Dallas) *Dallas Express,* July 9, 1966; (Austin) White, *Pictorial History of Black Policemen in Austin,* 129–131; (Charleston) *Charleston News and Courier,* September 6, 1971; (Houston) *Houston Post,* April 13, 1974.

TABLE 10
Year of First African-American Police Captain Appointment in Selected American Cities

City	*Year*
Chicago	1940
New York City	1952
Columbus, Ohio	1952
Philadelphia	1954
St. Louis	1956
Cleveland, Ohio	1960
Washington, D.C.	1965
Newark	1967
Atlanta	1968
Los Angeles	1969
St. Paul, Minnesota	1970

Sources: Dulaney, "Black Shields," 66; *Washington Star,* January 24, 1965.

TABLE 11

Year African-American Police Association Chartered or Founded in Selected Cities

City	*Association*	*Year*
Houston	Texas Negro Peace Officers' Association	1935
Miami	Colored Police Benevolent Association	1946
Cleveland	Shield Club	1946
New York City	Guardians Association	1949
North Carolina	Negro Law Enforcement Association	1953
Philadelphia	Guardians Civic League	1956
Detroit	The Guardians of Michigan	1963
Chicago	Afro-American Patrolmen's League	1967
San Francisco	Officers for Justice	1968
St. Louis	Ethical Police Society	1968
Los Angeles	Oscar Joel Bryant Association	1968
Atlanta	Afro-American Patrolmen's League	1969

Sources: Dulaney, "Black Shields," 67; *Norfolk Journal and Guide,* June 25, 1955.

TABLE 12

Year First African-American Police Chiefs Appointed in Selected American Cities

City	*Year*	*City*	*Year*
Portsmouth, Ohio	1962	Baltimore, Maryland	1984
Cleveland, Ohio*	1970	Miami, Florida	1985
Gary, Indiana	1970	New Orleans, Louisiana*	1985
Newark, New Jersey*	1973	Pittsburgh, Pennsylvania	1986
Atlanta, Georgia*	1974	Philadelphia, Pennsylvania*	1988
Detroit, Michigan	1976	Mobile, Alabama	1990
Washington, D.C.	1978	Columbus, Ohio	1990
Houston, Texas	1982	St. Louis, Missouri	1991
Charleston, South Carolina	1982	Los Angeles, California	1992
Chicago, Illinois*	1983	St. Paul, Minnesota	1992
Dayton, Ohio	1983	Jackson, Mississippi	1992
New York City*	1984		

Sources: (Portsmouth) "Portsmouth's Police Chief," 144–147; (Cleveland) "Lieutenant General B. O. Davis, Jr. Is Praised, Cited at Ceremony," 5; (Gary) Leavy, "Hail to the Chiefs," 115; (Newark) *New York Times,* December 11, 1972; (Atlanta) Raffauf, "Jackson v. Inman"; (Detroit) "Coleman Young Appoints Black Police Chief; Black Deputy Chief Kills Self," 8; (Washington, D.C.) *Washington Post,* May 31, 1979; (Houston) *Washington Post,* March 10, 1982; (Dayton, Ohio) Leavy, "Hail to the Chiefs," 120; (Charleston, South Carolina) "Charleston, S.C. Gets Its First Black Police Chief," 8; (New York City) "Veteran New York Cop Is Named City's First Black Commissioner of Police," 12; (Chicago) "Chicago Mayor Names City's First Black Police Superintendent," 8; (Baltimore) *Washington Post,* June 21, 1984; (Miami) "Miami's Finest," 24; (New Orleans) *Dallas Morning News,* December 29, 1984; (Pittsburgh) "Pittsburgh Gets First Black Chief of Police," 6; (Philadelphia) Reaves, *Black Cops,* 183; (Mobile, Alabama) *Dallas Morning News,* January 21, 1990; (Columbus, Ohio) *Columbus Dispatch,* June 16, 1990; (St. Louis) "Clarence Harmon Named First Black Police Chief for City of St. Louis, Mo.," 6; (Los Angeles) Herbert, "The Fruits of L.A.: New Chief, New Approach," 22; (Jackson, Mississippi) "Wilson Appointed Police Chief of Jackson, Miss.," 8; (St. Paul, Minnesota) "St. Paul Names First Black Police Chief," 8.

*Public safety directors, commissioners, or superintendents.

Table 13

Percentage of African Americans on Selected* American Police Forces, 1975 and 1985

City	*% on Police Force*		*% in Labor Force*	
	1975	*1985*	*1970*	*1980*
Atlanta	29.9	47.2	47.7	60.9
Detroit	22.3	41.2	41.2	60.0
Newark	21.9	26.4	48.9	54.7
New York City	8.1	12.5	18.6	23.1
Miami	11.2	16.7	20.3	22.8
Columbus, Ohio	4.1	5.7	16.9	19.3
Mobile, Alabama	11.2	17.4	29.9	30.7

Source: William G. Lewis, "Toward Representative Bureaucracy," 258.

*Black police chiefs were appointed in all of these cities from 1970 to 1990. See table 12.

Table 14

African-American Percentage on Selected Police Forces Compared to African-American Population, 1987

City	*% on Police Force*	*% in Population*
Washington, D.C.	54.8	70.2*
Atlanta	51.7	66.2
Detroit	48.0	64.2
Newark	25.4	57.7
Chicago	22.4	40.0
Baltimore	21.8	54.5
Cleveland	21.7	43.4
Philadelphia	19.2	37.6
Pittsburgh	18.8	24.1
Houston	13.5	27.5
New York City	11.0	25.0

Source: Andrew Hacker, *Two Nations,* 236.

*Washington's police force was the first to become 50 percent black.

TABLE 15

Longevity of African-American Police Executives

Name	*City*	*Tenure in Office*	*Total*
William Hart	Detroit	1976–1991	15 years
Hubert Williams	Newark	1974–1985	11 years
Reuben Greenberg	Charleston	1982–1993	11 years
Lee P. Brown	Houston	1982–1990	8 years
Benjamin Ward	New York City	1984–1989	5 years
Leroy Martin	Chicago	1987–1992	5 years
A. Reginald Eaves	Atlanta	1974–1978	4 years
Willie Williams	Philadelphia	1988–1992	4 years
Fred Rice	Chicago	1983–1987	4 years
Burtell Jefferson	Washington, D.C.	1978–1981	3 years
Clarence Dickson	Miami	1985–1988	3 years
William H. Moore	Pittsburgh	1986–1987	1 year

Sources: Leavy, "Hail to the Chiefs," 115; Narine, "Top Cops," 130; Ronald E. Childs, "Top Brass," 60–61; "New Cops on the Block," 22–25.

TABLE 16

Year of First African-American Policewoman Appointment in Selected Cities

City	*Year*
Los Angeles	1916
Chicago	1916
Indianapolis	1918
Pittsburgh	1919
New York City	1919
Washington, D.C.	1920
Detroit	1921
Toledo, Ohio	1922
Baltimore	1937
Columbus, Ohio	1938
Atlanta	1950
Houston	1953
Knoxville, Tennessee	1955
Dallas	1971

Sources: (Los Angeles) Coombs, "Colored Police for Colored People;" (Chicago) *Chicago Defender,* January 10, 1916; *The Crisis,* June 1918, 87; (Indianapolis) *Indianapolis Freeman,* June 22, 1918; *The Crisis,* August 1918, 190; (Pittsburgh) *Pittsburgh Sun,* February 11, 1919; (New York City) *Chicago Defender,* June 17, 1919; (Washington, D.C.) *Cleveland Advocate,* August 2, 1920; (Detroit) *Chicago Defender,* May 7, 1921; (Toledo, Ohio) *Cleveland Call,* March 18, 1922; (Baltimore) *Baltimore Afro-American,* December 11, 1937; (Columbus, Ohio) Department of Public Safety, *Minute Book,* 9, April 12, 1938, 70; (Atlanta) *Atlanta Daily World,* March 3, 1950; (Houston) "Houston, Texas Gets First Woman Officer," 8; (Knoxville) *Knoxville News-Sentinel,* October 6, 1955; (Dallas) *Dallas Morning News,* February 4, 1985. See also "Negro Policewomen," in *Negro Year Book, 1918–1919,* 53.

NOTES

Preface

1. Policeman's Benevolent Fund Association, *History of the Columbus Police Department* (Columbus, Ohio, 1900), 35; *Columbus Dispatch,* May 15, 1966. Gaston's service record can be found in Columbus, Ohio, Department of Public Safety, *Police and Fire Transfer Record,* Columbus, Ohio, City Hall Vault.

2. Robert Wintersmith, *Police and the Black Community* (Lexington, Mass.: D. C. Heath and Co., 1974), 2–39; Homer Hawkins and Richard Thomas, "White Policing of Black Populations: A History of Race and Social Control in America," in Ellis Cashmore and Eugene McLaughlin, eds., *Out of Order?: Policing Black People* (New York: Routledge, 1991), 65–86. For an analysis of the slave patrol and the elaborate police systems organized to police the behavior of African Americans during slavery, see H. M. Henry, *The Police Control of the Slave in South Carolina* (New York: Negro Universities Press, 1968), 28–52; Gladys-Marie Fry, *Night Riders in Black Folk History* (Knoxville: University of Tennessee Press, 1975), 82–109; Richard C. Wade, *Slavery in the Cities: The South, 1820–1860* (New York: Oxford University Press, 1964), 80–82, 98–106. See also chapter 1.

3. Dennis C. Rousey, "The New Orleans Police, 1805–1889: A Social History" (Ph.D. dissertation, Cornell University, 1978), 43; Police Mutual Benevolent Association, *1900 History of the New Orleans Police Department* (New Orleans: Graham Press, 1900), 23. An earlier ordinance had set the precedent for the participation by "des noirs libres et hommes libres de couleur" in the city militia. See *Moniteur de la Louisiane,* December 3, 1803. For the unique race relations in early New Orleans, see Donald E. Everett, "Free Persons of Color in Colonial Louisiana," *Louisiana History* 7 (1966): 21–50; Alice Dunbar-Nelson, "Free Persons of Color in Louisiana," Part I, *Journal of Negro History* 1 (October 1916): 359–376; and Dunbar-Nelson, "Free Persons of Color in Louisiana," Part II, *Journal of Negro History* 2 (January 1917): 51–78.

4. Walter Leavy, "Hail to the Chiefs," *Ebony,* November 1982, pp. 115–120; Dalton Narine, "Top Cops: More and More Black Police Chiefs Are Calling the Shots," *Ebony,* May 1988, pp. 130–136; "30-Year Veteran Neal Named to Top Police Job in Philadelphia," *Jet,* September 7, 1992, p. 4; Solomon J. Herbert, "The Fruits of L. A.: New Chief, New Approach," *Black Enterprise,* October 1992, p. 22.

5. James I. Alexander, *Blue Coats, Black Skins: The Black Experience in the New York City Police Department since 1891* (Hicksville, N.Y.: Exposition Press, 1978); Eugene J. Watts, "Black and Blue: Afro-American Police Officers in Twentieth Century St. Louis," *Journal of Urban History* 7 (February 1981): 131–168; James S. Griffin, "Blacks in the St. Paul Police Department: An Eighty-Year Survey," *Minnesota History* 45 (Fall 1975): 255–265; James N. Reaves, *Black Cops* (Philadelphia: Quantum Leap Publishers, 1991); Homer F. Broome, *LAPD's Black History, 1886–1976* (Los Angeles, 1976); Dennis C. Rousey, "Black Policemen in New Orleans during Reconstruction," *The Historian* 49 (February 1987): 223–243; May Walker, *The History of the Black Police Officers in the Houston Police Department, 1878–1988* (Dallas: Taylor Publishing Co., 1988); Rousey, "Yellow Fever and Black Policemen in Memphis: A Post Reconstruction Anomaly," *Journal of Southern History* 51 (August 1985): 357–374.

6. See, as examples, James F. Richardson, *The New York Police: Colonial Times to 1901* (New York: Oxford University Press, 1970); Roger Lane, *Policing the City: Boston, 1822–1885* (Cambridge, Mass.: Harvard University Press, 1967); Eric H. Monkkonen, *Police in Urban America, 1860–1920* (Cambridge: Cambridge University Press, 1981); Robert M. Fogelson, *Big-City Police* (Cambridge, Mass.: Harvard University Press, 1977); Elaine H. and Gene E. Carte, *Police Reform in the United States: The Era of August Vollmer, 1905–1932* (Berkeley: University of California Press, 1975); James F. Richardson, *Urban Police in the United States* (Port Washington, N.Y.: Kennikat Press, 1974).

7. A partial but representative listing of some of the studies on African-American police officers by sociologists and criminologists includes: Nicholas Alex, *Black in Blue: A Study of the Negro Policeman* (New York: Meredith Corp., 1969); William M. Kephart, *Racial Factors and Urban Law Enforcement* (Philadelphia: University of Pennsylvania Press, 1957); Eugene Beard, "The Black Police in Washington, D.C.," *Journal of Police Science and Administration* 5 (March 1977): 48–52; James D. Bannon and Marie G. Wilt, "Black Policemen: A Study of Self Images," *Journal of Police Science and Administration* 1 (March 1973): 21–29; William Kephart, "The Integration of Negroes into the Urban Police Force," *Journal of Criminal Law, Criminology, and Police Science* 40 (September–October 1954): 325–333; Edward Palmer, "Black Police in America," *The Black Scholar* 5 (October 1973): 19–27; Valencia Campbell, "Double Marginality of Black Policemen," *Criminology* 17 (February 1980): 477–484; Michael Wubnig, "Black Police Attitudes in the New York City Police Department: An Exploratory Study" (Ph.D. dissertation, City University of New York, 1975); Jon J. Daykin, "A Study of Negro Police Officers in Eleven Mid-South Cities" (M.A. thesis, University of Mississippi, 1965); John J. Grimes, "The Black Man in Law Enforcement: An Analysis of the Distribution of Black Men in Law Enforcement and Related Recruitment Problems" (M.A. thesis, John Jay College of Criminal Justice, 1969); James F. Scott, "A Study of Role Conflict among Policemen" (Ph.D. dissertation, Indiana University, 1968); Stephen H. Leinen, *Black Police, White Society,* (New York: New York University Press, 1984).

8. For a turn-of-the-century comment on this belief in the African-American community, see W. E. B. Du Bois, *The Souls of Black Folk,* in John Hope Franklin, ed., *Three Negro Classics* (New York: Avon Books, 1965), 329–331; Du Bois, "Some Notes on Negro Crime, Particularly in Georgia," *Atlanta University Publications,* Nos. 7–11, 1902–1906 (New York: Octagon Books, 1968), 1–9 and 55–56. See also Mackie C. Johnson, "Metropolitan Police Role in Our Society," *Negro History Bulletin* 26 (October 1962): 43–44, for a similar perspective on this belief.

Acknowledgments

1. For early examples of the argument for "colored police for colored people," see *New Orleans Tribune,* May 10, 1867; "Plea for a Negro Constabulary," *Southern Workman,* December 1906, pp. 646–648; Claire Chester Coombs, "Colored Police for Colored People," *Out West,* February 1917, p. 18; and "Negro Police Captains," *The Messenger,* July 1919, pp. 9–10.

2. The "classic" and often-cited description of white police officers as oppressors is found in James Baldwin, *Nobody Knows My Name* (New York: Dell Publishing Co., 1961), 61–63. After the 1967 "race riots" or civil disorders, depending on your perspective, President Lyndon B. Johnson appointed his National Advisory Commission on Civil Disorders chaired by Illinois governor Otto J. Kerner. Thus the Kerner Commission Report. See *Report of the National Advisory Commission on Civil Disorders,* Otto J. Kerner, Chairman (Washington, D.C.: Government Printing Office, 1968), 165–166. See also Cordell S. Thompson, "How Race Crisis Splits Black and White Policemen," *Jet,* October 16, 1969, pp. 14–19. Even recent articles have referred to the police as an occupying army in the nation's black communities. For example, see Mike Hudson, "Black and Blue," *Southern Exposure* 18 (Winter 1990): 16–19.

1. African-American History and American Policing

1. The quotes by Frank Gill and Polly Colbert are from the WPA Slave Narratives conducted in the 1930s. The quote by Marie Bing is from an interview by Gladys-Marie Fry, in Washington, D.C. March 6, 1964. All are cited in Fry, *Night Riders,* 105, 103, and 106, respectively.

2. Most scholars have dutifully traced the origins of the American police back to England and ignored the influences of the slave patrol and racism on the American police heritage. Two of the few writers of police history who accept the separate model thesis for American police forces are Patrick V. Murphy and Hubert Williams. See Patrick V. Murphy, "The Development of Urban Police," *Current History* 70 (June 1976): 245–248; and Hubert Williams and Patrick V. Murphy, "The Evolving Strategy of Policing: A Minority View," *Perspectives on Policing* 13 (January 1990): 1–16.

3. Harry A. Ploski and James Williams, eds., *Reference Library of Black America* II (Philadelphia: Gale Research, 1992), 483; Department of Commerce, Bureau of the Census, *Negro Population of the United States, 1790–1915* (Washington, D.C.: Government Printing Office, 1918), 25.

4. For examples, see especially Peter Wood, *Black Majority: Negroes in Colonial South Carolina from 1670 through the Stono Rebellion* (New York: W. W. Norton, 1975), 271–284; Harvey Wish, "American Slave Insurrections before 1861," *Journal of Negro History* 22 (July 1937): 299–320; William F. Cheek, *Black Resistance before the Civil War* (Beverly Hills, Calif.: Glencoe Press, 1970).

5. For the slave codes in South Carolina established in 1712 and 1740, see Henry, *Police Control of the Slave in South Carolina,* 4–18; and "An Act for the Better Ordering of Negroes and Slaves," in Leslie H. Fishel and Benjamin Quarles, eds., *The Negro American: A Documentary History* (Glenview, Ill.: Scott, Foresman and Co., 1967), 21–26.

6. Fry, *Night Riders,* 82–107; Henry, *Police Control,* 28–52; Wintersmith, *Police and the Black Community,* 13–20; "Poor White-Trash Paterollers," in Middleton Harris, *The Black Book* (New York: Random House, 1974), 19; Williams and Murphy, "The Evolving Strategy of Policing," 4.

7. Kenneth T. Jackson and Stanley Schultz, eds., *Cities in American History* (New York: Alfred A. Knopf, 1972), 41–49.

8. Lane, *Policing the City,* 3–13, 95–100; Richardson, *The New York Police,* 49–50; *History of the Columbus Police Department,* 21; Howard O. Sprogle, *The Philadelphia Police: Past and Present* (Philadelphia, 1887), 86; "Chicago Police, 1833–1976," *Chicago Police Star,* July 1976, p. 4; Richardson, *Urban Police in the United States,* 19–28. Eric Monk--konen discounts crime and disorder as the operative factors for the organization of formal police forces in the United States. He also theorizes that the adoption of police uniforms was more symbolic of the emergence of the "new police" than the legislative enactments that created these formal police forces. Monkkonen, *Police in Urban America,* 49–64 and Appendix A. See his reiteration of this position in "History of the Urban Police," in Michael Tonry and Norval Morris, eds., *Modern Policing* (Chicago: University of Chicago Press, 1992), 549–553.

9. For an example of how the elites created and controlled the police in Detroit, see John C. Schneider, "Public Order and the Geography of the City: Crime, Violence, and the Police in Detroit, 1845–1875," *Journal of Urban History* 4 (February 1978): 183–208. For the Irish dominance in American police forces, see Richardson, *Urban Police in the United States,* 53–54; Lane, *Policing the City,* 141, 196–197; Samuel Walker, *A Critical History of Police Reform: The Emergence of Professionalism* (Lexington, Mass.: Lexington Books, 1977), 10–11; Dennis C. Rousey, "Hibernanian Leatherheads: Irish Cops in New Orleans, 1830–1880," *Journal of Urban History* 10 (November 1983): 61–84; Fogelson, *Big City Police,* 36–37. H. Bruce Pierce noted that the Irish dominated the police in New York City so thoroughly that the police force was called the "Irish Mafia." Pierce, "Blacks and Law Enforcement: Toward Police Brutality Reduction," *The Black Scholar* 17 (May 1986): 50.

10. Williams and Murphy, "The Strategy of Policing," 4; Richard C. Wade, "The Negro in Cincinnati, 1800–1830," *Journal of Negro History* 39 (January 1954): 43–57; Gary B. Nash, *Forging Freedom: The Formation of Philadelphia's Black Community, 1720–1840* (Cambridge, Mass.: Harvard University Press, 1988), 275–277; Leonard P. Curry, *The Free Black in Urban America, 1800–1850: The Shadow of the Dream* (Chicago: University of Chicago Press, 1981), 96–110; Jerome H. Skolnick and Thomas C. Gray, *Police in America* (Boston: Little, Brown and Co., 1975), 18–19.

11. Victor Ullman, *Martin R. Delany: The Beginnings of Black Nationalism* (Boston: Beacon Press, 1971), 29–31; Frank A. Rollin, *Life and Public Services of Martin R. Delany* (New York: Kraus Reprint of the 1868 edition, 1969), 44.

12. Ploski and Williams, *Reference Library,* 483.

13. John Hope Franklin and Alfred A. Moss, *From Slavery to Freedom: A History of Negro Americans* (New York: Alfred A. Knopf, 1988), 136–157; Leon F. Litwack, *North of Slavery: The Negro in the Free States, 1790–1860* (Chicago: University of Chicago Press, 1969), 168.

14. Litwack, *North of Slavery,* chapters 4, 5, and 6; Nash, *Forging Freedom,* 217–223.

15. Charshee C. L. McIntyre, *Criminalizing a Race: Free Blacks during Slavery* (Queens, N.Y.: Kayode Publications, 1993), 71–86.

16. Wade, *Slavery in the Cities,* 248–252; Ira Berlin, *Slaves without Masters: The Free Negro in the Antebellum South* (New York: Pantheon Books, 1974), 108–114; Curry, *The Free Black in Urban America,* 17–33; Thomas Ingersoll, "Free Blacks in a Slave Society: New Orleans, 1718–1812," *William and Mary Quarterly* 48 (April 1991): 173–200.

17. Berlin, *Slaves without Masters,* xiv; McIntyre, *Criminalizing a Race,* 53. For the peculiar situation in Baltimore where free blacks outnumbered slaves, see Barbara J. Fields, *Slavery and Freedom on the Middle Ground: Maryland during the Nineteenth Century* (New Haven: Yale University Press, 1985), 40–62.

18. See William Stanton, "Less in Love with Freedom," in Barry N. Schwartz and Robert Disch, *White Racism: Its History, Pathology and Practice* (New York: Dell Publishing Co., 1970), 79–97; McIntyre, 8; and Winthrop Jordan's excellent study on the origins of Anglo-American racism, *White over Black: English Attitudes toward the Negro, 1550–1812* (Chapel Hill: University of North Carolina Press, 1968).

19. Aileen Kraditor, *Means and Ends in American Abolitionism: Garrison and His Critics on Strategy and Tactics, 1834–1850* (New York: Vintage Books, 1969), chapters 2 and 3; Franklin and Moss, *From Slavery to Freedom,* 164–172.

20. Williams and Murphy, "The Evolving Strategy of Policing," 3–4.

21. Ivan D. Steen, "Charleston in the 1850s: As Described by British Travelers," *South Carolina Historical Magazine* 71 (1970): 42; Laylon W. Jordan, "Police Power and Public Safety in Antebellum Charleston: The Emergence of a New Police, 1800–1860," in Samuel M. Hines and George W. Hopkins, eds., *South Atlantic Urban Studies* 3 (1979): 127; Rousey, "The New Orleans Police," 34; Wade, *Slavery in the Cities,* 98–102; John T. O'Brien, "Factory, Church, and Community: Blacks in Antebellum Richmond," *Journal of Southern History* 44 (November 1978): 516, 529.

22. G. S. Rowe, "Black Offenders, Criminal Courts, and Philadelphia Society in the Eighteenth Century," *Journal of Social History* 22 (Summer 1989): 697–702; Curry, *The Free Black in Urban America,* 110–119; Harris, *The Black Book,* 27.

2. *Black Pioneers*

1. Everett, "Free Persons of Color in Colonial Louisiana," 21–50; Donald E. Everett, "Emigres and Militiamen: Free Persons of Color in New Orleans, 1803–1815," *Journal of Negro History* 38 (October 1953): 377–412; Rousey, "The New Orleans Police," 43–44; Roland C. McConnell, *Negro Troops of Antebellum Louisiana: A History of the Battalion of Free Men of Color* (Baton Rouge: Louisiana State University Press, 1968), 3–32; James E.

Winston, "The Free Negro in New Orleans, 1803–1860," *Louisiana Historical Quarterly* 21 (1938): 1075–1076; Kimberly S. Hanger, "Avenues to Freedom Open to New Orleans' Black Population, 1769–1779," *Louisiana History* 31 (Summer 1990): 237–240. By 1810, "free persons of color" (5,727) together with African slaves (10,824) outnumbered whites (approx. 8,000) in New Orleans. See David Chandler, "An Experiment in Black and White: A Short history of Miscegenation in New Orleans," *New Orleans Magazine,* March 1974, pp. 70–79. The best and most recent source on the militia groups of "free men of color" in New Orleans is Kimberly S. Hanger, "A Privilege and Honor to Serve: The Free Black Militia of Spanish New Orleans," *Military History of the Southwest* 21 (Spring 1991): 59–86. Hanger notes that there were two "black" militia groups: one of *pardo* (light-skinned) blacks and one of *moreno* (dark-skinned) blacks.

2. Police Mutual Benevolent Association, *1900 History of the New Orleans Police Department,* 23; H. E. Sterkx, *The Free Negro in Antebellum Louisiana* (Cranbury, N.J.: Fairleigh Dickinson University Press, 1972), 186–187; Rousey, "The New Orleans Police," 27–30.

3. *1900 History of the New Orleans Police Department,* 23; Rousey, "The New Orleans Police," 34–46; Dunbar-Nelson, "People of Color in Louisiana," Part II, 51; *Moniteur de la Louisiane,* December 3, 1803; Earl E. Riley, "Historical Notes," *Law and Order,* April 1976, p. 61; Everett, "Emigres and Militiamen," 377 and 390–392; Henry Kmer, "They Also Served: Blacks in Defense of New Orleans," *New Orleans Magazine,* January 1972, pp. 65–76; McConnell, 33–49; Ira Berlin, in *Slaves without Masters,* 117–128, notes that when the United States assumed control of New Orleans, American whites sought not only to disband the "black" militia groups, but also to take away many of the rights that "free persons of color" had enjoyed under French and Spanish rule. See also Winston, "The Free Negro in New Orleans," 1079, who notes that when Claiborne officially recognized the black militia groups, he testified "to the zeal that they [free men of color] displayed for the public safety." The loyalty of free black militia in the 1811 insurrection is also supported by James H. Dormon, "The Persistent Specter: Slave Rebellion in Territorial Louisiana," *Louisiana History* 18 (1977): 402.

4. Sterkx, *The Free Negro,* 182–183; Winston, "The Free Negro," 1079–1080; Roger A. Fischer, "Racial Segregation in Antebellum New Orleans," *American Historical Review* 74 (February 1969): 926–937; Berlin, *Slaves without Masters,* 120–129; McConnell, *Negro Troops,* 99–104; James H. Dormon, "Louisiana's 'Creoles of Color': Ethnicity, Marginality, and Identity," *Social Science Quarterly* 73 (September 1992): 615–617; McIntyre, *Criminalizing a Race,* 69–70.

5. Rousey, "The New Orleans Police," 43 and 63–64; Rousey, "Black Policemen in New Orleans during Reconstruction," 223–227; Harry Gardner, "The History of Blacks in U.S. Law Enforcement" (Ph.D. dissertation, Union Graduate School, 1978), 10 and 13. David C. Rankin has argued, however, that "free men of color" in New Orleans always supported whites and the racial status quo against "blacks" because of their mixed race background, the ownership of slaves by some of them, and the benefits (although minimal) that their unique position provided them in New Orleans society. See Rankin, "The Impact of the Civil War on the Free Colored Community of New Orleans," *Perspectives in American History* 11 (1977–78): 379–418.

6. Curry, *The Free Black in Urban America,* 17; Rousey, "The New Orleans Police," 58, 63; Rousey, "Hibernanian Leatherheads: Irish Cops in New Orleans, 1830–1880," 61–84; Loren Schweninger, "Antebellum Free Persons of Color in Postbellum Louisiana," *Louisiana History* 30 (Fall 1989): 347; Robert C. Reinders, "The Free Negro in the New Orleans Economy, 1850–1860," *Louisiana History* 6 (1965): 273–285; Fischer, "Racial Segregation," 930–932. Both Rousey and Fischer note the decline in status of "free persons of color" in New Orleans after the acquisition of the Louisiana territory by the United States.

7. George C. Rable, *But There Was No Peace: The Role of Violence in the Politics of Reconstruction* (Athens: University of Georgia Press, 1984), 33–42 and 43–58; J. Paul Mitchell, ed., *Race Riots in Black and White* (Englewood Cliffs, N.J.: Prentice-Hall, 1970), 29–31 and 92–94; Herbert Shapiro, *White Violence and Black Response: From Reconstruction*

to Montgomery (Amherst: University of Massachusetts Press, 1988), 5–27; *New Orleans Tribune,* May 10, 1867; Leon Litwack, *Been in the Storm So Long: The Aftermath of Slavery* (New York: Alfred A. Knopf, 1979), 281–282 and 287–288. For a contemporary account of the 1866 New Orleans race riot, see Jean Jacque Houzeau, *My Life on the New Orleans Tribune: A Memoir of the Civil War Era* (Baton Rouge: Louisiana State University Press, 1984 [originally published in 1872]), 127–132.

8. *New Orleans Tribune,* May 10 and 12, 1867; Litwack, *Been in the Storm So Long,* 547; Rousey, "The New Orleans Police," 200 and 208. As we will see in chapter 7, the *Tribune*'s threat to elect a black mayor was prophetic; in the twentieth century, the election of a black mayor became the only way that African Americans obtained their fair share of police jobs.

9. *New Orleans Tribune,* May 28 and 31, 1867, June 1, 4, 6, 9, and 19, 1867; Rousey, "Black Policemen in New Orleans," 228; Rousey, "The New Orleans Police," 209. For a short biography of Octave Rey, see Rodolphe Lucien Desdunes, *Our People and Our History* (Baton Rouge: Louisiana State University Press, 1973), 114–123. Desdunes's book was originally published in 1911 as *Notre hommes et notre histoire.* According to Thomas Holt, during Reconstruction whites throughout the South coined a new verb, "to Africanize," in order to describe their fear of blacks allegedly taking over institutions in the South formerly and exclusively dominated by whites—especially the police and the military. See Thomas Holt, *Black over White: Negro Political Leadership in South Carolina during Reconstruction* (Urbana: University of Illinois Press, 1977), 95.

10. John W. Blassingame, *Black New Orleans, 1860–1880* (Chicago: University of Chicago Press, 1973), 31, 162–163; Rousey, "The New Orleans Police," 210; *New Orleans Tribune,* June 19, 1867, October 26, 1867, December 18, 1867.

11. John R. Ficklen, *History of Reconstruction in Louisiana* (Baltimore: Johns Hopkins University Press, 1910), 208–209; Rousey, "The New Orleans Police," 211–212; Rousey, "Black Policemen in New Orleans," 231; A. E. Perkins, "Oscar James Dunn," *Phylon* 4 (Second Quarter 1943): 110.

12. Rousey, "The New Orleans Police," 213; Melinda Meek Hennessey, "Race and Violence in Reconstruction New Orleans: The 1868 Riot," *Louisiana History* 20 (Winter 1979): 83–84; *Annual Report of the Board of Metropolitan Police, for the Year Ending September 30, 1869* (New Orleans, 1870), 7–10, Louisiana Room, New Orleans Public Library.

13. James G. Dauphine, "Knights of the White Camelia and the Election of 1868," *Louisiana History* 30 (Spring 1989): 173–190; Stuart O. Landry, *The Battle of Liberty Place: The Overthrow of Carpetbag Rule in New Orleans, September 14, 1874* (New Orleans: Pelican Publishing Co., 1955); Rable, *But There Was No Peace,* 77, 126–129; Hennessey, "Race and Violence," 77–91; Rousey, "The New Orleans Police," 261–267. For a recent analysis of the black opposition to the commemoration of Liberty Place and the removal of the monument, see the *Dallas Morning News,* November 3, 1991; and "New Orleans Removes Controversial Monument," *Jet,* August 16, 1993, p. 18.

14. Howard N. Rabinowitz, "The Conflict between Blacks and the Police in the Urban South, 1865–1900," *The Historian* 39 (November 1976): 64–66; Rousey, "The New Orleans Police," 216–217 and 330–331; *New Orleans Tribune,* July 3, 1867; Litwack, *Been in the Storm So Long,* 552; Vernon L. Wharton, *The Negro in Mississippi, 1865–1890* (New York: Harper and Row, 1965), 167; Howard N. Rabinowitz, *Race Relations in the Urban South, 1865–1890* (Urbana: University of Illinois Press, 1980), 41–43; Howard N. Rabinowitz, "Holland Thompson and Black Political Participation in Montgomery, Alabama," in Rabinowitz, ed., *Southern Black Leaders of the Reconstruction Era* (Urbana: University of Illinois Press, 1982), 254–255; Edwin P. Cantwell, "A History of the Charleston Police Force," *Charleston Yearbook* (Charleston, S.C., 1908), 7; Walker, *History of Black Police Officers in the Houston Police Department,* 5; Louie White, *A Pictorial History of Black Policemen Who Have Served in the Austin Police Department, 1871–1982* (Austin: Austin Police Department, 1982), 2; Nancy J. Potts, "Unfulfilled Expectations: The Erosion of Black Political Power in Chattanooga, 1865–1911," *Tennessee Historical*

Quarterly 49 (Summer 1990): 113; Kenneth G. Alfers, *Law and Order in the Capital City: A History of the Washington Police, 1800–1886,* GW Washington Studies, No. 5 (Washington, D.C.: George Washington University, 1976), 35.

15. Alfers, *Law and Order,* 35; Walter L. Fleming, *Civil War and Reconstruction in Alabama* (New York: Peter Smith, 1949), 765; Rabinowitz, "The Conflict between Blacks and the Police," 67; *New Orleans Tribune,* July 3, 1867.

16. Rousey, "The New Orleans Police," 241–251; Rabinowitz, *Race Relations in the Urban South,* 43–51. For a more comprehensive analysis of the impact of black officeholders in the Reconstruction South, see Eric Foner, *"The Tocsin of Freedom": The Black Leadership of Radical Reconstruction,* 31st Annual Robert Fortenbaugh Memorial Lecture (Gettysburg, Pa.: Gettysburg College, 1992), 10–23.

17. Rable, *But There Was No Peace,* 105–106; Ann Patton Baenziger, "The Texas State Police during Reconstruction," *Southwestern Historical Quarterly* 72 (April 1969): 470–491; Houston *Forward Times,* June 15, 1963; Samuel O. Young, "Ku Klux Days," in *True Stories of Old Houston and Houstonians* (Houston: Oscar Springer, 1913), 86; Otis Singletary, *Negro Militia and Reconstruction* (Austin: University of Texas Press, 1957), 145–147.

18. Robert A. Taylor, "Crime and Race Relations in Jacksonville, 1884–1892," *Southern Studies* 2 (Spring 1991): 27. The complaint of white citizens in Vicksburg about black police appeared in the *Cleveland Gazette,* September 28, 1884. Barksdale is quoted in Wharton, *The Negro in Mississippi,* 168. For an example of a race riot precipitated by a black deputy sheriff trying to exercise his duty as a law enforcement officer in Meridian, Mississippi, in 1870, see Dorothy Lee Chisolm, "The Black Response to White Violence in Four Southern States during Reconstruction, 1865–1877" (M.A. thesis, Howard University, 1979), 50.

19. Rousey, "Yellow Fever and Black Policemen," 364–366; W. Marvin Dulaney, "The Texas Negro Peace Officers' Association: The Origins of Black Police Unionism," *Houston Review* 12 (1990): 60–61; Taylor, "Crime and Race Relations in Jacksonville," 26–27; Edward N. Akin, "When a Minority Becomes the Majority: Blacks in Jacksonville Politics, 1887–1907," *Florida Historical Quarterly* 53 (October 1974): 128 and 136; Franklin and Moss, *From Slavery to Freedom,* 234; Eric Anderson, *Race and Politics in North Carolina: The Black Second* (Baton Rouge: Louisiana State University Press, 1981), 247–251.

20. James B. Crook, "Jacksonville in the Progressive Era: Responses to Urban Growth," *Florida Historical Quarterly* 65 (July 1986): 69; Akin, "When a Minority Becomes a Majority," 138–139; Taylor, "Crime and Race Relations in Jacksonville," 27–28.

21. Laylon W. Jordan, "Police and Politics: Charleston in the Gilded Age, 1880–1900," *South Carolina Historical Magazine* 81 (1980): 42–47; *Baltimore Afro-American,* February 22, 1896; *Nashville Banner,* April 25, 1905. An article in the *Charleston News-Times,* July 21, 1947, maintained that James Fordham and several African Americans retained their positions on the force after the 1876 "redemption" because they supported Wade Hampton and the Democrats. Whatever political clout Fordham had during the twenty years that he was on the force, he must have lost it after his dismissal in 1896.

22. Blassingame, *Black New Orleans,* 224, 226–227; Rousey, "Black Policemen in New Orleans," 240–241; *New Orleans Daily Picayune,* April 4, 1889; *1900 History of the New Orleans Police Department,* 93, 107, 115, 119, and 121; *New Orleans Item,* December 10, 1919; "New Orleans Gets Two Negro Police," press release, June 19, 1950, Associated Negro Press Clipping File, Claude A. Barnett Papers, Chicago Historical Society. Hereafter cited as the ANP Clipping File.

23. Department of Commerce, Bureau of the Census, *Negro Population in the United States, 1790–1915* (Washington, D.C.: Government Printing Office, 1918), 525; *East Tennessee News,* July 23, 1914.

24. Rousey, "The New Orleans Police," 338; Rousey, "Black Policemen in New Orleans," 242; Jordan, "Police and Politics," 42; Desdunes, *Our People and Our History,* 114–123; *New Orleans Daily Picayune,* April 21, 1886; *Baltimore Afro-American,* February 22, 1896. For Rey's and Fordham's demographic backgrounds, see United States Depart-

ment of Commerce, Bureau of the Census, *Tenth Census of the United States* (1880), Volume 9, E.D. #39, Sheet 32, and Volume 6, E.D. #75, Sheet 2, respectively. For Fordham, see also United States Department of Commerce, Bureau of the Census, *Twelfth Census of the United States* (1900) Volume 13, E.D. #110, Sheet 17; Eric Foner, *Freedom's Lawmakers: A Directory of Black Officeholders during Reconstruction* (New York: Oxford University Press, 1993), 181.

3. *The Politics of Tokenism*

1. For a discussion of how African Americans were still limited in their access to political patronage in the North, see David Gerber, "A Politics of Limited Options: Northern Black Politics and the Problem of Change and Continuity in Race Relations Historiography," *Journal of Social History* 14 (Winter 1980): 235–255.

2. Harold F. Gosnell, *Negro Politicians: The Rise of Negro Politics in Chicago* (Chicago: University of Chicago Press, 1935), 247.

3. Gosnell, *Negro Politicians,* 252–253; Ralph J. Bunche, "The Thompson-Negro Alliance," *Opportunity,* March 1929, pp. 78–80; City of Chicago Department of Development and Planning, *Chicago's Black Population: Selected Statistics* (Chicago, 1975), 5; Bruce Smith, *Chicago Police Problems: An Approach to Their Solutions* (New York: Institute of Public Administration, 1934), 17.

4. Smith, *Chicago Police Problems,* 18 and 45; Citizens' Police Committee, *Chicago Police Problems* (Chicago: University of Chicago Press, 1931), 3 and 41; Mark Haller, "Police Reform in Chicago, 1905–1935," *American Behavioral Scientist* 13 (May–August 1970): 649–665; Harry W. Morris, "The Chicago Negro and the Major Political Parties, 1940–1948" (M.A. thesis, University of Chicago, 1950), 37; "The Elections of 1940: Chicago's Machine Runs on Gratitude," *Life,* October 21, 1940, p. 94.

5. One source reports the number of African Americans on the Philadelphia police force at a high of 287 in 1917. See "General Race News," *Half-Century Magazine,* July 1917, p. 8. See also Reaves, *Black Cops,* 144–146; Roger Lane, *William Dorsey's Philadelphia and Ours: On the Past and Future of the Black City in America* (New York: Oxford University Press, 1991), 210–212; James Erroll Miller, "The Negro in Pennsylvania Politics with Special Reference to Philadelphia since 1932" (Ph.D. dissertation, University of Pennsylvania, 1945), 318–323, 381; W. E. B. Du Bois, *The Philadelphia Negro: A Social Study* (New York: Schocken Books, 1967 edition), 132; John A. Saunders, *100 Years After Emancipation: History of the Philadelphia Negro, 1787 to 1963* (Philadelphia: Philadelphia Tribune, 1963), 111–112, 157; *Philadelphia Independent,* November 19, 1939; Clara Hardin, *The Negroes of Philadelphia: The Cultural Adjustment of a Minority Group* (Fayetteville, Pa.: Craft Press, 1943), 15–16; "Philadelphia Police Detective Exam Up Soon; Force Continues Long Practice of Prejudice," press release, January 19, 1949, ANP Clipping File.

6. *Cleveland Plain Dealer,* June 3 1881; *Cleveland Leader,* June 4, 1881; *Cleveland Gazette,* January 9, 1886, and July 19, 1890; "Distinguished Negroes in Ohio," *Negro History Bulletin* 5 (May 1942): 174; Firemen's Pension Fund and Police Benevolent Association, *A Review of the Department of Public Safety of Columbus, Ohio* (Columbus, 1894), 77; David M. Katzman, *Before the Ghetto: Black Detroit in the Nineteenth Century* (Chicago: University of Illinois Press, 1973), 120; *St. Louis Star,* August 23, 1899; *St. Louis Globe-Democrat,* March 29, 1901. For the personnel records of Gordon, Wilkinson, and Allen (who was finally appointed in 1903), see St. Louis Board of Police Commissioners, *Metropolitan Police Record Book,* Book 4, pp. 93 and 109, St. Louis Police Archives, St. Louis Police Department, St. Louis, Missouri.

7. W. Marvin Dulaney, "Black and Blue: The Black Policemen of Columbus, Ohio, 1895–1974" (M.A. thesis, Ohio State University, 1974), 31; J. S. Himes, "Forty Years of Negro Life in Columbus, Ohio," *Journal of Negro History* 27 (April 1942): 136–137; Cleveland, Ohio, Department of Police, *Annual Report* (1904), 18; Carrie W. Clifford,

"Cleveland and Its Colored People," *Colored American Magazine*, July 1905, p. 371; *Chicago Defender*, December 30, 1922; *Cleveland Call and Post*, May 17, 1930; (Cleveland) *Plain Dealer*, September 19, 1974, and March 28, 1977; interview with Lynn R. Coleman, Cleveland, Ohio, September 17, 1977, audiotape; "Three Negro Specials Appointed," *St. Louis Police Journal*, June 8, 1912, p. 6. See Watts, "Black and Blue," 131–168, on how the reaffirmation of state control of the St. Louis Police Department may have limited the influence of local politics on the police department. But Watts still felt that the SLPD remained susceptible to political pressure.

8. Gosnell, *Negro Politicians*, 247 and 254; African Americans did not wear uniforms for the first twelve years that they served on the Chicago police force. Sprogle, *The Philadelphia Police*, 173; Lane, *Dorsey's Philadelphia*, 212–213; *Cleveland Gazette*, June 20, 1889, July 27, 1889, August 24, 1889, January 4, 1890; Katzman, *Before the Ghetto*, 120; Alexander, *Blue Coats, Black Skin*, 16–17; *St. Louis Globe-Democrat*, March 29–31, 1901; St. Louis Police Relief Association, *Souvenir History of the St. Louis Police Department, 1902* (St. Louis, 1902), pictures 10 and 13, show Gordon and Wilkinson in plainclothes. The St. Louis Police Department did not allow African-American police to wear uniforms until 1921.

9. For an example of the continuing southern repugnance toward black police officers, see the *Philadelphia Inquirer*, July 20, 1912, where Senator Hoke Smith of Georgia vowed to rid Washington, D.C. of African-American police officers. For assignment of African-American police officers to black communities, see Gosnell, *Negro Politicians*, 254–256; James J. Green and Alfred J. Young, *A History of the 28th Precinct* (New York, n.d.), 5, Schomburg Center for Research in Black Culture, New York Public Library. For prohibitions against arresting whites, see *St. Louis Globe-Democrat*, June 12, 1974, and my interviews with retired Cleveland police sergeant Lynn R. Coleman (1934–1977), September 17, 1977, and retired Columbus police officer Benjamin Eddings (1921–1946), December 7, 1973. For support of African-American police officers by white officers, see Sprogle, *The Philadelphia Police*, 173. For commendations for African-American police officers, see "Detective Ira Cooper Promoted to Detective Sergeant," *St. Louis Police Journal*, March 7, 1923, p. 9; *Mexico (Mo.) Ledger*, October 7, 1909; "Detective George Gaston," in *History of the Columbus Police Department*, 35; "Lt. Battle," in Green and Young, *A History of the 28th Precinct*, 2–3; Alexander, *Blue Coats, Black Skin*, 34; Samuel Johnson, *Often Back: The Tales of Harlem* (New York: Vantage Press, 1971), 204–205; *Pittsburgh Courier*, July 17 and 24, 1926.

10. *New York Times*, June 29, 1911, August 17 and 18, 1911; *New York Evening Mail*, July 1, 1911; "Troubles of a Black Policeman," *Literary Digest*, January 27, 1912, pp. 177–179; *Central Afro-American*, April 18, 1914; *Norfolk Journal and Guide*, July 25, 1931; *Amsterdam News*, January 12, 1935; "Lieutenant Battle," press release, June 26, 1941, ANP Clipping File.

11. Fogelson, *Big-City Police*, 98–118; Monkkonen, *Police in Urban America*, 155–156.

12. Fogelson, *Big-City Police*, 12, 36–37.

13. Rayford W. Logan, *The Betrayal of the Negro: From Rutherford B. Hayes to Woodrow Wilson* (New York: Collier Books, 1972). For a contemporary appraisal of early twentieth-century race relations, see Ray Stannard Baker, *Following the Color Line: American Negro Citizenship in the Progressive Era* (New York: Doubleday, Page and Co., 1908).

14. "Some 'Quirements' Lacking," *St. Louis Police Journal*, December 28, 1912, p. 7. See also the June 1, 1912, issue for another bad racial joke about "negroes" using razors for "professional or social purposes."

15. For the police role in early twentieth-century race relations, see Shapiro, *White Violence, Black Response*, 99, 107, 116–117, 150 and 152; and Mitchell, *Race Riots in Black and White*, 127–128. For excellent discussions of how the police participated in early twentieth-century race riots: for the Atlanta race riot of 1906, see John Dittmer, *Black Georgia in the Progressive Era, 1900–1920* (Urbana: University of Illinois Press, 1977), 125; and "Sentiment of the Northern Press on the Recent Criminal Outbreak in Atlanta," *Colored American Magazine*, November 1906, pp. 335–342; for police participation in the 1917

race riot in East St. Louis, see Elliott M. Rudwick, *Race Riot at East St. Louis, July 2, 1917!* (Cleveland, Ohio: Meridian Books, 1970), 74–94; for the police role in the Chicago race riot, see Carl Sandburg, *The Chicago Race Riots, July 1919* (New York: Harcourt, Brace and World, 1969). For a very critical assessment of the police role in the riot in Washington, D.C., see Cyril Briggs, "The Capital and Chicago Race Riots," *The Crusader,* September 1919, pp. 3–6. Briggs charged that in the Washington riot, black police were sent home so that white police, soldiers, and mobs would have free rein in attacking black neighborhoods. For the editorial on the racist behavior of white police officers in race riots, see "Get Colored Policemen," *Christian Recorder,* July 31, 1919, clipping, Tuskegee University Newspaper Clipping File. One-sided law enforcement by white police during civil disturbances remained a problem even in later riots. See Thurgood Marshall's account of the 1943 Detroit race riot, "The Gestapo in Detroit," *The Crisis,* August 1943, pp. 232–233 and 246–247.

16. Gosnell, *Negro Politicians,* 264–265; *New York Age,* January 2, 1913; Mark H. Haller, "Policy Gambling, Entertainment and the Emergence of Black Politics: Chicago from 1900–1940," *Journal of Social History* 24 (Summer 1991): 719–739. For a contemporary newspaper report critical of the link between crime, politics, and the police in Chicago's African-American community, see a special report by Junius B. Wood, "White Politics and Negro Crime Mixed—Leaders Held Responsible for Plague Spots in Colored Districts," *Chicago Daily News,* December 26, 1916.

17. Gosnell, *Negro Politicians,* 263–265; *Chicago Defender,* January 19, 1918, December 25, 1919, July 3, 1920. The first black desk sergeant in Chicago was appointed in 1905. See the *Nashville Banner,* April 25, 1905. According to the *Defender,* in 1923 Sergeant Lilburn Jackson became the first black police sergeant allowed to wear the sergeant's uniform. The *Defender* called the occasion "historic." See *Chicago Defender,* April 28, 1923.

18. *Chicago Defender,* September 18, 1915, June 24, 1922; *Baltimore Herald,* April 19, 1922.

19. Reaves, *Black Cops,* 147–148; *Baltimore Afro-American,* August 31, 1929, April 19, 1930.

20. Fogelson, *Big-City Police,* chapter VII; Walker, *A Critical History of Police Reform,* 165–166.

21. Morris, "The Chicago Negro and the Major Political Parties," 37; Christopher R. Reed, "Black Chicago Political Realignment during the Depression and New Deal," *Illinois Historical Journal* 78 (Winter 1985): 242–256; George F. Robinson, "The Negro in Politics in Chicago," *Journal of Negro History* 17 (April 1932): 190; *Chicago Defender,* August 17, 1940; Miller, "Negro in Pennsylvania Politics," 319–321; Reaves, *Black Cops,* 16–17, 47, 57–60; Guy W. Finney, *Angel City in Turmoil* (Los Angeles: Amer Press, 1945), 116–120; *Los Angeles Sentinel,* April 28, 1938; Victor J. Miller, President, St. Louis Board of Police Commissioners, to Governor Arthur M. Hyde, May 23, 1921, Correspondence, Governor's Files, Jefferson City, Mo.; *St. Louis Post-Dispatch,* August 18, 1921; *St. Louis Argus,* March 19, 1926, December 3, 1926, February 24, 1928, November 18, 1929; Watts, "Black and Blue," 138–141; Mary Welek, "Jordan Chambers: Black Politician and Boss," *Journal of Negro History* 57 (October 1972): 361; *St. Louis American,* November 11, 1943; Jordan W. Chambers to Governor Phil Donnelly, December 30, 1944, Governor's Files.

22. *St. Louis Post-Dispatch,* August 18, 1921, June 12, 1974; Watts, "Black and Blue," 138; *Cleveland Call and Post,* September 1, 1934; interview by author with Lynn R. Coleman; interview by author with retired Columbus police officer Edward Waller (1945–1970), Columbus, Ohio, November 20, 1973, transcript. On the Columbus, Ohio, Municipal Civil Service Commission, "Certification of Eligibles No. 98," Position: Patrolman (colored), May 27, 1941, Waller's name appeared on the list and was scratched out for no apparent reason. He waited another four years before he "passed" the physical examination and was appointed. Columbus, Ohio, Department of Public Safety, *Minute Book,* 11, August 13, 1945, p. 357. Alexander, *Blue Coats, Black Skin,* 30–31. The use of the physical examination to exclude African Americans from law enforcement seems to have remained a problem even in

the 1960s. See Richard J. Margolis, *Who Will Wear the Badge?: A Study of Minority Recruitment Efforts in Protective Services,* A Report of the United States Commission on Civil Rights (Washington, D.C.: U.S. Government Printing Office, 1971), 4 and 12.

23. For examples of the quota system in Columbus, see Columbus, Ohio, Department of Public Safety, *Minute Book,* 7, June 7, 1937, p. 391, and September 9, 1937, p. 463; *Minute Book,* 11, January 30, 1946, p. 445; and Columbus, Ohio, Municipal Civil Service Commission, "Certification of Eligibles No. 98," May 27, 1941, Position: Patrolman (colored). After 1946, the Civil Service Commission dropped the race designations but kept the lists of African Americans on the eligible lists separate from the lists of whites. See *Minute Books,* 9–13, November 26, 1937, to November 30, 1950. Robert Conot, *American Odyssey* (New York: William Morrow and Co., 1974), 413–414; *Detroit Independent,* February 25, 1927; *Houston Informer,* June 18, 1927, November 12, 1927; Watts, "Black and Blue," 138–141; Miller, "Negro in Pennsylvania Politics," 319; Hardin, *The Negroes of Philadelphia,* 15–16; *Philadelphia Independent,* November 19, 1939; William M. Kephart, "The Integration of Negroes into the Urban Police Force," *Journal of Criminal Law, Criminology and Police Science* 45 (September–October 1954): 326; Kephart, *Racial Factors and Urban Law Enforcement,* 138.

24. *Chicago Defender,* August 17, 1940; *Pittsburgh Courier,* July 20, 1940.

25. Columbus, Ohio, Department of Public Safety, *Minute Book,* 11, February 8, 1943, p. 29; Dulaney, "Black and Blue," 49; "Detective Ira Cooper Promoted to Detective Sergeant," *St. Louis Police Journal,* March 7, 1923, p. 9; *Mexico (Mo.) Ledger,* June 23, 1936; *St. Louis American,* November 11, 1943; Hardin, *The Negroes of Philadelphia,* 16; *Atlanta Daily World,* January 2, 1948; *Philadelphia Independent,* November 19, 1939; Reaves, *Black Cops,* 14–26; "'Negro Police Officers in Los Angeles,' by One of Los Angeles's Negro Police Officers, Who, For Obvious Reasons Remains Anonymous," *The Crisis,* August 1934, pp. 242 and 248; *Los Angeles Sentinel,* October 16, 1947.

26. Fogelson, *Big-City Police,* chapter VII; Walker, *Critical History of Police Reform,* xiv and 15. For example, in 1943 Edward Griffin, president of the Negro Labor Leaders in Columbus, Ohio, requested "capable Negro officers in Negro districts" to avoid confrontations between African Americans and the police, Edward S. Griffin to Roy B. Weed, Director of Public Safety, March 21, 1943, Correspondence, Department of Public Safety, Columbus, Ohio, City Hall Vault. Similarly, in 1948, African Americans requested the assignment of an all-black police platoon in St. Louis; *Chicago Defender,* December 18, 1948. There are numerous examples of these requests in other cities; for a full discussion of such requests in the South, see chapter 4.

27. Dulaney, "Black and Blue," 38–39; Gosnell, *Negro Politicians,* 256–258; Watts, "Black and Blue," 146–147; interview by author with retired St. Louis police sergeant James A. Taylor, July 13, 1977, St. Louis, Mo., audiotape; *Chicago Defender,* December 18, 1948; *Cleveland Call and Post,* April 20, 1946; interview by author with Lynn Coleman; *Cleveland Press,* November 4, 1976; *Los Angeles Sentinel,* May 25, 1939, October 30, 1947; Broome, *LAPD's Black History,* 90.

28. *Amsterdam News,* April 3, 1914; *Chicago Defender,* July 9, 1915; *Christian Recorder,* July 31, 1919; *Detroit Independent,* February 25, 1927; *Cleveland Call and Post,* May 17, 1930; *Ohio State News,* August 10, 1935. In New York City, African Americans had asked for the employment of black police periodically as early as 1899. See *The Ledger* (Baltimore), January 7, 1899, and *New York Times,* August 13, 1909.

29. *Chicago Defender,* January 19, 1918; *New York Evening World,* May 21, 1926; *Amsterdam News,* April 17, 1929; *Philadelphia Tribune,* October 17, 1940, November 7, 1940; *Chicago Bee,* October 27, 1940; *Philadelphia Independent,* November 19, 1939.

30. *Human Relations in Chicago,* Report for the Year 1946 of the Mayor's Commission on Human Relations (Chicago, 1946), 7, 73–75, 119–149; *The People of Chicago,* Five-Year Report, 1947–1951, of the Chicago Commission on Human Relations (Chicago, 1952), 14 and 21. The commission was composed of fourteen members appointed by the mayor and approved by the city council. Two notables among the African Americans on the commis-

sion were Ralph Metcalfe, the 1936 Olympic gold medalist and future U.S. congressman (1971–1978), and John H. Johnson, chief executive officer of Johnson Publishing Company and editor and publisher of *Ebony* magazine. Johnson was on the commission's Law and Order Committee, which made the recommendations for reforming the police department's racial policies.

4. The Second Coming in the South

1. For the statistics on the number of African-American police officers in the South in 1930 and 1940, see Gunnar Myrdal, *An American Dilemma: The Negro Problem and Modern Democracy* (New York: Harper and Row Publishers, 1944), 542–544; Elliott Rudwick, *The Unequal Badge: Negro Policemen in the South* (Atlanta: Southern Regional Council, 1962), 3; and the *Atlanta Daily World,* September 19, 1932.

2. Walker, *History of Black Police Officers in the Houston Police Department,* 5–9; Dulaney, "The Texas Negro Peace Officers' Association," 60–61; Louis J. Marchiafava, "The Houston Police, 1878–1948," *Rice University Studies* 63 (Spring 1977): 11–13; Monroe N. Work, ed., *Negro Yearbook, 1918–1919* (Tuskegee, Ala., 1919), 53; *Houston Observer,* June 16, 1918. See also an interesting perspective on the status of African-American police officers in the South during this period in a report on the shooting of a black police officer in Austin, Texas, in the *New York Age,* December 4, 1913.

3. For example, in the early twentieth century, Knoxville, Tennessee, was one of the few southern cities that allowed blacks to serve on the city police force. Although African Americans lost police jobs in the city following the end of Reconstruction, the 1908 election of a black alderman in Knoxville facilitated the appointment of five blacks to the police force in 1910. See *East Tennessee News* (Knoxville), July 23, 1914, January 26, 1922, March 9, 1922, April 13, 1922, December 21, 1922, April 23, 1930; Robert J. Booker, *The History of Blacks in Knoxville, Tennessee: The First One Hundred Years, 1791–1891* (Knoxville: Beck Cultural Exchange Center, 1990), 56–57.

4. See the *Cleveland Gazette,* March 15, 1890, for the dismissal of three of Memphis's post-Reconstruction African-American police officers. According to Rousey, the last one was dismissed in 1895. Rousey, "Yellow Fever and Black Policemen in Memphis," 373; *St. Louis Argus,* March 14, 1919; *Memphis Press,* March 19, 1919; *Dallas Express,* March 22, 1919; *Indianapolis Freeman,* August 16, 1919; *Chicago Defender,* March 22, 1919; *Memphis Commercial Appeal,* August 3, 1919; *Montgomery Advertiser,* September 9, 1927. For Robert R. Church, Jr.'s substantial influence on Memphis politics in the early twentieth century, see Annette and Roberta Church, *The Robert R. Churches of Memphis: A Father and Son Who Achieved in Spite of Race* (Ann Arbor: Privately published, 1974); and Roger Biles, "Robert R. Church, Jr. of Memphis: Black Republican Leader in the Age of Democratic Ascendancy, 1928–1940," *Tennessee Historical Quarterly* 42 (1983): 362–382.

5. George C. Wright, "The Billy Club and the Ballot: Police Intimidation of Blacks in Louisville, Kentucky, 1880–1930," *Southern Studies* 23 (1984): 20–23.

6. *Louisville News,* June 22, 1918; Wright, "The Billy Club and the Ballot," 32–33.

7. George C. Wright, "Black Political Insurgency in Louisville, Kentucky: The Lincoln Independent Party of 1921," *Journal of Negro History* 68 (Winter 1983): 8–23; and Wright, "The Billy Club and the Ballot," 33–34.

8. George C. Wright, *Life behind a Veil: Blacks in Louisville, Kentucky, 1865–1930* (Baton Rouge: Louisiana State University Press, 1985), 246–253; and Wright, "Black Political Insurgency in Louisville, Kentucky," 18–21. For contemporary accounts of the integration of the Louisville police force, see the *Louisville News,* July 14 and 21, 1923, and January 21, 1928; *Chicago Whip,* March 3, 1928; and *St. Louis Argus,* February 23, 1923, and March 2, 1928.

9. *Montgomery Advertiser,* December 7, 1913; "Petition to His Honor the Mayor of the City of Charleston, S.C., and the Honored Gentlemen of the City Council," July 26, 1921, City Archives, Charleston, South Carolina.

10. There are many examples of the argument by African Americans for police officers of their race to address crime in their communities. For some examples see *Charlotte (N. C.) Observer,* October 28, 1926; Atlanta NAACP et al., *Wanted: Negro Police for Negro Districts in Atlanta* (Atlanta Daily World and others, 1937), six pages; and *Atlanta Daily World,* August 1, 1937. In its semi-annual surveys of the number of African-American police officers in the South, the *Negro Year Book* also advocated the employment of "Negro police" as a crime prevention measure and method for improving race relations. See "Negro Policemen Are Urged as Means of Preventing Racial Friction," in Monroe N. Work, ed., *Negro Year Book,* 1921–22, 1925–26, and 1931–32 (Tuskegee, Ala.), 47, 57–58, and 82, respectively; and "Negro Policemen and Crime Prevention," in Jesse Parkhurst Guzman, ed., *Negro Year Book, 1941–1946* (Tuskegee, Ala.), 318. In the 1930s and 1940s, the *Negro Year Book*'s advocacy of the employment of "Negro police" was supported consistently by the Commission on Interracial Cooperation (CIC). See the following two articles in the CIC's official publication: "Negro Policemen Are Needed in Southern Cities," *Southern Frontier,* March 1943, p. 2; and "What Is the Objection to Negro Policemen?" *Southern Frontier,* January 1944, p. 3. When the Southern Regional Council succeeded the CIC in 1944, the SRC made the appointment of black police one of its main goals for improving race relations. This goal is very apparent in the Southern Regional Council's official publication, *New South.* See "SRC's Work and Plans," *New South,* December 1946, p. 6.

11. *The Ledger* (Baltimore), April 30, 1898, and June 18, 1898.

12. *Baltimore Herald,* April 13 and 26, 1920, July 7, 1920; *Baltimore Afro-American,* April 13, 1920. The antipathy toward black law enforcement officers was so bad in Baltimore that in 1919, police officials refused to release two prisoners to Chief Detective Orrie Ballard of Chester, Pennsylvania. Ballard, an African American and a sworn police officer on the Chester police force, appealed to the governor of Maryland to release the suspects, but to no avail. A white police officer had to come from Chester and accompany Ballard in order to gain release of suspects wanted in Chester. See the *Baltimore Afro-American,* March 14, 1919.

13. *Baltimore Afro-American,* October 10, 1931, May 14 and 21, 1932, November 5, 1932 (Gaither's quote); *Baltimore Morning Sun,* June 3, 1932.

14. *Baltimore Afro-American,* March 14, 1936. In response to a 1933 questionnaire from the Committee on Interracial Cooperation based in Atlanta, Gaither was even more dishonest. He said that Baltimore's police force was under civil service and blacks had never scored high enough to place them on the eligible list for the police department. Unfortunately, one of Gaither's underlings responded more truthfully to the questionnaire before it was brought to the attention of Gaither. Chief Inspector George C. Henry wrote that Baltimore had never had any black police, and "the citizens of this city prefer to continue as in the past." See Chief Inspector George G. Henry, Baltimore Police Department, to Mr. R. B. Eleazer, October 7, 1933; and Charles D. Gaither, Police Commissioner, Baltimore, Maryland, to R. B. Eleazer, October 9, 1933. Both letters are in the Committee on Interracial Cooperation Papers, Reel 51, Special Collections, Woodruff Library, Atlanta University Center.

15. *Baltimore Afro-American,* February 11, 1933, March 4, 1933, February 1, 1936, March 14, 1936, May 9, 1936. For an analysis of the role of the City-Wide Young People's Forum in achieving social justice in Baltimore, see Genna Rae McNeil, "African American Hopes and Tragic Realities," lecture delivered at the University of Texas at Arlington, March 14, 1991, photocopy.

16. *Baltimore Afro-American,* October 9, 1937; "Edward Lewis Writes in *Baltimore Sun* (On 'the Negro Police Question')," *Opportunity,* December 1937, p. 381.

17. "Colored Woman Named to Police Force in Baltimore, Maryland," *Opportunity,* March 1938, p. 91; *Baltimore Afro-American,* April 23, 1937, December 11, 1937, February 2, 1938, March 5, 1938, July 16, 1938, February 2, 1939, June 30, 1943, October 30, 1943; *Pittsburgh Courier,* August 6, 1938. The fact that only five African Americans qualified for the Baltimore police force is suspicious. According to the March 5, 1938, issue of the *Afro-American,* nearly 200 candidates graduated from the police school sponsored by the Maryland Republican League!

18. City of Dallas Council, *Minute Book,* 8, May 26, 1888, p. 150, and May 29, 1888, p. 174; *Minute Book,* 23, September 8, 1896, p. 260; *Dallas Morning News,* May 27 and 30, 1888, and December 26, 1896.

19. *Dallas Times Herald,* May 3, 1919; *Dallas Times Herald,* August 8, 1920; *Dallas Morning News,* January 25, 1927, and January 4, 1929; *Dallas Journal,* January 25, 1927; *Dallas Times Herald,* January 24 and 26, 1927; *Dallas Express,* February 2, 1927, and June 25, 1927.

20. *Dallas Morning News,* November 14 and 25, 1935; *Oklahoma Black Dispatch,* December 28, 1935; and *Dallas Journal,* November 15, 1935.

21. *Dallas Express,* October 17 and 31, 1936; *Houston Informer,* October 31, 1936; "Dallas Gets Two Negro Policemen," press release, October 25, 1936, ANP Clipping File; Dulaney, "Texas Negro Peace Officers' Association," 66.

22. Dulaney, "Texas Negro Peace Officers' Association," 66–67; *Dallas Express,* September 18, 1937, October 16 and 23, 1937, September 10 and 24, 1938, October 8, 15, and 22, 1938; *Atlanta Daily World,* October 8 and 10, 1937. See chapter 6 below for a full discussion of the origins of black police associations.

23. W. Marvin Dulaney, "The Progressive Voters League," *Legacies* 3 (Spring 1991): 27–35; *Dallas Express,* December 12 and 19, 1936, February 20, 1937, March 27, 1937, April 17, 1937, July 10, 17, and 24, 1937; *Dallas Morning News,* April 25, 1937.

24. City of Dallas Council, *Minute Book,* 47, September 10, 1937, p. 51; *Dallas Express,* September 18, 1937.

25. *Dallas Morning News,* September 12–22, 1937. For Butcher's "anti-Negro police" speech before the Dallas city council, see City of Dallas Council, *Minute Book,* 47, September 17, 1937, p. 67.

26. "White Dallas Cops Threaten Strike If Negro Police Are Appointed; Klan Takes It Up," press release, October 4, 1937, ANP Clipping File; *Dallas Morning News,* September 29, 1937, October 3, 1937; *Dallas Express,* October 23, 1937, January 21, 1939, and March 4, 1939; City of Dallas Council, *Minute Book,* 47, September 28, 1937, p. 117.

27. Minutes of the Dallas Council of Negro Organizations, November 27, 1944, December 11, 1944, January 8, 15, 1945, Negro Chamber of Commerce Collection, Box 7, Texas-Dallas Collection, Dallas Public Library; *Dallas Express,* January 23, 1943, January 19, 1946, February 16, 1946; *Dallas Morning News,* July 19 and 20, 1944, February 11, 13, and 26, 1945, October 21 and 30, 1946. For a short analysis of the Law and Crime Committee's report, see "The Conference of SRC Fellows," *New South,* December 1946, p. 21. For an example of the support that Smith's study and the Law and Crime Committee's report generated, see especially Lynn W. Landrum, "The Case for Negro Police," an editorial in the *Dallas Morning News,* October 21, 1946, where he called for a "Negro police detail in the Negro section of Dallas." Landrum's editorial was reprinted in *New South,* February 1947, pp. 3 and 5.

28. City of Dallas Council, *Minute Book,* 65, October 17, 1946, p. 367, and October 30, 1946, p. 467; *Dallas Express,* October 5, 12, and 19, 1946, November 9, 1946, March 29, 1947; *Dallas Morning News,* October 18 and 24, 1946, March 25, 1947. For the increase in the number of southern cities employing African-American police officers, see John H. McCray, "South Carolina Chief Praises Work of Negro Officers," *New South,* November 1946, pp. 3 and 5; and Guzman, *Negro Year Book, 1941–1946,* 318.

29. Clarence A. Bacote, "William A. Finch, Negro Councilman and Political Activities in Atlanta during Reconstruction," *Journal of Negro History* 40 (October 1955): 341–364; and James M. Russell and Jerry Thornbery, "William Finch of Atlanta: The Black Politician as Civic Leader," in Rabinowitz, *Southern Black Leaders of the Reconstruction Era,* 315–316. Two African Americans served as Atlanta city councilmen during Reconstruction. The white repugnance for African-American police in Atlanta was matched only by their repugnance for African-American city councilmen. Moreover, the same attitude was still present in the city in the 1930s. See Eugene M. Mitchell, "Atlanta during the 'Reconstruction Period,'" *Atlanta Historical Bulletin* 2 (November 1936): 21; and *Atlanta Centennial Yearbook, 1837–1937* (Atlanta: Gregg Murphy, 1937), 55.

30. Eugene J. Watts, "Black Political Progress in Atlanta, 1868–1895," *Journal of Negro History* 59 (July 1974): 268–286; and Clarence A. Bacote, "The Negro in Atlanta Politics," *Phylon* 16 (1955): 333–339; Charles L. Rosenzweig, "The Issue of Employing Black Policemen in Atlanta" (M.A. thesis, Emory University, 1980), 8.

31. For contemporary accounts of African-American arrests, police abuse, and the 1906 race riot in Atlanta, see "Here and There," *Colored American Magazine,* February 1903, pp. 284–285; Mary White Ovington, "Atlanta: A City Nursing Dead Ideals," *Colored American Magazine,* July 1905, pp. 389–390; "Sentiments of the Northern Press on the Recent Criminal Outbreak in Atlanta," *Colored American Magazine,* November 1906, pp. 335–342; and "Causes of Riots," *Southern Workman,* July 1907, pp. 371–373. See also Dittmer, *Black Georgia in the Progressive Era,* 88, 125–129, and 138–139. For a very critical history of the pattern of police abuse in Atlanta's black communities in the early twentieth century, see the *1975 Atlanta Bureau of Police Services Yearbook* (Atlanta, 1975), 20–98. For corroboration of this view, see Eugene J. Watts, "The Police in Atlanta, 1890–1905," *Journal of Southern History* 39 (May 1973): 171–172; and Rosenzweig, "Issue of Employing Black Policemen in Atlanta," 10–12. Rosenzweig also discusses Atlanta's "Pittsburg riot" of 1902 as a prelude to the 1906 riot.

32. *Atlanta Constitution,* January 24, 1922; *Atlanta Independent,* March 2, 1922. Earlier in 1919, African-American members of the city's NAACP branch presented a list of eight demands to the city council for improving city services in their community. They did not include the hiring of black police officers on this very succinct list. See "The Atlanta Negro Vote," *The Crisis,* June 1919, pp. 90–91.

33. For African Americans' support of Mayor Key in the 1932 recall election and the beginnings of their campaign for African-American police officers in the 1930s, see the *Atlanta World,* January 15, 1932, March 15–16, 1932; *Atlanta Daily World* (same newspaper, but it became a daily on March 18, 1932), May 20, 1932, November 23, 1932, July 18, 1933, August 29, 1933, October 5, 1933; *Atlanta Constitution,* October 5, 1933; *Macon (Ga.) Telegraph,* October 5, 1933; Rosenzweig, "Issue of Employing Black Policemen," 30; and Herbert T. Jenkins, *Keeping the Peace: A Police Chief Looks at His Job* (New York: Harper and Row Publishers, 1970), 6–7. In 1933 Jenkins was a young patrolman in Atlanta and Mayor Key's chauffeur. He was present at the 1933 meeting between Mayor Key and the delegation requesting African-American police officers. He first told this story in an interview with the *Birmingham News,* February 18, 1952.

34. Jesse Daniel Ames to Rev. John Moore Walker, October 10, 1933; R. B. Eleazer to "Dear Chief of Police," October 5, 1933; Minutes of the Committee of Citizens meeting, October 20, 1933. Both letters and the minutes are in the Committee on Interracial Cooperation (CIC) Papers, Reel 51. See also Appendix A for a copy of Eleazer's letter and a copy of the questionnaire.

35. *Atlanta Daily World,* October 21, 1933; Jesse Daniel Ames to A. T. Walden, November 21, 1933; "Memorandum of Meeting of the Citizens Committee Seeking the Appointment of Negro policemen in Atlanta," December 1, 1933; "Reasons For Employing Negro Police," undated. All of these documents are in the CIC Papers, Reel 51. The following cities responded to the questionnaire: Houston, Baltimore, Tulsa, Sarasota, Louisville, Knoxville, Galveston, Austin, St. Louis, Oklahoma City, Muskogee and Okmulgee, Oklahoma.

36. *Wanted: Negro Police for Negro Districts in Atlanta,* six pages; and *Atlanta Daily World,* August 1, 1937. The *World* first began its campaign against black-on-black homicides in 1932 when it released the figures showing that African-American homicides totaled 106 out of the 128 committed in the city in 1931. See *Atlanta Daily World,* May 20, 1932.

37. *Atlanta Daily World,* January 1, 1936, July 13, 1936, August 17 and 26, 1936, August 1, 1937, September 3, 1944, September 18, 1947. See editorial of November 26, 1947, for homicide statistics from 1938 to 1946. Interview by author with Mr. C. A. Scott, editor of the *Atlanta Daily World,* August 9, 1977, Atlanta, Georgia, audiotape.

38. "Crime and Police Administration," *Race Relations,* December 1943, p. 8; *Atlanta Daily World,* September 3, 1944, October 29, 1946; *Atlanta Constitution,* March 5, 1946; *Birmingham Herald,* March 6, 1946; *Baltimore Afro-American,* March 6, 1946. Ironically, the *Atlanta Daily World* did not support the demonstration by African-American veterans at city hall for police jobs. The *Daily World* editorialized that the veterans were "undoing good work," and instead urged them to allow the city's black leaders to "work through channels" to secure African-American police in the city. See the *Atlanta Daily World,* March 3, 5, and 8, 1946.

39. *Houston Informer,* June 3, 1944; Jack Walker, "Negro Voting in Atlanta, 1953–1961," *Phylon* 24 (Winter 1963): 379–387; Bacote, "The Negro in Atlanta Politics," 342–350; Glenn Sisk, "The Negro in Atlanta Politics (1870–1962)," *Negro History Bulletin* 28 (October 1964): 17–18; and *Atlanta Daily World,* July 1, 1934, August 29, 1934, October 23, 1934, November 25, 1934, December 7, 1934, and March 25, 1936.

40. *Savannah (Ga.) News,* May 1, 1947; *Atlanta Daily World,* May 6, 1947; *Baltimore Afro-American,* May 17, 1947; *New York Times,* June 26, 1947; "Savannah, Georgia," *New South,* May 1947, p. 7; "Thousands Witness Induction of Negro Police in Savannah," press release, May 14, 1947, ANP Clipping File. For the importance of the black vote in the police appointments in Savannah, see especially "Police Administration and Courts," *Race Relations,* June 1947, pp. 333–334; and Bushnell Eubanks, "The Negro South Goes to the Polls," *Negro Digest,* January 1949, pp. 20–22.

41. For examples of the numerous letters written in support of the employment of black police officers in Atlanta, see the *Atlanta Constitution,* May 15, 1947, October 2, 14, 1947; *Atlanta Journal,* May 15, 1947, July 9, 18, 1947, November 26, 1947; *Atlanta Daily World,* August 24, 1947, September 4, 11, 13, 18, 1947. For the support that the Negro Police Committee generated for the proposal, see the *Atlanta Daily World,* July 10, 20, 23, 1947, August 1, 21, 1947, October 1, 29, 1947. For the *Daily World's* ongoing editorial support for the proposal, see May 6, 1947, and September 16, 1947. For Mays's appearance before the Police Committee and his meeting with Mayor Hartsfield, see the *Daily World,* July 20 and 23, 1947.

42. *Atlanta Daily World,* October 22 and 23, 1947, November 19 and 26, 1947.

43. *Atlanta Daily World,* November 27, 1947. Two contemporary sources described the tension-filled nature of this hearing: Harold C. Fleming, "Race Hatred Gets a Hearing," in *Changing Patterns of the New South* (Atlanta: Southern Regional Council, 1955), 27–31 (reprint of an article first published in the January 1948 issue of *New South*); *Pittsburgh Courier,* December 27, 1947, an article written by Benjamin E. Mays, who attended the hearing. Also, see Mays's recountal of the hearing in Benjamin E. Mays, *Born to Rebel: An Autobiography* (New York: Charles Scribner's Sons, 1971), 276.

44. Fleming, 29–31; *Atlanta Daily World,* November 27, 1947. An even more detailed account of some of the race-baiting at the hearing was carried in the *Atlanta Constitution,* November 27, 1947.

45. Herbert Jenkins to the Atlanta City Council, December 1, 1947, quoted in Herbert T. Jenkins, *Forty Years on the Force, 1932–1972* (Decatur, Ga.: National Graphics, 1973), 148. The city council resolution and Jenkins's letter are in City of Atlanta, *Council Minutes,* 45, December 1, 1947, pp. 86–87; *Atlanta Daily World,* December 2, 1947. "Atlanta Approves Employing Negro Cops," press release, December 10, 1947, ANP Clipping File. In my interview with ex-police chief Herbert Jenkins, August 8, 1977, at Emory University in Atlanta, transcript, he indicated that he supported the appointment of blacks to the Atlanta police force in 1947 because he was "convinced that there was a place for blacks on the force," and the "police should be for all people."

46. *Atlanta Daily World,* December 11 and 12, 1947, January 28, 1948, April 2, 3, 4, 1948; *Atlanta Constitution,* February 26, 1948, April 4, 1948. A story in the *Atlanta Constitution,* March 29, 1992, quoted Mayor William B. Hartsfield as telling African-American leaders in 1945 that he would support the proposal for hiring black police officers only if they registered 10,000 black voters. Of course, African Americans achieved double this number of registered voters in 1946, but Hartsfield did not keep his promise until a year later.

47. For the lawsuit filed in Norfolk, see Tom Poston, "Law and Order in Norfolk," *New Republic,* October 7, 1940, pp. 472–473, *Richmond Times-Dispatch,* November 22, 1939, and *Norfolk Pilot,* March 18, 1940; for the lawsuit filed in New Orleans, see the *Pittsburgh Courier,* June 11, 1949; for the one in Mobile, see the *Montgomery Advertiser,* November 18, 1953; and for the one in Birmingham, see the *Oklahoma Black Dispatch,* October 26, 1956, and the *Birmingham World,* October 20, 1956. For sources for the police appointments cited in this paragraph, see the following: (Baltimore) *Baltimore Afro-American,* December 11, 1937; (Raleigh) *Norfolk Journal and Guide,* December 5, 1942; (Norfolk) *Richmond Times-Dispatch,* November 8, 1945, and *Kansas City Call,* November 23, 1945; (Durham) *Durham Herald,* July 2, 1944; (Richmond) *Richmond Times-Dispatch,* May 1 and June 4, 1946; (Dallas) *Dallas Morning News,* March 25, 1947; (Memphis) *Memphis Commercial Appeal,* September 10 and 11, 1948, and *Atlanta Daily World,* October 28, 1948; (Nashville) *Pittsburgh Courier,* April 24, 1948, and *Chicago Defender,* May 29, 1948; (Columbia, South Carolina) *Columbia Lighthouse and Informer,* December 19, 1948, and *Chicago Defender,* March 12, 1949; (Charleston) *Charleston News and Courier,* August 29, 1950, and *Chicago Defender,* September 9, 1950; (New Orleans) *Louisiana Weekly,* June 24, 1950; (Mobile) *Birmingham World,* February 12, 1954; (Montgomery) *Montgomery Advertiser,* May 1 and 9, 1954.

48. *New Orleans Times-Item,* December 10, 1919.

49. *New Orleans Times-Item,* March 29, 1929; *Houston Informer,* April 3, 1929; *Chicago Defender,* September 18, 1943; *Atlanta Daily World,* October 29, 1946; *Louisiana Weekly,* December 25, 1926, June 8, 1946, June 28, 1946, February 1, 1947, and September 2, 1948.

50. *Dallas Express,* February 8, 1947; *Birmingham News,* September 2, 1948; *Pittsburgh Courier,* June 11, 1949.

51. *Louisiana Weekly,* March 18, 1950, May 20, 1950, June 3 and June 24, 1950; "New Orleans Gets Negro Police," press release, June 19, 1950, ANP Clipping File. See also Brant Coopersmith and Helen Cohn, Executive Secretary of the New Orleans Committee on Race Relations, to A. P. Tureaud, February 24, 1950, Correspondence, Alexander Pierre Tureaud Papers, Box 20, Amistad Research Center, New Orleans, Louisiana.

5. Separate and Unequal

1. Interview by author with Major Claude Dixon, August 5, 1977, Atlanta, Georgia, audiotape.

2. Interview by author with former Atlanta police chief Herbert T. Jenkins, August 8, 1977, Atlanta, Georgia, transcript.

3. McCray, "South Carolina Police Chief Praises Work of Negro Officers," 3 and 5; Harold C. Fleming, "How Negro Police Worked Out in One Southern City," *New South,* October 1947, pp. 3–5 and 7; "Negro Police Successful in South," *Jet,* November 15, 1951, p. 8; "Southern Police Chiefs Comment (on Negro police)," *New South,* October–November 1953, pp. 7–8; "Survey Shows Negro Police Do Good Job in South," *Jet,* May 14, 1953, p. 10.

4. *Pittsburgh Courier,* February 10, 1945; *Chicago Defender,* September 9, 1947; *Baltimore Afro-American,* September 6, 1947; *Louisville Courier-Journal,* October 23, 1947; *Birmingham News,* September 20, 1955; Jenkins, *Keeping the Peace,* 31.

5. See Atlanta Police Department, *Annual Reports,* 1946–1953; *Atlanta Daily World,* January 6, 1950, February 23, 1950.

6. *Memphis Commercial Appeal,* August 20, 1942; *Atlanta Constitution,* April 4, 1948; *Atlanta Daily World,* September 3, 1944, January 30, 1948; *Dallas Express,* February 8, 1947; *Chicago Defender,* September 6, 1947; Fleming, "How Negro Police Worked Out in One Southern City," 3–5; John A. Harris, "How Charleston Got Negro Policemen," *New South,* September–October 1950, pp. 7–8; Elliott Rudwick, "The Negro Policeman in the South," *Journal of Criminal Law, Criminology and Police Science* 61 (July–August 1960): 274.

An especially enlightening article on the need for college-educated black police candidates appeared in the *Chicago Bee,* December 15, 1940, entitled "Should Negro College Graduates Be Policemen?" An article in the *Southern Frontier,* March 1943, p. 2, called black police officers in Charlotte, North Carolina, "the best of the Negro race." Compare the "care" taken in selecting black police officers with Gunnar Myrdal's assessment of the "average Southern policeman" in 1944: "The average Southern policeman is a promoted poor white with a legal sanction to use a weapon. His social heritage has taught him to despise the Negroes, and he has little education which could have changed him." Myrdal, *An American Dilemma,* 540–541.

7. *Birmingham News,* February 18, 1952; *Pittsburgh Courier,* June 24, 1950; *Chicago Defender,* September 6, 1947; *Atlanta Daily World,* January 4, 1950; Inspector Edward Preston to Dr. E. C. Estell, May 27, 1960, General Correspondence, Dallas Police Department Archives, Texas-Dallas Collection, Dallas Public Library.

8. *Dallas Express,* January 24, 1948, and February 14, 1948; "Tenn. Negro Police Guilty of Rights Violation," *Jet,* November 20, 1952, p. 12; "Blind Man Wins $1,000 for Police Brutality," *Jet,* January 1, 1953, p. 12; "Negroes Complain, N.C. Town Fires Negro Police," *Jet,* July 24, 1952, p. 6; *Pittsburgh Courier,* July 26, 1952, and May 2, 1959; *Dallas Express,* October 4, 1952; *Alabama Journal,* April 21, 1959; "Police Oust Last Negro from Force," press release, April 22, 1959, ANP Clipping File; "Montgomery Fires Last of 5 Negro Cops," *Jet,* May 14, 1959, p. 8. One of the more interesting and unusual dismissals of black police officers occurred in 1955, when Carlton Pecot and John Pitts were dismissed from the New Orleans police force for mishandling a homicide case and arresting the wrong man. *Louisiana Weekly,* May 21, 1955, and July 23, 1955.

9. Elliott Rudwick, "The Southern Negro Policeman and the White Offender," *Journal of Negro Education* 30 (Fall 1961): 426–431. According to Rudwick, prohibiting black officers from arresting whites was one way that southern police officials kept black police officers in their "place." The denial of the arrest power was "socially symbolic of the denial of race equality" and symbolized the second-class status of black police (and black citizens) in the South.

10. Margaret Price, "Survey Shows Increase of Negro Policemen in South," *New South,* September 1948, p. 8; Mrs. James S. Crate, "Texas Commission Works for Human Rights," *New South,* October 1948, pp. 14 and 20; *Oklahoma Black Dispatch,* September 25, 1948; "Suspend Negro Cop for Jailing White Woman," *Jet,* April 2, 1953, p. 10; *Dallas Express,* August 22, 1953. In 1948, a minor incident in Chattanooga, Tennessee, also demonstrated how precarious it was for black officers to violate the prohibition against arresting white offenders. The Chattanooga city commission suspended an unnamed black officer when he arrested a drunken white citizen who had "dared" the officer to arrest him. This prompted black citizens in Chattanooga to petition for the removal of the restrictions on the arrest powers of black officers. See "Civic Action for Negro Police," *Race Relations,* June–December 1948, p. 270.

11. *Birmingham World,* September 20, 1955; Preston to Estell, May 27, 1960, General Correspondence, Dallas Police Archives; *Dallas Morning News,* October 30, 1946; *Houston Informer,* April 26, 1947; Walker, *History of Black Police Officers in the Houston Police Department,* 55; *Atlanta Daily World,* April 2, 1948, and May 2, 1950; *Birmingham News,* February 17, 1952; "Police Administration and Courts," *Race Relations,* June 1947, p. 334; Ronald H. Bayor, "Race and City Services: The Shaping of Atlanta's Police and Fire Departments," *Atlanta History* 36 (Fall 1992): 21. In 1952, the headquarters for African-American police officers in Atlanta moved from the YMCA to the basement of the main police station. *Atlanta Journal,* March 10, 1952, and *Pittsburgh Courier,* March 22, 1952.

12. Paul S. George, "Colored Town: Miami's Black Community, 1896–1930," *Florida Historical Quarterly* 56 (April 1978): 432–447; Paul S. George, "Policing Miami's Black Community, 1896–1930," *Florida Historical Quarterly* 57 (April 1979): 434–450; A. George Igler, "History of the Miami Police Department," City of Miami, Department of Police Training Section, undated (mimeographed copy), p. 18.

13. George, "Colored Town," 441–442; George, "Policing Miami's Black Community," 436–439 and 447–448; Arthur Edward Chapman, "The History of the Black Police Force and Court in the City of Miami" (Ph.D. dissertation, University of Miami, 1986), 18–38.

14. Hugh D. Price, "The Negro and Florida Politics, 1944–1954," *Journal of Politics* 17 (May 1955): 198–220; H. D. Price, *The Negro and Southern Politics: A Chapter in Florida History* (Westport, Conn.: Greenwood Press, 1973), 23; "Miami Klan Tries to Scare Negro Vote," *Life*, May 15, 1939, p. 27; David H. Cohn, "The Development and Efficacy of the Negro Police Precinct and Court of the City of Miami" (M.A. thesis, University of Miami, 1951), 8. For the origins of the Progressive Voters League in Dallas, Texas, see chapter 4.

15. Chapman, "History of the Black Police Force," 45–46; *Miami Daily News*, August 29, 1944; *Miami Herald*, September 1, 1946; Cohn, "Negro Police Precinct of Miami," 12.

16. Cohn, "Negro Police Precinct of Miami," 14–18; Chapman, "History of the Black Police Force," 48–50; *Miami Herald*, September 2, 1945; *Baltimore Afro-American*, October 30, 1948; Walter Headley, "Utilization of Negro Police," *Traffic Review* 3 (March 1949): 10–13.

17. Chapman, "History of the Black Police Force," 52, 71–72; *Dallas Express*, April 29, 1950; *Los Angeles Sentinel*, April 27, 1950.

18. *Dallas Express*, April 29, 1950; Chapman, "History of the Black Police Force," 69–77; Cohn, "Negro Police Precinct of Miami," 37–40; *Los Angeles Sentinel*, April 27, 1950; *Miami News*, May 18, 1950; *Jackson (Miss.) Daily News*, November 2, 1951, and September 11, 1952. The police department's official history also called the court and station a "progressive step." Igler, "History of the Miami Police Department," pp. 21–22; and City of Miami Police Department, *Annual Report, 1953* (Miami, 1954), p. 12. Of course, no one described the rationale for the "Negro police station and court" better than O. D. Henderson, Miami's director of public safety in 1950:

> The use of a colored judge is a great step forward. He knows and understands their problems. He thinks their way; their way of life differs from ours. They are more closely related to their savage forefathers of the jungle. They are strongly influenced by the moon. When we have a full moon there is always more crime in the Negro areas because they are closely related to the jungle where they worshipped the moon. Statistics will prove that the rate of crime increases when there is a full moon.

Quoted without comment in Chapman, "History of the Black Police Force," 132.

19. *Miami Herald*, June 26, 1955, and January 29, 1962; "Negro Employment in Miami," *New South*, May 1962, p. 7; Chapman, "History of the Black Police Force," 77–85, 139–144; interview by author with retired Miami police major Leroy Smith, October 25, 1977, Miami, Florida, transcript.

20. *Miami Herald*, June 26, 1955, January 29, 1962, April 6, 1965, January 25, 1967; *Miami Times*, February 14 and 21, June 20, and July 18, 1969; Lieutenant Leroy A. Smith, Recruitment Officer for "Operation Badge," to Ted Nichols, Director, Community Affairs Division, City of Miami, September 15, 1969, Inter-office Memo, Miami Police Department, in Personal Papers of Lieutenant Leroy A. Smith; Margolis, *Who Will Wear the Badge*, 21–22. Margolis attributes the impetus for the "Operation Badge" black police recruitment campaign to the 1968 riot in Miami during the Republican National convention. After the campaign, in 1970 there were still only 70 blacks on a total force of more than 700. Forty–five percent of Miami's population was black, but only 14 percent of the city's police force was black.

21. *Miami Herald*, April 28, 1948, September 4, 1960; *Miami News*, March 27, 1957, May 10, 1960; *Sun-Reporter* (San Francisco), February 20, 1960.

22. *Miami Herald*, June 26, 1955, June 29, 1962; "Order Miami's Police Academy to Integrate," *Jet*, February 4, 1960, p. 8; "Miami's Finest," *Jet*, January 28, 1985, p. 24; interview by author with retired sergeant Jesse Nash, October 31, 1977, Miami, Florida, transcript; interview by author with Garth C. Reeves, Sr., editor and publisher of the *Miami Times*, October 27, 1977, Miami, Florida, transcript; Robert B. Ingram, "Brother Man," in *The Officer Victor Butler Benefit Souvenir Program* (Miami, 1971), p. 4.

23. International Association of Chiefs of Police, Field Services Division, *A Survey of the Police Division of Miami, Florida* (Miami, 1962), 70, 125–127.

24. *Miami Herald*, July 26, 1963; Ingram, "Brother Man," p. 4. A discussion of the significance of the closing of Miami's black police precinct follows in chapter 6.

25. Dulaney, "Texas Negro Peace Officers' Association," 74–77; Houston *Forward Times*, July 15, 1961; Walker, *History of Black Police Officers in the Houston Police Department*, 12–13; Chandler Davidson, *Biracial Politics: Conflict and Coalition in the Metropolitan South* (Baton Rouge: Louisiana State University Press, 1972), 121.

26. *Report to the Honorable Lewis Cutrer, Mayor City of Houston, The Houston Murder Problem: Its Nature, Apparent Causes and Probable Cure*, Henry A. Bullock, Chairman, Mayor's Negro Law Enforcement Committee (Houston, Texas, 1961), 81–111; Houston *Forward Times*, August 20, 1960, July 15, 1961. See also an earlier study by Bullock of Houston's homicide problem in "Urban Homicide in Theory and Fact," *Journal of Criminal Law, Criminology and Police Science* 45 (1955): 565–575.

27. Bullock, *The Houston Murder Problem*, 110–111.

28. *Houston Chronicle*, January 24, 1961, March 9, 1969; Houston *Forward Times*, February 16, 1963, April 22, 1967; and Walker, *History of Black Police Officers in the Houston Police Department*, 56.

29. Rudwick, *The Unequal Badge*, 10, 13–14; Rudwick, "Southern Negro Policeman and the White Offender," 430; *Baltimore Afro-American*, January 27, 1962; *Pittsburgh Courier*, February 3, 1962.

30. *Atlanta Daily World*, April 2, 1961, January 30, 1962; *Houston Informer*, April 15, 1961; *Baltimore Afro-American*, April 15, 1961; *Birmingham World*, May 5, 1962; Bayor, "Race and City Services," 24.

31. Daykin, "A Study of Negro Police in Eleven Mid-South Cities," 18, 103; *Pittsburgh Courier*, April 9, 1960, September 15, 1962; *Dallas Morning News*, July 15, 1960; *Dallas Express*, July 30, 1960; Bayor, "Race and City Services," 26.

6. The Rise of Black Police Unionism

1. For reference to the "second wave of police reform," see Fogelson, *Big-City Police*, chapter VII; and Walker, *A Critical History of Police Reform*, chapters 5 and 6. Also, see my discussion of this matter in regard to policies for black police in chapter 3 above.

2. See, for example, my interviews with retired Columbus police officer Benjamin Eddings, Columbus, Ohio, December 7, 1973, transcript; and Sergeant Robert Ingram, Miami, Florida, October 24 and 25, 1977, audiotape. See also Ingram, "Brother Man," p. 4.

3. "Meetings of the Executive Committee of the Police Relief Association," *St. Louis Police Journal*, July 9, 1924, p. 8; interview by author with retired St. Louis police sergeant James A. Taylor (1921–1962), St. Louis, July 12 and 13, 1977, audiotape.

4. "Detective Ira Cooper Promoted to Detective Sergeant," *St. Louis Police Journal*, March 7, 1923, pp. 8–9; W. Marvin Dulaney, "Sergeant Ira L. Cooper's Letter to the St. Louis Police Relief Association, May 25, 1924," *Journal of Negro History* 72 (Summer 1987): 84–86; "Meetings of the Relief Association."

5. Two cases illustrate how blacks were barred from rank-and-file police associations in the South. After African Americans had served four years on the Atlanta police force, Chief Jenkins reported to a survey conducted by the *Birmingham News* that there was a "mutual understanding" that "Negro officers would not participate" in the department's Police Relief Association. The *News* used this information to show that the appointment of blacks as police officers would not threaten the dominance of white officers in the South. *Birmingham News*, February 18, 1952. In the second case, on the fourth anniversary of the appointment of the city's first black officers since 1909, members of the New Orleans Police Benevolent Association voted 529 to 42 against changing the organization's bylaws to admit black officers. *Louisiana Weekly*, June 26, 1954.

6. *Houston Informer,* February 24, 1934, March 24, 1934; Dulaney, "Texas Negro Peace Officers' Association," 59–63. The six African Americans on the Houston police force were called the "negro police detail" because they were treated as a separate entity on the force. In the early twentieth century, the "detail" was called the "colored police brigade" to separate it from the regular police force. See "Police Time Book Entries," a 1910 clipping in Mrs. Patrick H. Campbell, "Scrapbook of Clippings, 1900–1923," p. 119, at the Houston Metropolitan Research Center, Houston, Texas.

7. Interview by author with retired Galveston police officer Leroy "Buster" Landrum (1935–1974), January 9, 1987, Galveston, Texas, transcript.

8. For a more complete discussion of the TNPOA's role in the campaign for black police officers in Dallas, 1936–1938, see chapter 4. Dulaney, "Texas Negro Peace Officers' Association," 64–67; *Dallas Express,* October 17, 31, 1936, October 23, 1937, October 22, 1938; "Dallas Gets Negro Police," press release, October 25, 1936, ANP Clipping File; *Norfolk Journal and Guide,* November 6, 1937.

9. For the objectives of the TNPOA, see the *Constitution of the Texas Negro Peace Officers' Association,* (Beaumont, 1949), Texas Negro Peace Officers' Association Collection, Personal Papers of Alvin V. Young, Houston, Texas. For the attempts by African-American police to organize in the South, see Dulaney, "Texas Negro Peace Officers' Association," 70–75; *Dallas Express,* October 8, 15, 1938, September 6, 1941; *Oklahoma Black Dispatch,* July 11, 1936; *St. Louis Argus,* November 11, 1938; *Los Angeles Sentinel,* July 13, 1950. For the problems African-American police officers had with white officers when they traveled outside their jurisdictions, see the *Atlanta Daily World,* August 17, 1948, June 16, 1959; *Dallas Express,* August 7, 1948; *Houston Informer,* August 21, 1948 and January 30, 1954.

10. Dulaney, "Texas Negro Peace Officers' Association," 70–72; *Dallas Express,* October 30, 1937, September 10, 1938, September 9, 1939, August 23, 1952; *Houston Informer,* May 1, 1954. Black police officers in Oklahoma appear to have formed the second statewide black police association. In July 1936 they formed the Oklahoma Colored Peace Officers' Association. This organization allied with the TNPOA in 1937 to form the Oklahoma and Texas association, which lasted until 1939. See the *Oklahoma Black Dispatch,* July 11, 1936.

11. The Miami Police Benevolent Association had a clause in its constitution that limited membership to "white members of the police force." The clause was not dropped from the PBA's constitution until January 1970. In December 1970, five blacks applied for membership in Miami's PBA, and all of them were rejected. See the *Miami Times,* January 22, 1971, February 19, 1971, and July 23, 1971.

12. Interview by author with retired Miami police officer Ralph White, Miami, Florida, October 31, 1977, audiotape; Ingram, "Brother Man," 4. For an excellent profile of Ralph White and his description of his first days on the Miami police force in 1944, see *Miami Herald,* July 19, 1976.

13. Ingram, "Brother Man"; Chapman, "History of the Black Police Force," 53–77; *Los Angeles Sentinel,* April 27, 1950. See also a complete discussion in chapter 5.

14. Chapman, "History of the Black Police Force," 223–230; interview by author with retired Miami police sergeant Jesse Nash, October 31, 1977, Miami, Florida, audiotape; *Miami News,* December 16, 1965.

15. Interviews by author with Otis Davis and George Adams, October 21 and 30, 1977, respectively, Miami, Florida, audiotape; Ingram, "Brother Man."

16. As noted in chapter 5, the black police units in Miami and Houston were treated as separate entities, and they were the two largest "negro police details" in the South: in 1948, Miami had twenty black police officers, Houston sixteen, and Louisville fifteen. See "Employment of Negro Policemen in Southern Towns and Cities," *New South,* September 1948, p. 7. See also chapter 5 for a full discussion of segregated assignments for African-American police officers in the South.

17. See chapter 3; and William Marvin Dulaney, "Black Shields: A Historical and Comparative Survey of Blacks in American Police Forces" (Ph.D. dissertation, Ohio State University, 1984), 37–38.

18. Mangum is quoted in Richard L. Bolden, "A Study of the Black Guardian Organization in the New York City Police Department from 1943–1978" (Ph.D. dissertation, Columbia University, 1980), 36.

19. Ibid., 35–38; *Baltimore Afro-American,* January 14, 1950, and February 13, 1954; interviews by author with retired members of the Guardians, Bill Johnson and Harold Respass, January 18, 1978, New York City, audiotape.

20. Interviews with Respass and Johnson. Arthur Niederhoffer, *Behind the Shield* (Garden City, N.J.: Doubleday and Co., 1967), 135, listed ethnic organizations in the New York City Police Department for Poles, Jews, Germans, Italians, Greeks, and Puerto Ricans. Forty-eight percent of the police department belonged to the largest ethnic association, the Emerald Association of the Irish.

21. Bolden, "A Study of the Black Guardian Organization," 38–39. Respass and Johnson discussed the "hooking" system and "rabbi" network with me. For a reference to the "hooking" system among the Irish on the Boston police force, see James Q. Wilson, "Generational and Ethnic Differences among Career Police Officers," *American Journal of Sociology* 69 (March 1964): 522–528.

22. Interviews with Respass and Johnson; Bolden, "A Study of the Black Guardian Organization," passim; Alexander, *Blue Coats, Black Skin,* 83–85; Leinen, *Black Police, White Society,* 243–246.

23. Interviews with Respass and Johnson; Alexander, *Blue Coats, Black Skin,* 82–108; *Atlanta Daily World,* July 28, 1964; Jimmie Briggs, "MLK's Protective 'Guardian': The Man in the White," *Emerge,* September 1993, pp. 55–56. For their stance against police violence against black citizens, the Guardians engendered a lot of hostility from white police officers. See Nicholas Alex, *New York Cops Talk Back: A Study of a Beleaguered Minority* (New York: John Wiley and Sons, 1976), 166.

24. *Cleveland Call and Post,* September 28, 1946, October 5, 1946; interview by author with retired Cleveland police sergeant Lynn R. Coleman, September 18, 1977, Cleveland, Ohio, audiotape.

25. A brief analysis of Coleman's role in the founding of the Shield Club is in City of Cleveland Council, "A Resolution Honoring Lynn R. Coleman," No. 2214–74, November 18, 1974. See also my interview with Lynn Coleman; *Cleveland Plain Dealer,* June 8, 1978. The *Plain Dealer* article reported that the Cleveland Moral Claims Commission had agreed to pay Coleman the sum of $21,800 in back pay for the discrimination he faced in the police department from 1934 to 1942 and for the pay that he lost after the Euclid Beach incident. In 1977, Coleman, eighty-one-year-old retired police officer Harrison Harney, and other black police veterans commented on the harassment that they had faced after forming the Shield Club; see *Cleveland Plain Dealer,* March 27, 1977. In the same article, Cleveland police chief Lloyd F. Garey called members of the Shield Club "unqualified malcontents."

26. Interview by author with retired policewoman Jean Clayton, September 10, 1977, Cleveland, Ohio, audiotape; interview with Lynn Coleman; *Cleveland Press,* June 7, 1977; *Cleveland Call and Post,* June 25, 1977; *Lynn R. Coleman et al. vs. Frank J. Schaefer, Cleveland Lodge, Fraternal Order of Police et al., Petition for Money, Declaratory Judgment and Further Relief,* County of Cuyahoga, Court of Common Pleas, October 20, 1969.

27. For the goals of the FOPs, PBAs, and other police unions, see Hervey A. Juris and Peter Feuille, *Police Unionism: Power and Impact in Public Sector Bargaining* (Lexington, Mass.: Lexington Books, 1973). For the pre-1960 reforms in New York City and Philadelphia, see *New York Herald Tribune,* June 20, 1959; Reaves, *Black Cops,* 64–75; Kephart, *Racial Factors and Urban Law Enforcement,* 138. Other cities where African Americans made progress toward integration and fair promotions in the 1940s and 1950s were Columbus, Cleveland, and Los Angeles. See Dulaney, "Blacks as Policemen in Columbus, Ohio," 15; Davis, *Black Americans in Cleveland,* 369–370; *Los Angeles Sentinel,* October 30, 1947.

28. For recruitment drives for African-American police in the 1960s, see the *Columbus Dispatch,* May 3, 1968; *Miami Times,* February 21, 1969; and Margolis, *Who Will Wear the Badge?* For the end of the "Negro Police Station" and "black police beats" in Miami and

Atlanta, see the *Miami Herald,* July 26, 1963, and the *Atlanta Journal,* May 13, 1969, respectively. See also chapter 5 above. For "race mixing" in police cars in Detroit and Houston, see "Detroit Now Mixes Car Crews," press release, February 5, 1959, ANP Clipping File, and *Houston Chronicle,* March 9, 1969, respectively. For O. W. Wilson's attempt to "reform" and "integrate" the Chicago police force, see William J. Bopp, *"O. W.": O. W. Wilson and the Search for a Police Profession* (Port Washington, N.Y.: Kennikat Press, 1977), 6, 85–95; "Name 23 New Negro Chicago Police Sergeants," *Jet,* January 19, 1961, p. 4; Jack Star, "Chicago Shows a Way to Police Reform," *Look,* October 9, 1965, pp. 43–49; *Chicago Tribune,* March 19, 1960, and April 1, 1965; *Chicago Defender,* January 19, 1963. For Spina's reforms in Newark, see *Baltimore Afro-American,* December 8, 1962; and New York *World-Telegram,* July 3, 1965. For the twenty-year resistance to the employment of African Americans on the Birmingham and Jackson police forces, see the *Weekly Review* (Birmingham), February 24, 1941; *Jackson (Miss.) News,* January 14, 1953; "Union Opposes Hiring of Negro Cops in Birmingham," press release, December 21, 1955, ANP Clipping File; *Chicago Defender,* March 26, 1966; *Jackson Daily News,* June 21, 1963.

29. Mark Haller, "Urban Crime and Criminal Justice: The Chicago Case," *Journal of American History* 57 (December 1970): 619–635; Haller, "Police Reform in Chicago: 1905–1935," *American Behavioral Scientist* 13 (May–August 1970): 649–665; "The Elections of 1940: Chicago's Machine Runs on Gratitude," *Life,* October 21, 1940, p. 94. For the appointment of John Scott as the first African-American police captain in Chicago, see the *Chicago Defender,* August 17, 1940.

30. Reaves, *Black Cops,* 73–75; *New York Times,* June 19, 1965; Edward D. Williams, *The First Black Captain* (New York: Vantage Press, 1974), 94–98. See chapter 7 for a full discussion of black police administrators.

31. A conclusion drawn from the Kerner Report and other sources. See *Report of the National Advisory Commission on Civil Disorders;* Paul Jacobs, "The Los Angeles Police: A Critique," *Atlantic Monthly,* December 1966, pp. 95–101; Paul Jacobs, *Prelude to Riot: A View of Urban America from the Bottom* (New York: Vintage Books, 1967), 18–60 and 270–276; Robert M. Fogelson, "From Resentment to Confrontation: The Police and the Outbreak of the Nineteen-Sixties Riots," *Political Science Quarterly* 83 (June 1968): 217–247.

32. Richard Hall, "Dilemma of the Black Cop," *Life,* September 18, 1970, pp. 60–70; Wallis W. Johnson, "Man in the Middle: The Black Policeman," *Civil Rights Digest,* Summer 1970, pp. 23–27; Alex Poinsett, "The Dilemma of the Black Policeman," *Ebony,* July 1971, pp. 122–124; Thompson, "How Race Crisis Splits Black, White Policemen," pp. 14–19.

33. Bolden, "A Study of the Black Guardian Organization," 83–116; Leonard Ruchelman, *Police Politics: A Comparative Study of Three Cities* (Cambridge, Mass.: Ballinger Publishing Co., 1974), 39–47; for the quote, see Niederhoffer, *Behind the Shield,* 175.

34. *New York Times,* July 30, 1968; Davis, *Black Americans in Cleveland,* 405–406; Carl B. Stokes, *Promises of Power: A Political Autobiography* (New York: Simon and Schuster, 1973), 206–224; Louis H. Masotti and Jerome R. Corsi, *Shoot-Out in Cleveland: Black Militants and the Police, July 23, 1968,* Report to the National Commission on the Causes and Prevention of Violence (New York: Frederick A. Praeger Publishers, 1969), 69–103; Estelle Zannes, *Checkmate in Cleveland: The Rhetoric of Confrontation during the Stokes Years* (Cleveland: Press of Case Western Reserve University, 1972), 140–148. Corsi and Masotti commend Stokes's decision to use only black police officers in the Glenville riot. Zannes, however, is critical of how Stokes handled the riot and even makes the unsubstantiated charge that "black militants" destroyed the Stokes administration (xii).

35. Robert McClory, *The Man Who Beat Clout City* (Chicago: Swallow Press, 1977), 13.

36. Quotes and position statement are in Renault A. Robinson, "Black Police: A Positive Means of Social Change," 25 pages, in the Afro-American Patrolmen's League Papers at the Chicago Historical Society. Hereafter cited as the AAPL Papers. See also Renault Robinson, "Black Police: A Positive Means of Social Change" (M.A. thesis, Roosevelt University, 1974).

37. These letters are in the AAPL Papers. I saw the show myself in April 1971 in a sociology class at Central State University, Wilberforce, Ohio.

38. McClory, *The Man Who Beat Clout City,*, 33–46; Hall, "Dilemma of the Black Cop," 64–70; Carol Morton, "Black Cops: Black and Blue Ain't White," *Ramparts,* May 1971, p. 25.

39. Stanley Robinson, *The Badge They Are Trying to Bury* (Bluff, Utah: Simon Belt Publishers, 1975), 70–85. Stanley Robinson identifies William O'Neal as the FBI informant who framed him—the same FBI informant who engineered the murders of Black Panthers Fred Hampton and Mark Clark in 1969 by the Chicago police. See Kenneth O'Reilly, *Racial Matters: The FBI's Secret File on Black America, 1960–1972* (New York: The Free Press, 1989), 310–315; "Stanley Robinson: Murderer or FBI Scapegoat?" *Encore American and Worldwide News,* December 8, 1975, pp. 14, 17.

40. McClory, *The Man Who Beat Clout City,*, 210–211; *Chicago Defender,* September 28, 1977; "Harassed Black Police Leader Wins $125,000, Reinstatement in Chicago," *Jet,* October 13, 1977, p. 16; "Chicago Police Superintendent Who Lost Discrimination Suit to Blacks Resigns His Post," *Jet,* October 27, 1977, p. 14.

41. McClory, *The Man Who Beat Clout City,*, 10–12. In 1965, while working as a rookie undercover officer, Renault Robinson reported observing two police officers accepting bribes. He was immediately transferred out of the assignment and into the academy. Ibid., 27. For an assessment of the AAPL's impact on the Chicago police force, see Leonard Sykes, Jr., "Black and Blue from Caring in Chicago," *The National Leader,* April 7, 1983, pp. 18–19.

42. Reaves, *Black Cops,* 124–131; (Phila.) *Evening Bulletin,* August 15, 1968; "NAACP Pushes Probe of Bias in Philly Police Department," *The Crisis,* September 1971, pp. 232–233; Linn Washington, Jr., "The City of Brotherly Love: The Sleeping Giant v. the White Crusader," *Encore: American and Worldwide News,* November 20, 1978, pp. 12–17; "Philly Mayor Orders Quota to Hire More Black Cops," *Jet,* April 12, 1982, p. 8; *Atlanta Constitution,* May 28, 1982; *Dallas Morning News,* August 13, 1983; Jerry M. Guess, "Alphonso Deal: Fighter to the End," *The Crisis,* June/July 1987, pp. 54–57. For information related to the founding of the GCL, see "The Guardians Civic League," membership brochure, ca. 1963, in the files of the Guardians Civic League, Philadelphia, Pennsylvania.

43. Terry S. Link, "Black and White in Blue," *San Francisco Magazine,* June 1970, p. 16. For assessments of the development of San Francisco's black community, see Albert S. Broussard, "Organizing the Black Community in the San Francisco Bay Area, 1915–1930," *Arizona and the West* 23 (Winter 1981): 335–354; Broussard, "Strange Territory, Familiar Leadership: The Impact of World War II on San Francisco's Black Community," *California History* 65 (March 1986): 18–25; Broussard, "The Politics of Despair: Black San Franciscans and the Political Process, 1920–1940," *Journal of Negro History* 69 (Winter 1984): 26–37; Douglas Henry Daniels, "Afro-San Franciscans: A Social History of Pioneer Urbanites, 1860–1930" (Ph.D. dissertation, University of California, Berkeley, 1975), 305–306. For the 1943 appointment of San Francisco's first black officer, William Glenn, who was a temporary appointment during World War II, see the *Kansas City Call,* July 6, 1945.

44. Link, "Black and White in Blue," pp. 17–18; *Sun-Reporter* (San Francisco), April 20, 1963; *San Francisco Examiner,* November 16, 1963, December 19, 1963, September 4, 1964, October 2 and 30, 1977. For the "race riot" in Hunter's Point, see Arthur E. Hibbler, *Hunter's Point: A Black Ghetto* (New York: Basic Books, 1974), 203–209.

45. Officers for Justice Peace Officers Association, *Why the Officers for Justice?* (San Francisco, 1968); *An Evening with the Officers for Justice,* Souvenir Benefit Program (San Francisco, 1971); *San Francisco Sunday Examiner and Chronicle,* October 6, 1968; Link, "Black and White in Blue," p. 18; interview with Chief of Police Richard Hongisto, Cleveland, Ohio, February 1, 1978.

46. *San Francisco Chronicle,* February 11, 1969, March 24, 1972, June 18, 1973, November 28, 1973, January 8, 1977; *San Francisco Examiner,* July 19, 1972, December 4, 1973, May 11, 1977, September 19, 1977; *The Officers for Justice, et al. v. The Civil Service Commission, et al.,* C-73-0657, November 14, 1977, U.S. District Court for the Northern District of California.

47. See footnotes 26 and 34 above; *Cleveland Plain Dealer,* September 30, 1968. The Shield Club also filed a racial discrimination suit against the Cleveland Police Department

in 1972. See *The Shield Club, et al. v. The City of Cleveland, et al.*, CA 72-1088, U.S. District Court, Northern District of Ohio; *Cleveland Plain Dealer,* May 7, 1974.

48. Ruchelman, *Police Politics,* 71; Bolden, "A Study of the Black Guardian Organization," passim; *Dallas Express,* December 31, 1966. For a full discussion of the white police opposition to minority police recruitment in New York City, see Alex, *New York Cops Talk Back,* 32–41.

49. Broome, *LAPD's Black History,* 216–217; Hall, "Dilemma of the Black Cop," pp. 60–64.

50. *Miami Herald,* March 29, 1966, July 28, 1966, December 15, 1971; *Miami News,* August 26, 1966, January 24, 1967; "Open Letter and Position Statement of the Community Police Benevolent Association," August 1971, photocopy.

51. National Black Police Association, *Fifth Annual Conference Program,* August 1977; *Atlanta Daily World,* May 17, 1970, October 22, 1973; *Atlanta Constitution,* April 3, 1973; *Atlanta Journal,* March 29, 1973; Bayor, "Race and City Services," 29. For more detail on the racial conflict in the Atlanta police force, see chapter 7.

52. For the national coverage given the conflict between black police officers and white-controlled police departments, see *New York Times,* September 28, 1969; *Wall Street Journal,* January 2, 1971; Paul Delaney, "Something That Had to Be Done: Black Cops in the South," *The Nation,* July 31, 1976, pp. 78–82. For the bid by blacks to control the police in Atlanta, Newark, and Washington, D.C., see Larry E. Moss, *Black Political Ascendancy in Urban Centers and Black Control of the Local Police Function: An Exploratory Analysis* (San Francisco: R and E Research Associates, 1977), chapters II, III, and IV. Moss argues that the key point of contention was whether whites would allow African Americans to control the police in cities where African Americans controlled city government. See also chapter 7.

53. This is a summary of information obtained from many sources and interviews. A partial list would include Robinson, "Black Police: A Positive Means to Social Change"; Lee P. Brown, *The Death of Police-Community Relations,* Occasional Paper, 1 (Washington, D.C.: Howard University Institute of Urban Affairs and Research, 1974); Lee P. Brown, ed., *The Administration of Justice: A View from Black America,* Occasional Paper, 2 (Washington, D.C.: Howard University Institute of Urban Affairs and Research, 1974); and Herrington J. Bryce, ed., *Black Crime: A Police View* (Washington, D.C.: Joint Center for Political Studies et al., 1977).

54. Norman Seay, Coordinator of the First National Conference of Black Policemen, to Colonel Delbert Miller, President, St. Louis Board of Police Commissioners, July 18, 1972, Correspondence, St. Louis Ethical Police Society files, St. Louis, Missouri; interview by author with Norman Seay, July 15, 1977, transcript.

55. National Black Police Association, "Fact Sheet," n.d.; see also the *Annual Conference Programs* for the 3rd through the 10th annual conferences, 1975–1982, all in the AAPL Papers.

7. *Black Police Administrators*

1. Eaves is quoted in Alex Poinsett, "Atlanta's Winning Fight against Black-on-Black Crime, *Ebony,* June 1976, p. 71. Sharpe James is quoted in Moss, *Black Political Ascendancy in Urban Centers,* 60. In 1986, James became Newark's second African-American mayor. For Harold Washington's campaign slogan, see Roger Biles, "Black Mayors: A Historical Assessment," *Journal of Negro History* 77 (Summer 1992): 120.

2. Moss, *Black Political Ascendancy in Urban Centers,* 1–3; Mack H. Jones, "Black Political Empowerment in Atlanta: Myth and Reality," *Annals of the American Academy of Political and Social Science* 439 (September 1978): 90–92. Former Cleveland, Ohio, mayor Carl Stokes made a similar observation in his autobiography. See Stokes, *Promises of Power,* 216.

3. For Shaw's appointment, see chapter 3. For Alston's career, see Columbus, Ohio, Department of Public Safety, *Minute Book,* 8, September 15, 1937, p. 463; *Minute Book,* 12, October 15, 1946, p. 86, and April 27, 1948, p. 377; Gale L. Reeder, Secretary, to Donald D.

Cook, Director of Public Safety, Columbus, Ohio, July 25, 1952, Correspondence, City Hall Vault; *Ohio State Sentinel,* May 9 and 16, 1959; "Good News," *The Crisis,* January 1955, p. 27.

4. *Pittsburgh Courier,* November 27, 1954; *Kansas City Call,* November 26, 1954; "Inspector of Police," *Ebony,* August 1956, pp. 60–64; Dulaney, "Black and Blue in America," 50–51; interview by author with retired police inspector Harvey Alston, November 26, 1973, Columbus, Ohio, transcript.

5. "Palmyra's Police Chief," *Ebony,* June 1959, pp. 61–64; *Pittsburgh Courier,* February 7, 1959; *Louisiana Weekly,* February 14, 1959; "Portsmouth's Police Chief," *Ebony,* April 1963, pp. 144–147; *Pittsburgh Courier,* July 28, 1962. See the *Springfield News-Sun,* July 26, 1987, for information on how James Burch became the first African-American police chief in Springfield, Ohio, in 1984.

6. "Mayor Names Negro Minister Police Chief in Illinois," *Jet,* May 28, 1959, p. 9; *Montgomery Advertiser,* July 17, 1965; *Birmingham News,* July 21, 1965; *New York Times,* July 17, 1965; *New York Herald Tribune,* July 22, 1965.

7. Several studies have attempted to assess how the presence of black mayors and black political power have influenced black access to municipal jobs and control of police policies. See Peter K. Eisinger, "Black Employment in Municipal Jobs: The Impact of Black Political Power," *American Political Science Review* 76 (June 1982): 380–392; Monte Piliawsky, "The Impact of Black Mayors on the Black Community: The Case of New Orleans," *Review of Black Political Economy* 13 (Spring 1985): 5–24; Grace H. Saltzstein, "Black Mayors and Police Policies," *Journal of Politics* 51 (1989): 525–544.

8. Richard Hatcher was elected mayor of Gary, Indiana on the same day that Stokes was elected mayor of Cleveland. Gary, however, was more than 50 percent black. Thus, in 1970 when Hatcher appointed Charles Boone as the city's first African-American police chief, there was little controversy about the appointment. Some black citizens thought that Hatcher's appointment of a black police chief was long overdue—since he had been in office for three years. See Alex Poinsett, *Black Power, Gary Style: The Making of Mayor Richard Gordon Hatcher* (Chicago: Johnson Publishing Co., 1970), 160.

9. Stokes, *Promises of Power,* 171–173; Carl Stokes, "My First Year in Office," *Ebony,* January 1969, p. 121; (Cleveland) *Plain Dealer,* January 27, 1970. In her 1989 study, Grace H. Saltzstein would find that most of the big-city black mayors who followed Stokes also pledged to "control" the police and to make them better serve the black community. See Saltzstein, "Black Mayors and Police Policies," 525–527. A similar conclusion is drawn by Biles in "Black Mayors," 109–125. For more evidence, see below.

10. Stokes, *Promises of Power,* 180–204; Benjamin O. Davis, Jr., *Benjamin O. Davis Jr., American: An Autobiography* (Washington, D.C.: Smithsonian Institution Press, 1991), 70, 84, 330–331, 332–335; "Lt. Gen. B. O. Davis, Jr. Is Praised, Cited at Ceremony," *Jet,* February 19, 1970, p. 5.

11. John H. Britton, "General Davis Begins to Make Cleveland Safest City," *Jet,* March 19, 1970, pp. 14–20; "A Cop-Panther Confrontation in Cleveland Raises Questions," *Jet,* July 30, 1970, pp. 20–22. Many blacks in Cleveland were put on guard about General Davis when they saw how he was embraced by the Cleveland Police Patrolmen's Association (CPPA), an organization of Cleveland police officers that had opposed the Shield Club and Stokes on almost every issue related to the reform of the police department. See "Davis, Coffey and the C.P.P.A.; Let's Keep It That Way," *Blue Line,* July 1970, p. 11. The *Blue Line* was the official monthly publication of the CPPA.

12. Stokes, *Promises of Power,* 180–204; Davis, *Black Americans in Cleveland,* 336–348; Zannes, *Checkmate in Cleveland,* 222–225; Emetra Black, "Why General Davis Quits Cleveland Police Force," *Jet,* August 13, 1970, pp. 14–19. Here I must note that there are vast differences between Stokes's account of Davis's tenure as public safety director and Davis's version. After reading both accounts and after witnessing these incidents myself (I grew up in a small town near Cleveland), I tend to believe Stokes's version of these events. One key incident seems to confirm my viewpoint: Collingwood. In his autobiography,

Davis distorted his role in handling the white-led protests at Collingwood High School. Thus, one wonders whether he is honest about any of his experiences as Cleveland's first African-American public safety director.

13. Stokes, *Promises of Power,* 232–235; Black, "Why General Davis Quit," p. 19; Davis, *Black Americans in Cleveland,* 412–413, 416. In his autobiography, Stokes said that his greatest frustration and failure was his inability to reform the police department. As a measure of his concern about this failure, he devoted an entire chapter in his book to the topic—the longest chapter in the book. See Stokes, *Promises of Power,* chapter 11, "The Police," 171–205.

14. Jerome H. Skolnick and David H. Bayley, *The New Blue Line: Police Innovation in Six American Cities* (New York: Free Press, 1986), 187; "Kenneth Gibson," *Current Biography Yearbook, 1971* (New York: H. W. Wilson Co., 1971), 151; Williams, *The First Black Captain,* 94–97.

15. Skolnick and Bayley, *The New Blue Line,* 187; *New York Times,* November 29, 1972, December 1, 1972; Moss, 56–60.

16. Two examples, sixty years apart, make this point. In 1899, Columbus, Ohio, mayor Samuel Swartz appointed James W. Dusenbury as that city's public safety director. Dusenbury was just a ward boss who turned out the vote on election day to get Swartz elected to office. See the *Ohio State Journal,* April 20, 1899. In 1958, the mayor of San Francisco appointed *Patrolman* Thomas Cahill as chief of police. Cahill's "qualifications" were that he was the mayor's best friend. Cahill served as chief of the SFPD for twelve years and even became president of the International Association of Chiefs of Police (IACP). In 1970, however, when it appeared that several black officers were going to be skipped several ranks to lieutenant and captain to compensate them for past discrimination, the San Francisco POA placed a proposition on the city ballot preventing officers with lower ranks from being appointed to administrative positions. The proposition passed. See San Francisco Police Department, Planning and Research Division, "A History of the San Francisco Police Department," May 1972, p. 7 (photocopy); Link, "Black and White in Blue," p. 34.

17. *New York Times,* December 11, 1972, July 12, 1973, July 25, 1973.

18. Skolnick and Bayley, *The New Blue Line,* 187; *New York Times,* July 25, 1973, June 28, 1974.

19. *New York Times,* May 15, 1974, June 28, 1974, July 1, 1974.

20. Williams also had to abide by a federal court order to hire and promote more black officers. Three months after he became police director, a federal court ordered the city of Newark to fill at least one-third of its new police positions with minority officers. *New York Times,* October 8, 1974; "Newark: The Promise of Survival," *The Nation,* December 14, 1974, p. 621.

21. *New York Times,* August 8, 1974, and November 15, 1974; Skolnick and Bayley, *The New Blue Line,* 188–209; Julie Lewin, "Future Cop," *Parade Magazine,* March 21, 1982, pp. 4–5. The author is aware that crime statistics are not a true indication of whether crime goes up or down; they also are not a fair means of evaluating how well a police department (or police administrator) is "controlling" or "reducing" crime. Such statistics measure only "reported crime." The statistics are used here only to indicate how the local press in each city evaluated the performance of black police chiefs and administrators.

22. *New York Times,* February 8, 1985; "The New Black Police Chiefs," *Time,* February 18, 1985, p. 84.

23. "New Men for Atlanta and Detroit," *Time,* January 14, 1974, pp. 13–14; *Columbus Call and Post,* May 24, 1974; *Atlanta Constitution,* February 28, 1973; Mike Raffauf, "Jackson v. Inman," *Creative Loafing,* August 24, 1974, clipping; Moss, *Black Political Ascendancy in Urban Centers,* 21–24; Jones, "Black Political Empowerment in Atlanta," 110.

24. "A City Learning to Hate," *Newsweek,* July 8, 1974, p. 34; Raffauf, "Jackson v. Inman"; Jones, "Black Political Empowerment in Atlanta," 111; "Atlanta: A Mayor Learning on the Job," *Time,* April 21, 1975, p. 33.

25. Raffauf, "Jackson v. Inman"; Moss, *Black Political Ascendancy in Urban Centers,* 26–27; Jones, "Black Political Empowerment in Atlanta"; Poinsett, "Atlanta's Winning Fight against Black-on-Black Crime," p. 68; Bayor, "Race and City Services," 30–31. According to Raffauf, Jackson allegedly cut a deal with John Inman: if Inman supported Jackson's choice of a black public safety commissioner (which he did in August 1974), Inman would be left alone to collect his salary for doing nothing as director of police services for one year. Either the deal failed or it was never made, because Inman remained as director of police services through 1979, literally collecting a salary for five years for doing nothing! In August 1979, Inman balked at being forced to earn his income when he was ordered by Commissioner Brown to develop a handgun control policy. Inman's resistance to the order prompted Jackson to call him "a parasite at the public trough." *Atlanta Journal,* August 15, 1979.

26. "Eaves Wins Council Support for City Post," *Jet,* September 5, 1974, p. 12; "The Black Crime Buster," *Time,* March 22, 1976, p. 41; Poinsett, "Atlanta's Winning Fight against Black-on-Black Crime," pp. 68–70; "Atlanta's Businessmen Fight City Hall," *Business Week,* September 2, 1974, pp. 36–37; Jones, "Black Political Empowerment in Atlanta," 112. Jones also maintains that Atlanta's white businessmen were upset with Jackson not only because he was allowing a black man to take over the police department, but also because he had mandated that blacks share in the city funds allocated to renovate the airport, and because he had stated that the new airport would be built in South Atlanta to aid the economic development of Atlanta's black communities rather than in North Atlanta close to the city's major white communities. In other words, Jackson was mandating that black Atlantans be allowed to share in the spoils of city government that had historically benefited only whites. Jones, "Black Political Empowerment in Atlanta," 111.

27. Poinsett, "Atlanta's Winning Fight against Black-on-Black Crime," p. 67; "The Black Crime Buster," p. 41; "Atlanta: A Mayor Learning on the Job," p. 33; "Violence Solves Problems? TV Says Yes; Public Safety Chief Says No," *Jet,* December 30, 1976, p. 44; *Atlanta Constitution,* December 5, 1974, and March 29, 1976; *Boston Globe,* August 5, 1976; *Atlanta Journal,* August 5, 1976; *Omaha World-Herald,* August 6, 1976; Jones, "Black Political Empowerment in Atlanta," 113; Milton Viorst, "Black Mayor, White Power Structure," *The Nation,* June 7, 1975, pp. 9–11; interview by author with Commissioner A. Reginald Eaves, Atlanta, Georgia, August 11, 1977, audiotape; Eisinger, "Black Employment in Municipal Jobs," 384–385; Biles, "Black Mayors," 118–120.

28. See the quote at the beginning of this chapter.

29. Jones, "Black Political Empowerment in Atlanta," 109, 115; Poinsett, "Atlanta's Winning Fight against Black-on-Black Crime," 70; *Atlanta Constitution,* August 22, 1974, September 23, 1974, November 25, 1975, June 16, 1976; City of Atlanta, City Council, "Equal Opportunities for Minorities within the Bureau of Police Services in Atlanta: An Analysis," Public Safety Committee Report, July 1974, p. 1; William G. Lewis, "Toward Representative Bureaucracy: Blacks in City Police Organizations, 1975–1985," *Public Administration Review* 49 (May/June 1989): 263–265; Eisinger, "Black Employment in Municipal Jobs," 391; Bruce Cory, "In Atlanta, a Furor over Cheating," *Police Magazine,* March 1979, p. 16.

30. *Atlanta Constitution,* November 25, 1975, March 13, 1976, June 16, 1976, September 23, 1976; Bayor, "Race and City Services," 31–32; Lewis, "Blacks in City Police Organizations," 263–264; Cory, "In Atlanta, a Furor over Cheating," pp. 16–17.

31. Cory, "In Atlanta, a Furor over Cheating," pp. 18–19; *Atlanta Journal,* March 10, 1978; *Atlanta Journal and Constitution,* March 11 and 12, 1978; *Atlanta Constitution,* March 14 and 20, 1978. See chapters 2 and 4 above for the charges that the police would be "Africanized" if too many blacks served as police officers.

32. To compare the careers of O. W. Wilson and Patrick V. Murphy with Brown's, see Bopp, *"O. W.": O. W. Wilson and the Search for a Police Profession;* and Patrick V. Murphy and Thomas Plate, *The Commissioner* (New York: Simon and Schuster, 1977).

33. "If You're Brown," *Black Enterprise,* June 1982, pp. 46–47; Skolnick and Bayley, *The New Blue Line,* 91–92; Peter Blauner, "The Rap Sheet on Lee Brown," *New York,* January

22, 1990, pp. 32–38; "Dr. Lee Brown Appointed Atlanta's New Police Chief," *Jet,* April 20, 1978, p. 6.

34. Blauner, "The Rap Sheet on Lee Brown," p. 36; *Dallas Morning News,* March 28, 1982; "Lee Brown Is Appointed Police Chief of Houston," *Jet,* March 29, 1982, p. 7.

35. *Columbus Dispatch,* September 22, 1977; Alex Poinsett, "Houston: Golden City of Opportunity," *Ebony,* July 1978, pp. 132–142; Tom Curtis, "Support Your Local Police—or Else!" *Texas Monthly,* September 1977, pp. 82–89; David Blum, "Houston's Illness," *New Republic,* July 8 and 15, 1978, pp. 12–14; "Police Story: Two Hard Towns," *Time,* September 19, 1977, pp. 29–30; *Dallas Morning News,* March 11, 1980, and March 28, 1982; "Lee Brown Is Appointed Police Chief of Houston"; "Brown Confirmed to Head Houston's Police Department," *Jet,* April 12, 1982, p. 29; *Washington Post,* March 10, 1982; "If You're Brown"; Tom Curtis, "The Lawman," *Texas Monthly,* January 1986, p. 266; Walker, *History of Black Police Officers in the Houston Police Department,* 56–58.

36. *Dallas Morning News,* April 15, 1984, and September 20, 1987; Skolnick and Bayley, *The New Blue Line,* 81–116; Walker, *History of Black Police Officers in the Houston Police Department,* 61–75; Lee P. Brown, "Neighborhood-Oriented Policing," *American Journal of Police* 9 (1990): 197–207.

37. *Dallas Morning News,* December 3, 1989; Blauner, "The Rap Sheet on Lee Brown," p. 32; *New York Times,* December 19, 1989.

38. "Benjamin Ward," *Current Biography Yearbook, 1988* (New York: H. W. Wilson Co., 1988), 597–601; *New York Times,* September 26, 1989; *Dallas Morning News,* December 17, 1989. It is interesting to note that Mayor Dinkins was lobbied by New York Governor Mario Cuomo and John Cardinal O'Connor to choose "in-house" and politically expedient candidate Deputy Police Commissioner Richard Condon as his police commissioner, rather than the "best-qualified" candidate, Lee P. Brown. *New York Times,* December 19, 1989.

39. "Benjamin Ward," 600; *New York Times,* March 24, 1989, October 2, 1989.

40. *New York Times,* January 23, 1990, March 22, 1990, April 27, 1990, April 29, 1991; *Dallas Morning News,* October 20, 1990, August 26, 1991; *USA Today,* November 26, 1990.

41. *Dallas Morning News,* August 26, 1990; *New York Times,* August 14, 1991; "Lee Brown's New York Blues," *Newsweek,* October 8, 1990, p. 33; George M. Daniels, "The Crisis Interview: Dr. Lee P. Brown," *The Crisis,* August–September 1991, p. 36. The text of Brown's "Code of Values":

> In partnership with the community, we pledge to: protect the lives and property of fellow citizens and impartially enforce the law; fight crime both by preventing it and by aggressively pursuing violators of the law; maintain a higher standard of integrity than is generally expected of others because so much more is expected of us; and value human life, respect the dignity of each individual and render our services with courtesy and civility.

42. *New York Times,* August 4, 1992, October 8, 1992; *Dallas Morning News,* August 4, 1992; "N.Y. Has Worst Cop to Resident Ratio for Blacks," *Jet,* November 2, 1992, p. 32.

43. *New York Times,* September 19, 1992; *Dallas Morning News,* October 18, 1992, April 4, 1993.

44. As noted in chapter 2, the first African American to chair a police board was Oscar J. Dunn, who chaired the Metropolitan Police Board of New Orleans from 1868 to 1871. A. R. Jones chaired the police commission in Jacksonville, Florida, from 1887 to 1888. The first African American to serve on a police commission in the twentieth century was Charles Matthew, who served on the Los Angeles Police Commission from 1946 to 1948. Attorney Elbert T. Hudson served as president of the Los Angeles Police Commission during his term on the commission from 1963 to 1970. Unlike the commission in St. Louis, however, the Los Angeles Police Commission did not have direct oversight over appointments, firings, and promotions. See Broome, *LAPD's Black History,* 37–42.

45. *St. Louis Sentinel,* December 19, 1972; *St. Louis Argus,* March 20, 1970, and December 20, 1972; "Policing the Police: Former State Solon Heads St. Louis Board," *Ebony,* May 1973, pp. 43–50; Ernest Calloway, *The T. D. McNeal Story* (St. Louis, 1966), six pages; interview by author with former St. Louis Board of Police Commissioners president Theodore D. McNeal, St. Louis, Missouri, July 20, 1977, audiotape; "Biography of Theodore D. McNeal," mimeographed.

46. Watts, "Black and Blue," 132–133; St. Louis Metropolitan Police Department, *Annual Report, 1974* (St. Louis, 1975), p. 6; *Souvenir History St. Louis Police Department,* n.p.; interview with McNeal.

47. *St. Louis Globe-Democrat,* September 7, 1974, October 4, 1974; *St. Louis Post-Dispatch,* December 12, 1971; Sergeant James Buchanan, "Minority Police Recruiting: A Move toward a Better Community," Recruiting Division, St. Louis Metropolitan Police Department, February 1977, n.p.; Watts, "Black and Blue," 152; John Egerton, "Minority Police: How Many Are There?" *Race Relations Reporter* 5 (November 1974): 19–21.

48. *St. Louis Argus,* November 11, 1974, December 19, 1974; *St. Louis Globe-Democrat,* October 31, 1974, August 21, 1975; *St. Louis American,* November 7, 1974, January 29, 1976; *St. Louis Post-Dispatch,* January 10, 1974, January 8, 1975, August 1, 1975, August 21, 1975, January 22 and 23, 1976; interview with McNeal; interview by author with Norman Seay, July 15, 1977, St. Louis, Missouri.

49. *St. Louis Argus,* November 11, 1974, June 23, 1977; *St. Louis American,* November 7, 1974, February 18, 1977; *St. Louis Globe-Democrat,* October 31, 1974, January 24, 1977; *St. Louis Post-Dispatch,* April 29, 1976, February 14, 1977; interview with McNeal; interview by author with Captain Gay Carraway, director of the St. Louis Team Policing project, July 14, 1977. For Harmon's appointment, see table 12 above.

50. Wilbur C. Rich, *Coleman Young and Detroit Politics: From Social Activist to Power Broker* (Detroit: Wayne State University Press, 1989), 105–107, 205–208; "Mayor: A Tale of Two Cities," *Newsweek,* October 15, 1973, p. 35; "New Men for Atlanta and Detroit," pp. 13–14; "Detroit," *Race Relations Law Reporter* 7 (Summer 1962): 621–623; "Negro Gets No. 3 Spot in Detroit Police Dept.," *Jet,* November 2, 1967, p. 5; John Hersey, *The Algiers Motel Incident* (New York: Bantam Books, 1968); Conot, *American Odyssey,* 413–415; *New York Times,* January 3, 1974, and March 10, 1974. See also Albert J. Reiss, *The Police and the Public* (New Haven: Yale University Press, 1971), 35–36, where two white officers in Detroit deprecated the ability of black police officers in the city.

51. "Black on Black," *Newsweek,* January 14, 1974, p. 20; *New York Times,* January 22, 1975, and October 9, 1976; Remer Tyson, "Detroit Hangs in There: Mayor Young a Year Later," *The Nation,* March 1, 1975, p. 238; "Detroit to Hire 1,000 Black Policemen in '75," *Jet,* April 17, 1975, p. 7.

52. Rich, *Coleman Young,* 217–224; *New York Times,* May 10, 1975, May 15, 1975, March 6, 1976; Margo Williams, "What Happens When the Police Department Goes from White to Black: The Changing Face of the Detroit Police Department," *The Crisis,* December 1991, pp. 15–17; Bruce Cory, "Detroit: Paying for the Sins of the Past," *Police Magazine,* March 1979, pp. 9–11; Lawrence W. Sherman, "Minority Quotas for Police Promotions: A Comment on *Detroit Police Officers Association v. Young,*" *Criminal Law Bulletin* 15 (January–February 1979): 79–84.

53. *New York Times,* August 19, 1976, October 9, 1976, September 29, 1976; Rich, "Coleman Young," 213–215; "Coleman Young Appoints Black Police Chief; Black Deputy Chief Kills Himself," *Jet,* October 14, 1976, p. 8; "Key Detroit Policeman Takes Sudden Leave," *Jet,* November 4, 1976, p. 6.

54. *New York Times,* January 22, 1975; Bruce Babiar, "Police Chief Changes Detroit's Crime Image," *The National Leader,* August 25, 1983, p. 21; Phil W. Petrie, "Do Black Mayors Make a Difference?" *Black Enterprise,* July 1979, p. 28; *Dallas Morning News,* December 22, 1983; Skolnick and Bayley, *The New Blue Line,* 58–80; Williams, "What Happens," 16.

55. *New York Times,* February 12, 13, and 14, 1991; *Dallas Morning News,* February 17, 1991; "Detroit Police Chief Quits after Conviction," *Jet,* June 15, 1992, p. 28; Williams, "What Happens," 17.

56. Simeon Booker, "D.C. Mayor Sworn In," *Jet,* October 12, 1967, pp. 6–8; Moss, *Black Political Ascendancy in Urban Centers,* 98; *Washington Post,* May 31, 1979.

57. *Washington Post,* May 25, 1979, May 26, 1979, May 30, 1979, June 19, 1979. For the number and ranks of blacks on the D.C. force in 1975, see Lee P. Brown, Lawrence Gary, and Eugene Beard, *Final Report: Attitudes and Perceptions of Black Police Officers of the District of Columbia Metropolitan Police Department* (Washington, D.C.: Howard University Institute of Urban Affairs and Research, 1976), 32 and 34. For the percentage of blacks on the force in 1979, see the *Washington Post,* August 31, 1981.

58. *Washington Post,* May 31, 1979, June 3, 1979, June 19, 1979, July 1, 1981; Leavy, "Hail to the Chiefs," p. 115. After less than one year, Barry also clashed with Turner over policy in the police department. See *Washington Post,* April 14, 1982.

59. Ironically, in 1982 during Harold Washington's campaign to become Chicago's first black mayor, police superintendent Fred J. Brzeczek campaigned for Mayor Jane Byrne and tried to scare whites by stating that the streets would not be safe if Washington were elected. Brzeczek said: "I guarantee that it [the police department] will be a circus." Washington, of course, won the race and, to prove Brzeczek wrong, appointed Fred Rice as the city's first African-American police superintendent. See Dempsey J. Travis, *"Harold" the People's Mayor: An Authorized Biography of Mayor Harold Washington* (Chicago: Urban Research Press, 1989), 174.

60. Leavy, "Hail to the Chiefs," p. 115; Narine, "Top Cops," p. 130; Ronald E. Childs, "Top Brass," *Ebony Man,* May 1989, pp. 60–61; "New Cops on the Block," *U.S. News and World Report,* August 2, 1993, pp. 22–25.

61. A number of sources analyze how the combination of black mayors and black police chiefs has changed the quality of law enforcement in African-American communities. See Saltzstein, "Black Mayors and Police Policies," 525–544; Walter Leavy, "Can Black Mayors Stop Crime?" *Ebony,* December 1983, pp. 116–122; *Dallas Morning News,* December 22, 1983; *Dallas Times Herald,* April 27, 1988; Frederick H. Lowe, "Policing the Police: Spotlight on Black Top Cops," *Northstar News and Analysis,* May 1992, p. 5. For an assessment of the community policing concept that emerged in the 1980s in big-city police departments, see Lee P. Brown, "Community Policing: A Practical Guide for Police Officials," *Perspectives on Policing* 12 (September 1989): 1–12. For the advocacy of tough law enforcement in black communities by a black police chief, see Reuben Greenberg, "Let's Take Back Our Streets," *Ebony,* April 1991, pp. 106–108.

8. Three Generations

1. The categories defined in the first paragraph are based on the author's extensive research on the African-American experience in law enforcement. Walker, *A Critical History of Police Reform,* 41–43 and 61–66; Fogelson, *Big-City Police,* 110–114. New York City police officer Alexander "Clubber" Williams has been cited as the epitome of the brutal and corrupt police officers of the pre-Progressive era. See Thomas A. Reppetto, *The Blue Parade* (New York: Free Press, 1978), 49–57.

2. Broome, *LAPD's Black History,* 27, 29, and 43; *St. Louis Post-Dispatch,* August 14, 1899; *St. Louis Star,* August 14, 1899; *St. Louis Republic,* August 16, 1899. St. Louis police examiners were surprised to find that Allen also had the intellectual aptitude for police work. St. Louis police chief Campbell called Allen "one of the most intelligent men I have ever met." Nevertheless, as noted in chapter 3, Allen did not win an appointment to the force because he was not a registered Democrat. See *St. Louis Star,* August 23, 1899. For the repeated listing of Battle's height and weight, see *New York Evening Mail,* July 1, 1911; press release, June 6, 1941, ANP Clipping File; *Baltimore Afro-American,* January 14, 1956; Green and Young, *A History of the 28th Precinct,* 3. The *Evening Mail* did attempt to go beyond Battle's physique by observing that "he is undoubtedly the best type of Negro, a type that promises much for the future of the race." In his autobiographical novel, Jesse Kimbrough, who joined the LAPD in 1916, described the "ideal policeman" of his

generation as "a burly two-fisted knuckle-buster who could flatten a [law] violator with one blow." Jesse Kimbrough, *Defender of the Angels: A Black Policeman in Old Los Angeles* (London: Macmillan Co., 1969), 16.

3. *Houston Informer,* October 11, 1919. For Gilbert's police career, see Columbus, Ohio, Department of Public Safety, *Police and Fire Transfer Record,* n.p.; Columbus Police Benevolent Association, *History of the Police Department in Columbus, Ohio, 1908* (Columbus, Ohio, 1908), 143; *East Tennessee News,* April 16, 1929. For Garrison's career, see *History of the Columbus Police Department, 1821–1945,* 63; interview by author with James Watson, Columbus, Ohio, March 3, 1974, transcript; Columbus, Ohio Department of Public Safety, *Minute Record,* 3, October 5, 1920, p. 87; *Minute Book,* 5, November 14, 1931, p. 498; *Columbus Dispatch,* February 20, 1954, March 4, 1954.

4. The St. Louis Police Library has several unreferenced newspaper clippings on Cooper dated October 7, 1909, October 2, 1911, and June 23, 1936. See also St. Louis Metropolitan Board of Police Commissioners, *Official Record Book of Officers,* Book No. 1, p. 298; *Mexico (Mo.) Ledger,* March 20, 1919; "Detective Ira Cooper Promoted to Detective Sergeant," *St. Louis Police Journal,* March 7, 1923, p. 9; "Lt. Ira L. Cooper," *St. Louis Police Journal,* December 1965, p. 8; *St. Louis Argus,* February 28, 1930; *Baltimore Afro-American,* March 29, 1930; *Dallas Express,* February 25, 1939; Joseph J. Boris, ed., *Who's Who in Colored America* (New York: Who's Who in Colored America Corp., 1931–1932, 1933–1934).

5. Sylvester "Two-Gun Pete" Washington, "Why I Killed 11 Men," *Ebony,* January 1950, pp. 51–57; Burleigh Hines, "No More 'Two Gun Pete,'" *The Chicagoan,* February 1974, pp. 77–79.

6. *New York Herald Tribune,* January 1946 (clipping in the Tuskegee Collection); *Cincinnati Union,* January 24, 1946; *Baltimore Afro-American,* March 23, 1946; Herbert T. Klein, *The Police: Damned If They Do—Damned If They Don't* (New York: Crown Publishers, 1968), 206–207; Green and Young, *A History of the Twenty-eighth Precinct,* 5–6. Of course, there was some truth to Klein's charges about the reaction of blacks to white police actions in Harlem. See "White Policemen in Harlem," *The Crisis,* January 1945, pp. 16–17.

7. *American Ledger,* March 13, 1915; Claire Coombs, "Colored Police for Colored People," *Out West,* February 1917, p. 18; Broome, *LAPD's Black History,* 203; "Lady Cops," *Ebony,* September 1954, p. 32; Walker, *A Critical History of Police Reform,* 85–94; Samuel Walker, "The Rise and Fall of the Policewomen's Movement, 1905–1975," in Joseph M. Hawes, ed., *Law and Order in American History* (Port Washington, N.Y.: Kennikat Press, 1979), 101–111. According to Walker, the first white "policewoman" with actual police duties was appointed in Portland, Oregon, in 1905, while Los Angeles is considered to have appointed the first sworn policewoman in 1910. See Joseph Balkin, "Why Policemen Don't Like Policewomen," *Journal of Police Science and Administration* 16 (March 1988): 29.

8. Sources for the this paragraph: (Los Angeles) Coombs, "Colored Police for Colored People"; (Chicago) *Chicago Defender,* January 10, 1916; *The Crisis,* June 1918, p. 87; (Indianapolis) *Indianapolis Freeman,* June 22, 1918; *The Crisis,* August 1918, p. 190; (Pittsburgh) *Pittsburgh Sun,* February 11, 1919; (New York City) *Chicago Defender,* June 17, 1919; (Washington, D.C.) *Cleveland Advocate,* August 2, 1920; (Detroit) *Chicago Defender,* May 7, 1921; (Toledo, Ohio) *Cleveland Call,* March 18, 1922; (Baltimore) *Baltimore Afro-American,* December 11, 1937; (Columbus, Ohio) Department of Public Safety, *Minute Book,* 9, April 12, 1938, p. 70; (Atlanta) *Atlanta Daily World,* March 3, 1950; (Houston) "Houston, Tex. Police Gets First Woman Police Officer," *Jet,* July 30, 1953, p. 8; (Knoxville) *Knoxville News-Sentinel,* October 6, 1955. See also "Negro Policewomen," *Negro Year Book, 1918–1919* (Tuskegee, Ala., 1919), 53.

9. *Indianapolis Star,* April 3, 1919; clipping dated February 2, 1929, in "Policemen-Policewomen" file, Woodruff Library Special Collections, Atlanta University Center; "America's Most Glamorous Negro Cop," *Jet,* September 2, 1955, pp. 54–55; *Cleveland Call and Post,* June 25, 1977; Jean Clayton to Sgt. Matula, June 9, 1976, personal papers of Jean Clayton, Cleveland, Ohio.

10. Myron E. Moorehead, "An Evaluation of the Friendly Service Bureau in Its Crime Prevention among Negroes in the City of Columbus, Ohio, 1921 to 1930" (M.A. thesis,

Ohio State University, 1935); Richard C. Minor, "The Negro in Columbus, Ohio" (Ph.D. dissertation, Ohio State University, 1936), 123–135; Edward R. Lentz, "Rationalization and Reform: The Columbus Urban League, 1942–1962" (M.A. thesis, Ohio State University, 1969), 36–38; Leslie M. Shaw, Director, "Report of the Crime Prevention Work of the Columbus Police Department through the Friendly Service Bureau for 1934," in the Columbus Urban League and Departments, *Seventeenth Annual Report,* January 1935, Columbus Urban League Papers, Ohio Historical Society. Nine of Shaw's eighteen annual reports on the work of the Friendly Service Bureau are also available in the correspondence of the Columbus, Ohio, Department of Public Safety, 1933–1937, and the Columbus, Ohio Police Department's *Annual Reports,* 1941–1943. The Friendly Service Bureau was also cited and praised in the Urban League's official journal. See "Negro Crime Rate," *Opportunity,* June 1927, p. 160.

11. *Dallas Express,* November 4, 1950.

12. During the 1960s and 1970s, a number of black officers raised this question. Here is just a sampling: Brown, *Death of Police Community Relations,* 18–22; Lee P. Brown, "A Time for Change," *Police,* February 1970, p. 4; Palmer, "Black Police in America," 19–25; Gwynne Peirson, "The Role of Police in Reducing Crime," in Bryce, *Black Crime,* 83–84; Benjamin Ward, "The Need for Black Police Officers," in Brown, *The Administration of Justice,* 3–7; Jimmy Hargrove, "Stress—Above and Beyond of Black Police Officers," unpublished FBI National Police Academy paper, dated 1977; Renault Robinson, "The Police and the Community," n.d., AAPL Papers; Renault Robinson, President, AAPL, to Jay A. Miller, Executive Director, ACLU, June 19, 1969, AAPL Papers.

13. "Black Police Group Wants In on War against Crime," *Jet,* November 4, 1976, p. 31; "Chicago Conference Explores Black-on-Black Crime," *Jet,* December 1, 1986, pp. 32–33; "History of the National Organization of Black Law Enforcement Executives (NOBLE), September 1976–June 1977," six pages, mimeographed; *New York Times,* April 23, 1990; National Organization of Black Law Enforcement Executives, First Annual Conference, Atlanta, Georgia, June 21–25, 1977, Convention Program. One reason that the members of NOBLE began to overshadow the 15,000-member IACP in the advocacy of progressive police policies was that the latter organization continued to defend all police at all costs. In 1982, for example, the IACP tried to expel Patrick Murphy for saying that the police were "racist." See "Blue Funk," *Time,* July 26, 1982, p. 43, and "Outspoken Police Reformist Vows to Fight," *Officers for Justice Journal,* September 1982, p. 19. In 1990, the IACP finally recognized the contributions of Lee Brown to the police profession by making him its first African-American president. Of course, he had been recognized by the NBPA and NOBLE earlier. See "NOBLE Honors Lee Brown," *Jet,* August 3, 1987, p. 40; and Karen Osborne, "Leading the Top Cops," *Black Enterprise,* December 1990, p. 18.

14. "Declaration under Penalty of Perjury of Wilbert Battle, President of Officers for Justice," October 20, 1977, Supplemental Brief, Exhibit D, *The Officers for Justice, et al. v. The Civil Service Commission of the City and County of San Francisco, et al.,* Civil Action No. C-73-0657, U.S. District Court, Northern District of California, pp. 1–4; interview by author with Wilbert K. Battle, San Francisco, California, December 18, 1977, audiotape; Wilbert Battle, President, Officers for Justice, to W. Marvin Dulaney, November 29, 1977, May 6, 1978, November 9, 1978; Wilbert K. Battle, Chairman, NBPA, to W. Marvin Dulaney, February 21, 1980; Wilbert K. Battle, Vice Chairman, Region V, NBPA, to W. Marvin Dulaney, January 28, 1982; Wilbert K. Battle, "Governor's Task Force on Civil Rights," *Officers for Justice Journal,* September 1982, p. 11; Wilbert K. Battle, "Can This Happen Here?" *Officers for Justice Journal,* First Quarter 1983, p. 1; *San Francisco Examiner,* March 21, 1988.

15. Author's notes, National Black Police Association Fifth Annual Conference, "Women in Policing" Session, August 24, 1977, New Orleans, Louisiana. The author has copies of the old "Policemen's" stationery (Renault Robinson to U.S. Attorney General Griffin Bell, April 25, 1977, AAPL Papers), and the new "Police" stationery (Howard Saffold, National Chairman, to NBPA Members, August 20, 1978, AAPL Papers), which show the change made after the women's complaint.

16. Peggy Triplett, "Women in Policing," *Police Chief,* December 1976, pp. 46–47; *Baltimore Afro-American,* August 27, 1955, January 11, 1958; "Ambassador of Goodwill for the Police Department," *Ebony,* March 1964, pp. 40–46; Broome, *LAPD's Black History,* 202–206. As you will recall from chapter 4, in 1937 Whyte was the first African American appointed to the Baltimore police force.

17. Triplett, "Women in Policing," p. 47; Regina Jones, "Women in Law Enforcement," *The Crisis,* August–September 1991, p. 19; Balkin, "Why Policemen Don't Like Policewomen," 31; Daniel J. Bell, "'Policewomen: Myths and Reality," *Journal of Police Science and Administration* 10 (1982): 112–120.

18. Bill Berry, "Do Women Make Good Cops?" *Ebony,* February 1981, pp. 104–108; Jones, "Women in Policing," 38; Ellen Hochstedler et al., "Changing the Guard in American Cities: A Current Empirical Assessment of Integration in Twenty Municipal Police Departments," *Criminal Justice Review* 9 (1984): 11–13; *New York Times,* April 25, 1991; Karima A. Haynes, "How Good Are Women Cops?" *Ebony,* September 1993, p. 66.

19. Claudia Dreifus, "Why Two Women Cops Were Convicted of Cowardice," *Ms.,* April 1981, p. 57; Hochstedler et al., "Changing the Guard in American Cities," 12; "Black Firemen, Black Police Have Increased Significantly," *Jet,* February 11, 1991, p. 24; Carroll Peterson Horton and Jessie Carney Smith, eds., *Statistical Record of Black America* (Detroit: Gale Research, 1990), 417.

20. Roxanne Brown, "Is Jackie Davis the Best Homicide Detective in New Orleans History?" *Ebony,* May 1991, pp. 133–136; Peter Michelmore, "From Outcast to Supercop," *Reader's Digest,* November 1992, pp. 179–186.

21. Jones, "Women in Law Enforcement," 26; "Billie Holliday of the NYPD: The Deputy Police Commissioner Is Not Singing the Blues," *Ebony,* September, 1985, pp. 46–50; "D. C. Cop Is City's First Female Deputy Chief," *Jet,* January 28, 1985, p. 24.

22. See, for example, Elsie L. Scott, "Black Attitudes toward Crime and Crime Prevention," in Lee P. Brown and Lawrence E. Gary, eds., *Crime and Its Impact on the Black Community* (Washington, D.C.: Howard University Institute of Urban Affairs and Research, 1975), 13–30. With this analysis I am making a comparison to earlier police reformers such as Bruce Smith and August Vollmer.

23. "Dr. Elsie Scott Is New Deputy Commissioner of New York Police Department," *Jet,* April 8, 1991, p. 32.

24. *New York Times,* October 8, 1992; Haynes, "How Good are Women Cops?" 68.

SELECTED BIBLIOGRAPHY

Archival Sources and Manuscript Collections

Afro-American Patrolmen's League Papers. Chicago Historical Society, Chicago, Illinois.
Charleston Police Collection. Charleston City Archives, Charleston, South Carolina.
Cleveland Urban League Papers. Western Reserve Historical Society, Cleveland, Ohio.
Columbus, Ohio, Department of Public Safety Archives. City Hall Vault, Columbus, Ohio.
Columbus, Ohio Urban League Papers. Ohio Historical Society, Columbus, Ohio.
Commission on Interracial Cooperation Papers. Woodruff Library Special Collections, Atlanta University Center, Atlanta, Georgia.
Dallas Negro Chamber of Commerce Collection. Texas-Dallas Collection, Dallas Public Library, Dallas, Texas.
Dallas Police Archives. Texas-Dallas Collection, Dallas Public Library, Dallas, Texas.
Governors' Files. Missouri State Archives, Jefferson City, Missouri.
Chief Reuben Greenberg Collection. Avery Research Center for African American History and Culture, Charleston, South Carolina.
Guardians Civic League Files. Office of the Guardians Civic League, Philadelphia, Pennsylvania.
R. R. Herrick Papers, 1875–1882. Western Reserve Historical Society, Cleveland, Ohio.
St. Louis Ethical Police Society Files. St. Louis, Missouri.
St. Louis Police Department Archives. St. Louis Police Library, St. Louis, Missouri.
Personal Papers of Major Leroy Smith. Miami, Florida.
Sergeant James A. Taylor Papers. Author's Personal Files.
Texas Commission on Interracial Cooperation Papers. Houston Metropolitan Research Center, Houston, Texas.
Texas Negro Peace Officers Collection. Personal Papers of Mr. A. V. Young, Houston, Texas.
Alexander Pierre Tureaud Papers. Amistad Research Center, Tulane University, New Orleans, Louisiana.

Books

Alex, Nicholas. *Black in Blue: A Study of the Negro Policeman.* New York: Meredith Corporation, 1969.
———. *New York Cops Talk Back: A Study of a Beleaguered Minority.* New York: John Wiley and Sons, 1976.
Alexander, James I. *Blue Coats, Black Skin: The Black Experience in the New York City Police Department since 1891.* Hicksville, New York: Exposition Press, 1978.
Alfers, Kenneth G. *Law and Order in the Capital City: A History of the Washington Police, 1800–1886.* GW Washington Studies, No. 5. Washington, D.C.: George Washington University, 1976.
Anderson, Eric. *Race and Politics in North Carolina: The Black Second.* Baton Rouge: Louisiana State University Press, 1981.
Astor, Gerald. *The New York City Police: An Informal History.* New York: Charles Scribner's Sons, 1971.
Bailey, Richard. *Neither Carpetbaggers nor Scalawags: Black Officeholders during the Reconstruction of Alabama, 1867–1878.* Montgomery, Alabama: Richard Bailey Publishers, 1991.

Baker, Ray Stannard. *Following the Color Line: American Negro Citizenship in the Progressive Era.* New York: Doubleday, Page and Company, 1908.

Baldwin, James. *Nobody Knows My Name.* New York: Dell Publishing Company, 1961.

Banton, Michael. *The Policeman in the Community.* New York: Basic Books, 1964.

Barr, Alwyn. *Black Texans: A History of Negroes in Texas, 1528–1971.* Austin, Texas: Jenkins Publishing Company, 1973.

Bayley, David H., and Harold Mendelsohn. *Minorities and the Police: Confrontation in America.* New York: The Free Press, 1968.

Beasely, Delilah. *The Negro Trail Blazers of California.* Los Angeles: By the author, 1979.

Berlin, Ira. *Slaves without Masters: The Free Negro in the Antebellum South.* New York: Pantheon Books, 1974.

Blassingame, John W. *Black New Orleans, 1860–1880.* Chicago: University of Chicago Press, 1973.

Booker, Robert. *The History of Blacks in Knoxville, Tennessee: The First One Hundred Years, 1791–1891.* Knoxville, Tennessee: Beck Cultural Exchange Center, 1990.

Bopp, William J. *"O. W.": O. W. Wilson and the Search for a Police Profession.* Port Washington, New York: Kennikat Press, 1977.

Brown, Letitia Woods. *Free Negroes in the District of Columbia, 1790–1846.* New York: Oxford University Press, 1972.

Bryce, Herrington J, ed. *Black Crime: A Police View.* Washington, D.C.: Joint Center for Political Studies et al., 1977.

Carte, Elaine H., and Gene E. Carte. *Police Reform in the United States: The Era of August Vollmer, 1905–1932.* Berkeley: University of California Press, 1975.

Cashmore, Ellis, and Eugene McLaughlin, eds. *Out of Order?: Policing Black People.* New York: Routledge, 1991.

Changing Patterns of the New South. Atlanta: Southern Regional Council, 1955.

Cheek, William F. *Black Resistance before the Civil War.* Beverly Hills, California: Glencoe Press, 1970.

Church, Annette, and Roberta Church. *The Robert R. Churches of Memphis.* Ann Arbor, Michigan: Privately published, 1974.

Cohen, Bernard, and Jan M. Chaiken. *Police Background Characteristics and Performance.* Lexington, Massachusetts: Lexington Books, 1973.

Conot, Robert. *American Odyssey.* New York: William Morrow and Company, 1974.

Curry, Leonard P. *The Free Black in Urban America, 1800–1850: The Shadow of the Dream.* Chicago: University of Chicago Press, 1981.

Davidson, Chandler. *Biracial Politics: Conflict and Coalition in the Metropolitan South.* Baton Rouge: Louisiana State University Press, 1972.

Davis, Benjamin O. Jr. *Benjamin O. Davis, Jr., American: An Autobiography.* Washington, D.C.: Smithsonian Institution Press, 1991.

Davis, Russell. *Memorable Negroes in Cleveland's Past.* Cleveland, Ohio: Western Reserve Historical Society, 1969.

Davis, Russell H. *Black Americans in Cleveland.* Washington, D.C.: Associated Publishers, 1972.

Desdunes, Rodolphe Lucien. *Our People and Our History.* Baton Rouge: Louisiana State University Press, 1973.

Dittmer, John. *Black Georgia in the Progressive Era, 1900–1920.* Urbana: University of Illinois Press, 1977.

Du Bois, W. E. B. *Some Notes on Negro Crime Particularly in Georgia.* In W. E. B. DuBois, ed., *Atlanta University Publications,* Volume 2. New York: Octagon Books, 1968.

———. *The Philadelphia Negro: A Social Study.* New York: Schocken Books, 1967.

———. *The Souls of Black Folk.* In John Hope Franklin, ed., *Three Negro Classics.* New York: Avon Books, 1965.

Edwards, George. *The Police on the Urban Frontier.* New York: Institute of Human Relations Press, 1968.

Ershkowitz, Miriam, and Joseph Zikmund II, eds. *Black Politics in Philadelphia.* New York: Basic Books, 1973.

Fields, Barbara J. *Slavery and Freedom on the Middle Ground: Maryland during the Nineteenth Century.* New Haven: Yale University Press, 1985.

Finney, Guy W. *Angel City in Turmoil.* Los Angeles: Amer Press, 1945.

Fishel, Leslie, and Benjamin Quarles. *The Negro American: A Documentary History.* Glenview, Illinois: Scott, Foresman and Company, 1967.

Fitzgerald, Michael W. *The Union League Movement in the Deep South: Politics and Agricultural Change during Reconstruction.* Baton Rouge: Louisiana State University Press, 1989.

Fleming, Walter L. *Civil War and Reconstruction in Alabama.* New York: Peter Smith, 1949.

Fogelson, Robert M. *Big-City Police.* Cambridge, Massachusetts: Harvard University Press, 1977.

Foner, Eric. *Freedom's Lawmakers: A Directory of Black Officeholders during Reconstruction.* New York: Oxford University Press, 1993.

Fosdick, Raymond B. *American Police Systems.* Montclair, New Jersey: Patterson Smith, 1969.

Franklin, John Hope, and Alfred A. Moss. *From Slavery to Freedom: A History of Negro Americans.* 6th ed. New York: Alfred A. Knopf, 1988.

Friedman, Ina R. *Black Cop.* Philadelphia: Westminster Press, 1974.

Fry, Gladys Marie. *Night Riders in Black Folk History.* Knoxville: University of Tennessee Press, 1975.

Gary, Lawrence E., and Lee P. Brown, eds. *Crime and Its Impact on the Black Community.* Washington, D.C.: Howard University Institute for Urban Affairs and Research, 1975.

Gober, Dom. *Black Cop.* Los Angeles: Holloway House Publishing, 1974.

Gosnell, Harold F. *Negro Politicians: The Rise of Negro Politics in Chicago.* Chicago: University of Chicago Press, 1935.

Hacker, Andrew. *Two Nations: Black, White, Separate, Hostile, Unequal.* New York: Charles Scribner's Sons, 1992.

Hardin, Clara A. *The Negroes of Philadelphia: The Cultural Adjustment of a Minority Group.* Fayetteville, Pennsylvania: The Craft Press, 1943.

Harris, Middleton. *The Black Book.* New York: Random House, 1974.

Hawes, Joseph M, ed. *Law and Order in American History.* Port Washington, New York: Kennikat Press, 1979.

Haynes, Robert V. *A Night of Violence: The Houston Riot of 1917.* Baton Rouge: Louisiana State University Press, 1976.

Henry, H. M. *The Police Control of the Slave in South Carolina.* New York: Negro Universities Press, 1968.

Hersey, John. *The Algiers Motel Incident.* New York: Bantam Books, 1968.

Hippler, Arthur E. *Hunter's Point: A Black Ghetto.* New York: Basic Books, 1974.

Holt, Thomas. *Black over White: Negro Political Leadership in South Carolina during Reconstruction.* Urbana: University of Illinois Press, 1977.

Horton, Carroll Peterson, and Jesse Carney Smith, eds. *Statistical Record of Black America.* Detroit: Gale Research, 1990.

Houzeau, Jean Jacque. *My Life on the New Orleans Tribune: A Memoir of the Civil War Era.* Baton Rouge: Louisiana State University Press, 1984.

Jackson, Kenneth T., and Stanley Schultz, eds. *Cities in American History.* New York: Alfred A. Knopf, 1972.

Jacobs, Paul. *Prelude to Riot: A View of Urban America from the Bottom.* New York: Vintage Books, 1967.

Jenkins, Herbert T. *Forty Years on the Force, 1932–1972.* Decatur, Georgia: National Graphics, 1973.

———. *Keeping the Peace: A Police Chief Looks at His Job.* New York: Harper and Row Publishers, 1970.

Johnson, Samuel M. *Often Back: The Tales of Harlem.* New York: Vantage Press, 1971.
Jordan, Winthrop. *White over Black: English Attitudes toward the Negro, 1550–1812.* Chapel Hill: University of North Carolina Press, 1968.
Juris, Hervey A., and Peter Feuille. *Police Unionism: Power and Impact in Public Sector Bargaining.* Lexington, Massachusetts: Lexington Books, 1973.
Katzman, David M. *Before the Ghetto: Black Detroit in the Nineteenth Century.* Chicago: University of Illinois Press, 1973.
Kephart, William M. *Racial Factors and Urban Law Enforcement.* Philadelphia: University of Pennsylvania Press, 1957.
Kimbrough, Jesse. *Defender of the Angels: A Black Policeman in Old Los Angeles.* London: Macmillan Company, 1969.
King, Charles. *Fire in My Bones.* Grand Rapids, Michigan: Eerdmans Publishing Company, 1983.
Kirkham, George. *Signal Zero: The True Story of a Professor Who Became a Street Cop.* Philadelphia and New York: J. B. Lippincott Company, 1976.
Klein, Herbert T. *The Police: Damned If They Do—Damned If They Don't.* New York: Crown Publishers, 1968.
Klockars, Carl B., ed. *Thinking about Police: Contemporary Readings.* New York: McGraw-Hill, 1983.
Kolchin, Peter. *First Freedom: The Responses of Alabama's Blacks to Emancipation and Reconstruction.* Westport, Connecticut: Greenwood Press, 1972.
Kraditor, Aileen. *Means and Ends in American Abolitionism: Garrison and His Critics on Strategy and Tactics, 1834–1850.* New York: Vintage Books, 1969.
Landry, Stuart Omer. *The Battle of Liberty Place: The Overthrow of Carpet-Bag Rule in New Orleans, September 14, 1874.* New Orleans: Pelican Publishing Company, 1955.
Lane, Roger. *Policing the City: Boston, 1822–1885.* Cambridge, Massachusetts: Harvard University Press, 1967.
———. *William Dorsey's Philadelphia and Ours: On the Past and Future of the Black City in America.* New York: Oxford University Press, 1991.
Leinen, Stephen H. *Black Police, White Society.* New York: New York University Press, 1984.
Lewis, Earl. *In Their Own Interests: Race, Class and Power in Twentieth Century Norfolk, Virginia.* Berkeley: University of California Press, 1991.
Litwack, Leon F. *Been in the Storm So Long: The Aftermath of Slavery.* New York: Alfred A. Knopf, 1979.
———. *North of Slavery: The Negro in the Free States, 1790–1860.* Chicago: University of Chicago Press, 1961.
Locke, Alain, ed. *The New Negro.* Chicago: Johnson Reprint Corporation, 1968.
Logan, Rayford W. *The Betrayal of the Negro: From Rutherford B. Hayes to Woodrow Wilson.* New York: Collier Books, 1972.
McClory, Robert. *The Man Who Beat Clout City.* Chicago: Swallow Press, 1977.
McConnell, Roland C. *Negro Troops of Antebellum Louisiana: A History of the Battalion of Free Men of Color.* Baton Rouge: Louisiana State University Press, 1968.
McIntyre, Charshee C. L. *Criminalizing a Race: Free Blacks during Slavery.* Queens, New York: Kayode Publications, 1993.
Mann, Coramae Richey. *Unequal Justice: A Question of Color.* Bloomington: Indiana University Press, 1993.
Mays, Benjamin E. *Born to Rebel: An Autobiography.* New York: Charles Scribner's Sons, 1971.
Mills, A. B. Hartsfield. *The Old Stentorians.* Los Angeles: Privately published, 1973.
Mitchell, J. Paul, ed. *Race Riots in Black and White.* Englewood Cliffs, New Jersey: Prentice-Hall, 1970.
Monkkonen, Eric H. *Police in Urban America, 1860–1920.* Cambridge: Cambridge University Press, 1981.
Moss, Larry E. *Black Political Ascendancy in Urban Centers and Black Control of the Local Police Function: An Exploratory Analysis.* San Francisco: R and E Research Associates, 1977.

Mosse, George L., ed. *Police Forces in History.* Beverly Hills: Sage Publications, 1975.
Murphy, Patrick V., and Thomas Plate. *Commissioner.* New York: Simon and Schuster, 1977.
Myrdal, Gunnar. *An American Dilemma: The Negro Problem and Modern Democracy.* New York: Harper and Row Publishers, 1974.
Nash, Gary B. *Forging Freedom: The Formation of Philadelphia's Black Community, 1720–1840.* Cambridge, Massachusetts: Harvard University Press, 1988.
Newby, I. A. *Black Carolinians: A History of Blacks in South Carolina from 1895–1968.* Columbia: University of South Carolina Press, 1973.
Niederhoffer, Arthur. *Behind the Shield.* Garden City, New Jersey: Doubleday and Company, 1967.
O'Reilly, Kenneth. *Racial Matters: The FBI's Secret File on Black America, 1960–1972.* New York: The Free Press, 1989.
Ploski, Harry A., and James Williams, eds. *Reference Library of Black America.* Vol. II. Philadelphia: Gale Research, 1992.
Poinsett, Alex. *Black Power, Gary Style: The Making of Mayor Richard Gordon Hatcher.* Chicago: Johnson Publishing Company, 1970.
Price, Hugh D. *The Negro and Southern Politics: A Chapter of Florida History.* Westport, Connecticut: Greenwood Press, 1973.
Rabinowitz, Howard N. *Race Relations in the Urban South, 1865–1890.* Urbana: University of Illinois Press, 1980.
Rabinowitz, Howard N., ed. *Southern Black Leaders of the Reconstruction Era.* Urbana: University of Illinois Press, 1982.
Rable, George C. *But There Was No Peace: The Role of Violence in the Politics of Reconstruction.* Athens: University of Georgia Press, 1984.
Reaves, James N. *Black Cops.* Philadelphia: Quantum Leap Publishers, 1991.
Reiss, Albert J. *The Police and the Public.* New Haven: Yale University Press, 1971.
Reppetto, Thomas A. *The Blue Parade.* New York: Free Press, 1978.
Rich, Wilbur C. *Coleman Young and Detroit Politics: From Social Activist to Power Broker.* Detroit: Wayne State University Press, 1989.
Richardson, James F. *The New York Police: Colonial Times to 1901.* New York: Oxford University Press, 1970.
———. *Urban Police in the United States.* Port Washington, New York: Kennikat Press, 1974.
Robinson, Stanley. *The Badge They Are Trying to Bury.* Bluff, Utah: Simon Belt Publishers, 1975.
Rollin, Frank A. *Life and Public Services of Martin R. Delany.* New York: Kraus Reprint Company, 1969.
Ruchelman, Leonard. *Police Politics: A Comparative Study of Three Cities.* Cambridge, Massachusetts: Ballinger Publishing Company, 1974.
Rudwick, Elliott M. *Race Riot at East St. Louis, July 2, 1917!.* Cleveland, Ohio: Meridian Books, 1970.
———. *The Unequal Badge: Negro Policemen in the South.* Atlanta: Southern Regional Council, 1962.
Runnels, Gerald D. *Blacks Who Wear Blue.* Forney, Texas: Alexander Publications, 1989.
Sandburg, Carl. *The Chicago Race Riots, July 1919.* New York: Harcourt, Brace and World, 1969.
Saunders, John A. *100 Years after Emancipation: History of the Philadelphia Negro, 1787 to 1963.* Philadelphia: Philadelphia Tribune, 1963.
Scheiner, Seth M. *Negro Mecca: A History of the Negro in New York City, 1865–1920.* New York: New York University Press, 1965.
Schneider, John C. *Detroit and the Problem of Order, 1830–1880.* Lincoln: University of Nebraska Press, 1980.
Schwartz, Barry N., and Robert Disch. *White Racism: Its History, Pathology and Practice.* New York: Dell Publishing Company, 1970.

Shapiro, Herbert. *White Violence and Black Response: From Reconstruction to Montgomery.* Amherst: University of Massachusetts Press, 1988.

Singletary, Otis A. *Negro Militia and Reconstruction.* Austin: University of Texas Press, 1957.

Skolnick, Jerome H., and David H. Bayley. *The New Blue Line: Police Innovation in Six American Cities.* New York: The Free Press, 1986.

Skolnick, Jerome H., and Thomas C. Gray. *Police in America.* Boston: Little, Brown and Company, 1975.

Smith, Bruce. *Chicago Police Problems: An Approach to Their Solutions.* New York: Institute of Public Administration, 1934.

Snibbe, John R. and Homa M. *The Urban Policeman in Transition: A Psychological and Sociological Review.* Springfield, Illinois: Charles C. Thomas, 1973.

Somerville, Dr. J. Alexander. *Man of Color: An Autobiography.* Los Angeles: Louis J. Morrison, 1949.

Sterkx, H. E. *The Free Negro in Antebellum Louisiana.* Cranbury, New Jersey: Fairleigh Dickinson University Press, 1972.

Stokes, Carl B. *Promises of Power: A Political Autobiography.* New York: Simon and Schuster, 1973.

Sullivan, Charles T. *Snitching Niggers.* New York: Vantage Press, 1974.

Tonry, Michael, and Norval Morris, eds. *Modern Policing.* Chicago: University of Chicago Press, 1992.

Travis, Dempsey J. *"Harold" the People's Mayor: An Authorized Biography of Mayor Harold Washington.* Chicago: Urban Research Press, 1989.

Ullman, Victor. *Martin R. Delany: The Beginnings of Black Nationalism.* Boston: Beacon Press, 1971.

Vincent, Charles. *Black Legislators in Louisiana during Reconstruction.* Baton Rouge: Louisiana State University Press, 1976.

Vollmer, August. *The Police and Modern Society.* Montclair, New Jersey: Patterson Smith, 1971.

Wade, Richard C. *Slavery in the Cities: The South, 1820–1860.* New York: Oxford University Press, 1964.

Walker, Samuel. *A Critical History of Police Reform: The Emergence of Professionalism.* Lexington, Massachusetts: Lexington Books, 1977.

———. *Popular Justice: A History of American Criminal Justice.* New York: Oxford University Press, 1980.

———. *The Police in America: An Introduction.* New York: McGraw-Hill, 1983.

Weinberg, Kenneth G. *Black Victory: Carl Stokes and the Winning of Cleveland.* Chicago: Quadrangle Books, 1968.

Wharton, Vernon Lane. *The Negro in Mississippi, 1865–1890.* New York: Harper and Row, 1965.

Williams, Edward D. *The First Black Captain.* New York: Vantage Press, 1974.

Wintersmith, Robert F. *Police and the Black Community.* Lexington, Massachusetts: D. C. Heath and Company, 1974.

Wood, Peter H. *Black Majority: Negroes in Colonial South Carolina from 1670 through the Stono Rebellion.* New York: Alfred A. Knopf, 1974.

Wright, George C. *Life behind a Veil: Blacks in Louisville, Kentucky, 1865–1930.* Baton Rouge: Louisiana State University, 1985.

Young, Samuel O. *True Stories of Old Houston and Houstonians.* Galveston, Texas: Oscar Springer, 1913.

Zannes, Estelle. *Checkmate in Cleveland: The Rhetoric of Confrontation during the Stokes Years.* Cleveland: The Press of Case Western Reserve University, 1972.

Journal Articles

Akin, Edward N. "When a Minority Becomes the Majority: Blacks in Jacksonville Politics, 1887–1907." *Florida Historical Quarterly* 53 (October 1974): 123–145.

Bacote, Clarence A. "The Negro in Atlanta Politics." *Phylon* 16 (1955): 333–350.
———. "William Finch, Negro Councilman and Political Activities in Atlanta during Early Reconstruction." *Journal of Negro History* 40 (October 1955): 341–364.
Baenziger, Ann Patton. "The Texas State Police during Reconstruction: A Re-examination." *Southwestern Historical Quarterly* 72 (April 1969): 470–491.
Balkin, Joseph. "Why Policemen Don't Like Policewomen." *Journal of Police Science and Administration* 16 (March 1988): 29–38.
Bannon, James D., and G. Marie Wilt. "Black Policemen: A Study of Self Images." *Journal of Police Science and Administration* 1 (March 1973): 21–29.
Bayor, Ronald H. "Race and City Services: The Shaping of Atlanta's Police and Fire Departments." *Atlanta History* 36 (Fall 1992): 19–35.
Beard, Eugene. "The Black Police in Washington, D.C." *Journal of Police Science and Administration* 5 (1977): 48–51.
Bell, Daniel J. "Policewomen: Myths and Reality." *Journal of Police Science and Administration* 10 (1982): 112–120.
Biles, Roger. "Black Mayors: A Historical Assessment." *Journal of Negro History* 77 (Summer 1992): 109–125.
———. "Robert R. Church, Jr. of Memphis: Black Republican Leader in the Age of Democratic Ascendancy, 1928–1940." *Tennessee Historical Quarterly* 42 (1983): 362–382.
"The Black Cop." *Negro History Bulletin* 34 (October 1971): 138.
Blassingame, John W. "Before the Ghetto: The Making of the Black Community in Savannah, Georgia, 1865–1880." *Journal of Social History* 6 (Summer 1973): 463–488.
Broussard, Albert S. "Organizing the Black Community in the San Francisco Bay Area, 1915–1930." *Arizona and the West* 23 (Winter 1981): 335–354.
———. "The Politics of Despair: Black San Franciscans and the Political Process, 1920–1940." *Journal of Negro History* 69 (Winter 1984): 26–37.
———. "Strange Territory, Familiar Leadership: The Impact of World War II on San Francisco's Black Community." *California History* 65 (March 1986): 18–25.
Brown, Lee P. "Neighborhood-Oriented Policing." *American Journal of Police* 9 (1990): 197–207.
Bullock, Henry A. "Urban Homicide in Theory and Fact." *Journal of Criminal Law, Criminology and Police Science* 45 (1955): 565–575.
Cameron, Diane Maher. "Historical Perspectives on Urban Police." *Journal of Urban History* 5 (November 1978): 125–132.
Campbell, Valencia. "Double Marginality of Black Policemen." *Criminology* 17 (February 1980): 477–484.
Crook, James B. "Jacksonville in the Progressive Era: Responses to Urban Growth." *Florida Historical Quarterly* 65 (July 1986): 52–71.
Cross, Granville J. "The Negro, Prejudice and the Police." *Journal of Criminal Law* 55 (September 1964): 405–411.
Crouch, Barry A. "A Spirit of Lawlessness: White Violence; Texas Blacks, 1865–1868." *Journal of Social History* 18 (Winter 1984): 217–232.
Cuban, Larry. "A Strategy for Racial Peace: Negro Leadership in Cleveland, 1900–1919." *Phylon* 28 (Fall 1967): 299–311.
Dauphine, James G. "Knights of the White Camelia and the Election of 1868." *Louisiana History* 30 (Spring 1989): 173–190.
De Graaf, Lawrence B. "The City of Black Angels: Emergence of the Los Angeles Ghetto, 1890–1930." *Pacific Historical Review* 39 (August 1970): 323–352.
DeLatte, Carolyn E. "The St. Landry Riot: A Forgotten Incident of Reconstruction Violence." *Louisiana History* 17 (Winter 1976): 41–49.
"Detroit." *Race Relations Law Reporter* 7 (Summer 1962): 621–623.
"Distinguished Negroes in Ohio." *Negro History Bulletin* 5 (May 1942): 174–176 and 184–186.
Dormon, James H. "Louisiana's Creoles of Color: Ethnicity, Marginality and Identity." *Social Science Quarterly* 73 (September 1992): 615–626.

———. "The Persistent Specter: Slave Rebellions in Territorial Louisiana." *Louisiana History* 18 (1977): 389–404.

Douglass, Melvin I. "Dr. Louis Tompkins Wright: The First Black Police Surgeon of New York City." *Afro-Americans in New York Life and History* 17 (January 1993): 57–64.

Doyle, Judith K. "Maury Maverick and Racial Politics in San Antonio, Texas, 1938–1941." *Journal of Southern History* 53 (May 1987): 194–224.

Dulaney, W. Marvin. "The Progressive Voters League: A Political Voice for African Americans in Dallas." *Legacies* 3 (Spring 1991): 27–35.

———. "Sergeant Ira L. Cooper's Letter to the St. Louis Police Relief Association, May 25, 1924." *Journal of Negro History* 72 (Summer–Fall 1987): 84–86.

———. "The Texas Negro Peace Officers' Association: The Origins of Black Police Unionism." *Houston Review* 12 (1990): 59–78.

Dunbar-Nelson, Alice. "People of Color in Louisiana, Part I." *Journal of Negro History* 1 (October 1916): 359–376.

———. "People of Color in Louisiana, Part II." *Journal of Negro History* 2 (January 1917): 51–78.

Egerton, John. "Minority Police: How Many Are There?" *Race Relations Reporter* 5 (November 1974): 19–21.

Eisinger, Peter K. "Black Employment in Municipal Jobs: The Impact of Black Political Power." *American Political Science Review* 76 (June 1982): 380–392.

Everett, Donald E. "Emigres and Militiamen: Free Persons of Color in New Orleans, 1803–1815." *Journal of Negro History* 38 (October 1953): 377–402.

———. "Free Persons of Color in Colonial Louisiana." *Louisiana History* 7 (1966): 21–50.

Fischer, Roger A. "Racial Segregation in Antebellum New Orleans." *American Historical Review* 74 (February 1969): 926–937.

Fishel, Leslie H. "The Negro in Northern Politics, 1870–1900." *Mississippi Valley Historical Review* 42 (December 1955): 466–489.

Fisher, John A. "The Political Development of the Black Community in California, 1850–1950." *California Historical Quarterly* 50 (September 1971): 256–266.

Fitchett, E. Horace. "The Tradition of the Free Negro in Charleston, South Carolina." *Journal of Negro History* 25 (April 1940): 139–152.

———. "The Origin and Growth of the Free Negro Population in Charleston, South Carolina." *Journal of Negro History* 26 (October 1941): 421–437.

Fogelson, Robert M. "From Resentment to Confrontation: The Police and the Outbreak of the Nineteen-Sixties Riots." *Political Science Quarterly* 83 (June 1968): 217–247.

Fyffe, James J. "Who Shoots? A Look at Officer Race and Police Shooting." *Journal of Police Science and Administration* 9 (December 1981): 367–382.

George, Paul S. "Colored Town: Miami's Black Community, 1896–1930." *Florida Historical Quarterly* 56 (April 1978): 432–447.

———. "Policing Miami's Black Community, 1896–1930." *Florida Historical Quarterly* 57 (April 1979): 434–450.

Gerber, David. "A Politics of Limited Options: Northern Black Politics and the Problem of Change and Continuity in Race Relations Historiography." *Journal of Social History* 14 (Winter 1980): 235–255.

Gordon, Rita Werner. "The Change in the Political Alignment of Chicago's Negroes during the New Deal." *Journal of American History* 56 (December 1969): 584–603.

Griffin, James S. "Blacks in the St. Paul Police Department: An Eighty-Year Survey." *Minnesota History* 45 (Fall 1975): 255–265.

Hahn, Harlan. "A Profile of Urban Police." *Law and Contemporary Problems* 36 (Autumn 1971): 449–466.

Haller, Mark H. "Policy Gambling, Entertainment, and the Emergence of Black Politics: Chicago from 1900–1940." *Journal of Social History* 24 (Summer 1991): 719–739.

———. "Police Reform in Chicago, 1905–1935." *American Behavioral Scientist* 13 (May–August 1970): 649–665.

———. "Urban Crime and Criminal Justice: The Chicago Case." *Journal of American History* 57 (December 1970): 619–635.
Hanger, Kimberly S. "Avenues to Freedom Open to New Orleans' Black Population, 1769–1779." *Louisiana History* 31 (Summer 1990): 237–264.
———. "A Privilege and Honor to Serve: The Free Black Militia of Spanish New Orleans." *Military History of the Southwest* 21 (Spring 1991): 59–86.
Headley, Walter. "Utilization of Negro Police." *Traffic Review* 3 (Fall 1949): 10–13.
Hennessey, Melinda Meek. "Race and Violence in Reconstruction New Orleans: The 1868 Riot." *Louisiana History* 20 (Winter 1975): 77–91.
Himes, James S. "Forty Years of Negro Life in Columbus, Ohio." *Journal of Negro History* 27 (April 1942): 133–154.
Hindus, Michael. "Black Justice under Law: Criminal Prosecution of Blacks in Antebellum South Carolina." *Journal of American History* 63 (December 1976): 575–599.
Hochstedler, Ellen; Robert M. Regoli; and Eric Poole. "Changing the Guard in American Cities: A Current Empirical Assessment of Integration in Twenty Municipal Police Departments." *Criminal Justice Review* 9 (1984): 8–14.
Hudson, Mike. "Black and Blue." *Southern Exposure* 18 (Winter 1990): 16–19.
Ingersoll, Thomas N. "Free Blacks in a Slave Society: New Orleans, 1718–1812." *William and Mary Quarterly* 48 (April 1991): 173–200.
Jacobs, James B., and Jay Cohen. "The Impact of Integration on the Police." *Journal of Police Science and Administration* 6 (June 1978): 168–183.
Johnson, Mackie C. "Metropolitan Police Role in Our Society." *Negro History Bulletin* 26 (October 1962): 43–44.
Jones, Mack H. "Black Political Empowerment in Atlanta: Myth and Reality." *Annals of the American Academy of Political and Social Science* 439 (September 1978): 90–117.
Jones, Terry. "The Police in America: A Black Viewpoint." *The Black Scholar* 9 (October 1977): 22–39.
Jordan, Laylon W. "Police and Politics: Charleston in the Gilded Age, 1880–1900." *South Carolina Historical Magazine* 81 (1980): 35–50.
Kephart, William M. "The Integration of Negroes into the Urban Police Force." *Journal of Criminal Law, Criminology, and Police Science* 45 (September–October 1954): 325–333.
Lewis, William G. "Toward Representative Bureaucracy: Blacks in City Police Organizations, 1975–1985." *Public Administration Review* 49 (May/June 1989): 257–267.
Littlefield, Daniel Jr., and Lonnie E. Underhill. "Negro Marshals in the Indian Territory." *Journal of Negro History* 56 (April 1971): 77–87.
Miller, James E. "The Negro in Present Day Politics with Special Reference to Philadelphia." *Journal of Negro History* 33 (1948): 303–343.
Mitchell, Eugene M. "Atlanta during the 'Reconstruction Period.'" *Atlanta Historical Bulletin* 2 (November 1936): 20–35.
Murphy, Patrick V. "The Development of Urban Police." *Current History* 70 (June 1976): 245–248 and 272–273.
Nieman, Donald G. "Black Political Power and Criminal Justice: Washington County, Texas, 1868–1884." *Journal of Southern History* 55 (August 1989): 391–420.
O'Brien, John T. "Factory, Church, and Community: Blacks in Antebellum Richmond." *Journal of Southern History* 22 (Summer 1989): 509–536.
Palmer, Edward. "Black Police in America." *The Black Scholar* 5 (October 1973): 19–27.
Perkins, A. E. "Oscar James Dunn." *Phylon* 4 (Second Quarter 1943): 105–118.
Pierce, H. Bruce. "Blacks and Law Enforcement: Toward Police Brutality Reduction." *The Black Scholar* 17 (May/June 1986): 49–54.
Piliawsky, Monte. "The Impact of Black Mayors on the Black Community: The Case of New Orleans." *Review of Black Political Economy* 13 (Spring 1985): 5–24.
Potts, Nancy J. "Unfulfilled Expectations: The Erosion of Black Political Power in Chattanooga, 1865–1911." *Tennessee Historical Quarterly* 49 (Summer 1990): 112–128.

Price, Hugh D. "The Negro in Florida Politics, 1944–1954." *Journal of Politics* 17 (May 1955): 198–220.
Rabinowitz, Howard N. "The Conflict between Blacks and the Police in the Urban South, 1865–1900." *The Historian* 39 (November 1976): 62–76.
Rafky, David M. "Racial Discrimination in Urban Police Departments." *Crime and Delinquency* 21 (July 1975): 233–242.
Rankin, David C. "The Impact of the Civil War on the Free Colored Community of New Orleans." *Perspectives in American History* 2 (1977–78): 379–418.
Reed, Christopher Robert. "Black Chicago Political Realignment during the Depression and New Deal." *Illinois Historical Journal* 78 (Winter 1985): 242–256.
Reinders, Robert C. "The Free Negro in the New Orleans Economy, 1850–1860." *Louisiana History* 6 (1965): 273–285.
Robinson, George F. "The Negro in Politics in Chicago." *Journal of Negro History* 17 (April 1932): 180–229.
Rousey, Dennis C. "Black Policemen in New Orleans during Reconstruction." *The Historian* 49 (February 1987): 223–243.
———. "Hibernanian Leatherheads: Irish Cops in New Orleans, 1830–1880." *Journal of Urban History* 10 (November 1983): 61–84.
———. "Yellow Fever and Black Policemen in Memphis: A Post-Reconstruction Anomaly." *Journal of Southern History* 51 (August 1985): 357–374.
Rowe, G. S. "Black Offenders, Criminal Courts, and Philadelphia Society in the Late Eighteenth Century." *Journal of Social History* 22 (Summer 1989): 685–712.
Rudwick, Elliott M. "Negro Police Employment in the Urban South." *Journal of Negro Education* 30 (Spring 1961): 102–108.
———. "The Negro Policeman in the South." *Journal of Criminal Law, Criminology and Police Science* 51 (July–August 1960): 273–276.
———. "Police Work and the Negro." *Journal of Criminal Law, Criminology and Police Science* 50 (March–April 1960): 596–599.
———. "The Southern Negro Policeman and the White Offender." *Journal of Negro Education* 30 (Fall 1961): 426–431.
Saltzstein, Grace H. "Black Mayors and Police Policies." *Journal of Politics* 51 (1989): 525–544.
Sax, Richard M. "Why It Hurts to Be Black and Blue." *Issues in Criminology* 4 (Fall 1968): 1–11.
Schneider, John C. "Public Order and the Geography of the City: Crime, Violence and the Police in Detroit, 1845–1875." *Journal of Urban History* 4 (February 1978): 183–208.
Schiesl, Martin J. "Progressive Reform in Los Angeles under Mayor Alexander, 1909–1913." *California Historical Quarterly* 44 (Spring 1975): 37–56.
Schweninger, Loren. "Antebellum Free Persons of Color in Postbellum Louisiana." *Louisiana History* 30 (Fall 1989): 345–364.
Scott, James F. "Racial Group Membership, Role Orientation, and Police Conduct among Urban Policemen." *Phylon* 31 (Spring 1970): 5–15.
Sherman, Lawrence W. "Minority Quotas for Police Promotions (A Comment on *Detroit Police Officers Association v. Young*)." *Criminal Law Bulletin* 15 (January–February 1979): 79–84.
Sisk, Glenn. "The Negro in Atlanta Politics (1870–1962)." *Negro History Bulletin* 28 (October 1964): 17–18.
Somers, Dale A. "Black and White in New Orleans: A Study in Urban Race Relations, 1865–1900." *Journal of Southern History* 40 (February 1974): 19–42.
Steen, Ivan D. "Charleston in the 1850s: As Described by British Travelers." *South Carolina Historical Magazine* 71 (1970): 36–45.
Stokes, Larry D., and James F. Scott. "Affirmative Action Policy Standard and Employment of African Americans in Police Departments." *Western Journal of Black Studies* 17 (1993): 135–142.

Taylor, Robert A. "Crime and Race Relations in Jacksonville, 1884–1892." *Southern Studies* 2 (Spring 1991): 17–37.
Thomas, David Y. "The Free Negro in Florida before 1865." *South Atlantic Quarterly* 10 (1911): 335–345.
"252 Cities Hire Negro Police." *American City* 65 (March 1950): 19.
Vandal, Gilles. "The Policy of Violence in Caddo Parish, 1865–1884." *Louisiana History* 32 (Spring 1991): 159–182.
Wade, Richard C. "The Negro in Cincinnati, 1800–1830." *Journal of Negro History* 39 (January 1954): 43–57.
Walker, Donald B. "Black Police Values and the Black Community." *Police Studies* 5 (1983): 20–28.
Walker, Jack. "Negro Voting in Atlanta, 1953–1961." *Phylon* 24 (Winter 1963): 379–387.
Walker, Samuel. "The Urban Police in American History: A Review of the Literature." *Journal of Police Science and Administration* 4 (September 1976): 252–260.
Watts, Eugene J. "Black and Blue: Afro-American Police Officers in Twentieth Century St. Louis." *Journal of Urban History* 7 (February 1981): 131–168.
———. "Black Political Progress in Atlanta, 1868–1895." *Journal of Negro History* 59 (July 1974): 268–286.
———. "Continuity and Change in Police Careers: A Case Study of the St. Louis Police Department." *Journal of Police Science and Administration* 11 (June 1983): 217–224.
———. "The Police in Atlanta, 1890–1905." *Journal of Southern History* 39 (May 1973): 165–182.
———. "Police Priorities in Twentieth Century St. Louis." *Journal of Social History* 14 (Summer 1981): 649–673.
———. "Police Response to Crime and Disorder in Twentieth Century St. Louis." *Journal of American History* 70 (September 1983): 340–358.
Welek, Mary. "Jordan Chambers: Black Politician and Boss." *Journal of Negro History* 57 (October 1972): 352–369.
Williams, Hubert. "Trends in American Policing: Implications for Executives." *American Journal of Police* 9 (1990): 139–149.
Williams, Nudie E. "Bass Reeves: Lawman in the Ozarks." *Negro History Bulletin* 42 (April–June 1979): 37–39.
———. "United States vs. Bass Reeves: Black Lawman on Trial." *Chronicles of Oklahoma* 68 (Summer 1990): 154–167.
Wilson, C. E. "The System of Police Brutality." *Freedomways* 8 (Winter 1968): 47–56.
Wilson, James Q. "Generational and Ethnic Differences among Career Police Officers." *American Journal of Sociology* 69 (March 1964): 522–528.
Winston, James E. "The Free Negro in New Orleans, 1803–1860." *Louisiana Historical Quarterly* 21 (1938): 1075–1085.
Wish, Harvey. "American Slave Insurrections before 1861." *Journal of Negro History* 22 (July 1937): 299–320.
Wright, George C. "Black Political Insurgency in Louisville, Kentucky: The Lincoln Independent Party of 1921." *Journal of Negro History* 68 (Winter 1983): 8–23.
———. "The Billy Club and the Ballot: Police Intimidation of Blacks in Louisville, Kentucky, 1880–1930." *Southern Studies* 23 (1984): 20–41.

Commemorative Histories and Souvenir Programs

Advancement: Negroes' Contributions in Franklin County, 1803–1953. Columbus, Ohio: Columbus, Ohio Chapter of the Frontiers of America, 1954.
Brewer, J. Mason. *One Hundred Years of Negro Progress in Texas.* An Historical and Pictorial Souvenir of the Negro in Texas History. Dallas: Mathis Publishing Company, 1936.
Broome, Homer F. *LAPD's Black History, 1886–1976.* Los Angeles: By the author, 1976.

Calloway, Ernest. *The T. D. McNeal Story.* St. Louis, 1966.
An Evening with the Officers for Justice. San Francisco, 1971.
Firemen's Pension Fund and the Police Benevolent Association. *A Review of the Department of Public Safety of Columbus, Ohio.* Columbus, Ohio: Hann and Adair Printers, 1894.
Flinn, John J. *History of the Chicago Police: From the Settlement of the Community to the Present Time, under the Authority of the Mayor and Superintendent of the Force.* Chicago: The Police Book Fund, 1887.
Green, James J., and Alfred J. Young. *A History of the 28th Precinct.* New York: New York City Police Department, n.d.
History of the Columbus Police Department. Columbus, Ohio: Policeman's Benevolent Fund Association, 1900.
History of the Columbus Police Department, 1821–1945. Columbus, Ohio, 1945.
History of the Metropolitan Police Department of St. Louis, 1810–1910. St. Louis: Board of Police Commissioners, 1911.
History of the Police Department of Columbus, Ohio, 1908. Columbus, Ohio: Police Benevolent Association, 1908.
Knight, Thomas A. *History of the Cleveland Police Department, 1898.* Cleveland: n.p., 1898.
National Black Police Association. *5th Annual Conference Program.* New Orleans, Louisiana, August 1977.
National Black Police Association. *1978 Conference Program.* Chicago, Illinois, August 1978.
National Black Police Association. *Tenth Anniversary Conference Program.* Houston, Texas, August 1982.
National Black Police Association. *3rd Annual Conference Program.* Boston, Massachusetts, October 1975.
Officer Victor Butler Souvenir Program. Miami: Miami Community Police Benevolent Association, 1971.
Police Mutual Benevolent Association. *1900 History of the New Orleans Police Department.* New Orleans: Graham Press, 1900.
Policeman's Relief Association. *1898 History of the Atlanta Police Department.* Atlanta: Reissued by the Center for Research in Social Change, Emory University, 1976.
St. Louis Police Relief Association. *Souvenir History St. Louis Police Department, 1902.* St. Louis, 1902.
Sprogle, Howard O. *The Philadelphia Police: Past and Present.* Philadelphia, 1887.
Walker, May. *The History of the Black Police Officers in the Houston Police Department, 1878–1988.* Dallas: Taylor Publishing Company, 1988.
White, Louie. *A Pictorial History of Black Policemen Who Have Served in the Austin Police Department, 1871–1982.* Austin: Austin Police Department, 1982.

Unpublished Materials

Alfers, Kenneth G. "The Washington Police: A History, 1800–1886." Ph.D. dissertation, George Washington University, 1975.
Ball, James III. "A Study of Negro Policemen in Selected Florida Municipalities." Master's thesis, Florida State University, 1954.
Bolden, Richard Lee. "A Study of the Black Guardian Organization in the New York City Police Department from 1943–1978." Ph.D. dissertation, Columbia University, 1980.
Bond, J. Max. "The Negro in Los Angeles." Ph.D. dissertation, University of Southern California, 1936.
Campbell, Valencia Preuitt. "A Reexamination of the Marginal Status of Black Policemen in the Washington, D.C. Metropolitan Area." Master's thesis, Howard University, 1977.
Chapman, Arthur Edward. "The History of the Black Police Force and Court in the City of Miami." Ph.D. dissertation, University of Miami, 1986.

Chisolm, Dorothy Lee. "The Black Response to White Violence in Four Southern States during Reconstruction, 1865–1877." Master's thesis, Howard University, 1979.

Cohn, David H. "The Development and Efficacy of the Negro Police Precinct and Court of the City of Miami." Master's thesis, University of Miami, 1951.

Daniels, Douglas Henry. "Afro–San Franciscans: A Social History of Pioneer Urbanites, 1860–1930." Ph.D. dissertation, University of California, Berkeley, 1975.

Daykin John J. "A Study of Negro Police Officers in Eleven Major Mid-South Cities." Master's thesis, University of Mississippi, 1965.

Dulaney, William Marvin. "Black and Blue in America: The Black Policemen of Columbus, Ohio, 1895–1974." Master's thesis, Ohio State University, 1974.

———. "Black Shields: A Historical and Comparative Survey of Blacks in American Police Forces." Ph.D. dissertation, Ohio State University, 1984.

Gardner, Harry. "The History of Blacks in U.S. Law Enforcement." Ph.D. dissertation, Union Graduate School, 1978.

Grimes, John J. "The Black Man in Law Enforcement: An Analysis of the Distribution of Black Men in Law Enforcement Agencies and Related Recruitment Problems." Master's thesis, John Jay College of Criminal Justice, 1969.

Hargrove, Jimmy. "Stress—Above and Beyond of Black Police Officers." FBI Police Academy Paper, 1978. Photocopy.

"A History of the National Organization of Black Law Enforcement Executives (NOBLE), September 1976–June 1977." Mimeographed.

"A History of the San Francisco Police Department." San Francisco Division of Planning and Research, 1972. Photocopy.

Igler, A. George. "History of the Miami Police Department." Police Training Section, City of Miami, Florida. Undated.

Jones, Leroy Vernell. "The Black Police Officer: A Study in Re-Education." Master's thesis, San Francisco State College, 1970.

Lentz, Edward R. "Rationalization and Reform: The Columbus Urban League, 1942–1962." Master's thesis, Ohio State University, 1969.

Mays, Carl F. "An Exploratory Dichotomy of the Black Policeman: Role Perception and Profile." Master's thesis, Pepperdine University, 1974.

Merseberger, Marion. "A Political History of Houston, Texas, during the Reconstruction Period as Recorded by the Press, 1868–1873." Master's thesis, Rice University, 1950.

Miller, James Errol. "The Negro in Pennsylvania Politics with Special Reference to Philadelphia since 1932." Ph.D. dissertation, University of Pennsylvania, 1945.

Minor, Richard C. "The Negro in Columbus, Ohio." Ph.D. dissertation, Ohio State University, 1936.

Moorehead, Myron E. "An Evaluation of the Friendly Service Bureau in Its Crime Prevention among Negroes in the City of Columbus, Ohio, 1921 to 1930." Master's thesis, Ohio State University, 1935.

Morris, Harry W. "The Chicago Negro and the Major Political Parties, 1940–1948." Master's thesis, University of Chicago, 1950.

"Open Letter and Position Statement of the Community Police Benevolent Association." Miami, 1977. Photocopy.

Robinson, James Lee. "Tom Bradley: Los Angeles's First Black Mayor." Ph.D. dissertation, University of California at Los Angeles, 1976.

Robinson, Renault. "Black Police: A Positive Means of Social Change." Master's thesis, Roosevelt University, 1972.

Rosenzweig, Charles L. "The Issue of Employing Black Policemen in Atlanta." Master's thesis, Emory University, 1980.

Rousey, Dennis C. "The New Orleans Police, 1805–1889: A Social History." Ph.D. dissertation, Cornell University, 1978.

Rouzan, Joseph T. "Attitudinal Factors Affecting Recruitment of Blacks into the Los Angeles Police Department." Master's thesis, Pepperdine University, 1973.

Scott, James F. "A Study of Role Conflict among Policemen." Ph.D. dissertation, Indiana University, 1968.
Stoltz, Mary Welek. "Jordan Chambers: Black Politician." Master's thesis, St. Louis University, 1964.
Williams, Willie Samuel. "Attitudes of Black and White Policemen toward the Opposite Race." Ph.D. dissertation, Michigan State University, 1970.
Wubnig, Michael. "Black Police Attitudes in the New York City Police Department: An Exploratory Study." Ph.D. dissertation, City University of New York, 1975.

Magazine Articles

"Acquittal Not Enough for Black Chicago Law Enforcer." *Jet,* December 23, 1976, p. 16.
"Albany, New York Police Chief Says Community Effort Is Key to Solving Crime." *Jet,* February 25, 1991, p. 13.
Alves, Anthony. "Essence Men." *Essence,* August 1977, p. 9.
"Ambassador of Goodwill for the Police Department." *Ebony,* March 1964, pp. 40–46.
"America's Most Glamorous Negro Cop." *Jet,* September 2, 1954, pp. 54–55.
"The Anguish of Blacks in Blue." *Time,* November 23, 1970, pp. 13–14.
Armbrister, Trevor. "The Lonely Struggle of the Black Cop." *Reader's Digest,* March 1971, pp. 123–127.
"Art Matthews, Philadelphia's Black Homicide Captain." *Sepia,* November 1970, pp. 32–37.
"Atlanta: A Mayor Learning on the Job." *Time,* April 21, 1975, p. 33.
"Atlanta Businessmen Fight City Hall." *Business Week,* September 25, 1974, pp. 36–37.
"The Atlanta Negro Vote." *The Crisis,* June 1919, pp. 90–91.
"Atlanta Officials Upset over 'Crime Capital' Tag." *Jet,* November 29, 1979, p. 7.
"Atlanta Policeman Earns Law Degree." *Jet,* April 20, 1961, p. 6.
"Atlantan May Become 1st Black Female Sheriff in U.S." *Jet,* August 31, 1992, p. 2.
"Authorities Charge Bias in Los Angeles Police Dept." *Jet,* February 25, 1991, p. 31.
Babiar, Bruce. "Police Chief Changes Detroit's Crime Image." *National Leader,* August 25, 1983, p. 21.
Bailey, Peter. "You Can't Tell the Cops from the Robbers." *Ebony,* December 1974, pp. 114–122.
"Baltimore Gets Its First Black Police Commissioner." *Jet,* July 9, 1984, p. 37.
Berry, Bill. "Do Women Make Good Cops?" *Ebony,* February 1981, pp. 104–108.
"Billie Holliday of the NYPD: The Deputy Police Commissioner Is Not Singing the Blues." *Ebony,* September 1985, pp. 46–50.
"Billy Rowe Resigns New York Police Job." *Jet,* February 11, 1954, p. 4.
Black, Emetra. "Why General Davis Quits Cleveland Police Force." *Jet,* August 13, 1970, pp. 14–19.
"Black Appointed to LAPD Assistant Chief Post." *Jet,* January 11, 1988, p. 30.
"The Black Cop." *Newsweek,* August 4, 1969, p. 54.
"The Black Cop: A Man Caught in the Middle." *Newsweek,* August 16, 1971, pp. 19–20.
"The Black Cop: Man on a Tightrope." *Sepia,* February 1971, pp. 58–62.
"The Black Crime Buster." *Time,* March 22, 1976, p. 41.
"Black Firemen, Black Police Have Increased Significantly." *Jet,* February 11, 1991, p. 24.
"Black Man Leads Illinois Crime Fight." *Ebony,* May 1971, pp. 64–70.
"Black Named President of Chicago Police League." *Jet,* August 3, 1975, p. 5.
"Black Named to Top Philadelphia Police Post." *Jet,* June 20, 1988, p. 8.
"Black New York Police Officer Turns Down a Promotion: Says He's No 'Quota Cop.'" *Jet,* March 23, 1987, p. 25.
"Black on Black." *Newsweek,* January 14, 1974, p. 20.
"Black on Black Crime: The Causes, the Consequences and the Cures." *Ebony,* August 1979, Special Issue.

"Black Police: A Long Way to Go." *The Economist,* March 28, 1987, pp. 62–63.
"Black Police Execs Honor Pioneers in Atlanta." *Jet,* April 14, 1986, p. 10.
"Black Police Execs Meet To Build Trust between Cops and Community." *Jet,* August 13, 1984, pp. 36–37.
"Black Police Group Wants In on War against Crime." *Jet,* November 4, 1976, p. 31.
"Black Sheriff Victimized, Says NAACP Leader." *The Crisis,* April 1971, p. 100.
"Black, White, Blue." *The Economist,* March 26, 1988, pp. 25–28.
Blauner, Peter. "The Rap Sheet on Lee Brown." *New York,* January 22, 1990, pp. 32–38.
"Blue Funk." *Time,* July 26, 1982, p. 43.
Blum, David. "Houston's Illness." *New Republic,* July 8 and 15, 1978, pp. 12–14.
Booker, Simeon. "D.C. Mayor Sworn In, LBJ Names Mostly Negro Council." *Jet,* October 12, 1967, pp. 6–8.
Briggs, Cyril V. "The Capital and Chicago Race Riots." *The Crusader,* September 1919, pp. 3–6.
Briggs, Jimmie. "MLK's Protective 'Guardian':The Man in White." *Emerge,* September 1993, pp. 55–56.
Britton, John H. "General Davis Begins to Make Cleveland Safest City." *Jet,* March 19, 1970, pp. 14–20.
Brown, Lee P. "A Time for Change." *Police,* January–February 1970, p. 4.
———. "Evaluation of Police Community Relations Programs." *Police,* November–December 1969, pp. 27–31.
———. "Handling Complaints against the Police." *Police,* May–June 1968, pp. 74–81.
Brown, Roxanne. "Is Jackie Davis the Best Homicide Detective in New Orleans' History?" *Ebony,* May 1991, pp. 133–136.
"Brown Confirmed to Head Houston's Police Department." *Jet,* April 12, 1982, p. 29.
Bunche, Ralph J. "The Thompson-Negro Alliance." *Opportunity,* March 1929, pp. 78–80.
"By the People." *New South,* June 1947, pp. 3–30.
"Capt. Marion Bass, Commander." *Ebony,* March 1980, pp. 60–64.
"Causes of Race Riots." *Southern Workman,* July 1907, pp. 371–373.
Chandler, David. "An Experiment in Black and White: A Short History of Miscegenation in New Orleans." *New Orleans Magazine,* March 1974, pp. 70–79.
"Charleston, S.C. Gets Its First Black Police Chief." *Jet,* April 12, 1982, p. 8.
Chesnutt, Charles W. "The Negroes in Cleveland." *Clevelander,* November 1930, pp. 3–4, 24, 26–27.
"Chicago Agrees to Court-Ordered Minority Hiring." *Jet,* February 24, 1977, p. 12.
"Chicago Conference Explores Black-on-Black Crime in U.S." *Jet,* December 1, 1986, pp. 32–33.
"Chicago Mayor Complies with Order for Black Cops." *Jet,* March 4, 1976, p. 7.
"Chicago Mayor Names City's First Black Police Superintendent." *Jet,* September 12, 1983, p. 8.
"Chicago Mayor Names City's Second Black Police Chief." *Jet,* November 16, 1987, p. 5.
"Chicago Police Superintendent Who Lost Discrimination Suit to Blacks Resigns His Post." *Jet,* October 27, 1977, p. 14.
"Chicagoan Named Police Captain." *Jet,* April 29, 1954, p. 18.
"Chicago's Black Police League Is in Deep Debt." *Jet,* June 9, 1977, p. 12.
"Chicago's Top Black Policeman Indicted." *Jet,* August 12, 1976, p. 12.
Childs, Ronald E. "Top Brass: Black Police Chiefs Are Making Their Mark across the Country." *Ebony Man,* May 1989, pp. 60–61.
"A City Learning to Hate." *Newsweek,* July 8, 1974, p. 34.
"Civic Action for Negro Police." *Race Relations: A Monthly Summary of Events and Trends,* June–December 1948, pp. 269–270. (Hereafter this periodical will be cited as *Race Relations.*)
"Clarence Harmon Named First Black Police Chief for City of St. Louis, Mo." *Jet,* September 16, 1991, p. 6.
Clifford, Carrie W. "Cleveland and Its Colored People." *Colored American Magazine,* July 1905, pp. 365–380.

Clowers, Norman L. "Prejudice and Discrimination in Law Enforcement." *Police,* January–February 1964, pp. 42–45.
"Coleman Young Appoints Black Police Chief; Black Deputy Chief Kills Self." *Jet,* October 14, 1976, p. 8.
Coles, Robert. "A Policeman Complains." *New York Times Magazine,* June 13, 1971, pp. 78–80.
Collier, Aldore. "High Noon in L.A.: Willie Williams, the City's First Black Chief, Confronts Massive Challenges." *Ebony,* December 1992, pp. 71–74 and 132.
"Colored Woman Named to Police Force in Baltimore, Maryland." *Opportunity,* March 1938, p. 91.
"Columbia, Missouri Gets First Black Police Chief." *Jet,* January 10, 1983, p. 57.
"The Conference of SRC Fellows." *New South,* December 1946, pp. 16–22.
"Cook County Crime Fighter." *Ebony,* December 1963, pp. 101–107.
Coombs, Claire Chester. "Colored Police for Colored People." *Out West,* February 1917, p. 18.
"A Cop-Panther Confrontation in Cleveland Raises Questions." *Jet,* July 30, 1970, pp. 20–22.
"Corruption, Laxity Out: Deputy Inspectors Help Bring 'New' Respect for Chicago Police." *Jet,* January 19, 1961, pp. 12–14.
Cory, Bruce. "In Atlanta, a Furor over Cheating." *Police Magazine,* March 1979, pp. 15–19.
———. "Minority Police: Trampling through a Racial Minefield." *Police Magazine,* March 1979, pp. 4–14.
"Court Sets Racial Quota for New Orleans Police." *Jet,* January 10, 1983, p. 5.
Crate, Mrs. James S. "Texas Commission Works for Human Rights." *New South,* October 1948, pp. 14 and 20.
"Crime and Police Administration." *Race Relations,* December 1943, pp. 8–9.
"Crime and Police Administration." *Race Relations,* January 1944, p. 27.
"Crime and Punishment." *Race Relations,* February 1946, p. 205.
Curtis, Tom. "The Lawman." *Texas Monthly,* January 1986, p. 266.
———. "Support Your Local Police—Or Else." *Texas Monthly,* September 1977, pp. 82–89, 156–164.
Daniels, George M. "The Crisis Interview: Dr. Lee P. Brown." *The Crisis,* August–September 1991, pp. 20–22, 36.
Davis, Dowdal H. "They Forced the Chief Out." *The Crisis,* October 1941, pp. 314–316.
Davis, Edgar. "A Method of Approach to the Tasks of a Human Relations Officer." *Police,* January-February 1971, pp. 61–64.
"D.C. Cop Is City's 1st Female Deputy Chief." *Jet,* January 28, 1985, p. 24.
"D.C. Police Chief Fulwood Announces Resignation." *Jet,* September 28, 1992, p. 7.
"D.C. Police Chief Quits, Mulls GOP Run for Mayor." *Jet,* August 14, 1989, p. 4.
Delaney, Paul. "'Something That Had to Be Done': Black Cops in the South." *The Nation,* July 31, 1976, pp. 78–82.
"Detroit Police Chief Quits after Conviction." *Jet,* June 15, 1992, p. 28.
"Detroit Police Union Must Have Black Leaders." *Jet,* August 27, 1984, p. 34.
"Detroit to Hire 1,000 Black Policemen in 1975." *Jet,* April 17, 1975, p. 7.
"Dr. Elsie Scott Is New Deputy Commissioner of New York Police Department." *Jet,* April 8, 1991, p. 32.
"Dr. Lee P. Brown Appointed Atlanta's New Police Chief." *Jet,* April 20, 1978, p. 6.
"Dr. Louis Tompkins Wright." *Jet,* July 25, 1994, p. 24.
Dorfman, Ron. "Daley's Bluff." *Chicago,* April 1976, pp. 123–129.
Dreifus, Claudia. "Why Two Women Cops Were Convicted of Cowardice." *Ms.,* April 1981, pp. 57–64.
Dulaney, W. Marvin. "A Long Road to Blue." *Our Texas,* Summer 1992, pp. 14–15.
"Earl Buford, Jr. Named Pittsburgh's Police Chief." *Jet,* July 20, 1992, p. 32.
"Eaves Wins Council Support for City Post." *Jet,* September 5, 1974, p. 12.
"Edward Lewis Writes in the Baltimore *Sun* (on 'The Negro Police Question')." *Opportunity,* December 1937, p. 381.

"The Elections of 1940: Chicago's Machine Runs on Gratitude." *Life,* October 21, 1940, p. 94.
Elias, Marilyn K. "The Urban Cop: A Job for a Woman." *Ms.,* June 1984, p. 17.
"Employment of Negro Policemen in Southern Towns and Cities." *New South,* September 1948, pp. 7–8.
Eubanks, Bushnell. "The Negro South Goes to the Polls." *Negro Digest,* January 1949, pp. 20–22.
"First Black Police Chief Hired in Greenville, Miss." *Jet,* August 31, 1987, p. 10.
"First Black Police Chief Named in Natchez, Miss." *Jet,* October 17, 1988, p. 8.
Fleetwood, Martha. "The NAACP Response to Police Violence." *The Crisis,* April 1982, pp. 27–29.
Fleming, Harold C. "How Negro Police Worked Out in One Southern City." *New South,* October 1947, pp. 3–5, 7.
Gayle, Stephen. "Tom Bradley's California Quest." *Black Enterprise,* May 1982, pp. 46–49.
"General Race News." *Half-Century Magazine,* July 1917, p. 8.
"Georgia's First Black Police Officer Retires." *Jet,* October 8, 1984, p. 5.
Gettinger, Stephen. "The Lonely Labor of Sheriff Hulett." *Police Magazine,* July 1976, pp. 41–46.
"Good News." *The Crisis,* January 1955, p. 27.
Goodrich, James. "West Coast Crime Fighter." *Negro Digest,* February 1951, pp. 62–65.
Gray, Ernest A. Jr. "How to Prevent Race Riots." *Negro Digest,* February 1946, pp. 21–28.
Greenberg, Reuben M. "Let's Take Back Our Streets." *Ebony,* April 1991, pp. 106–108.
Grogan, Leander Jackie. "Houston's SuperCop." *Players,* January 1984, pp. 18–21 and 64.
Guess, Jerry M. "Alphonso Deal: Fighter to the End." *The Crisis,* June–July 1987, pp. 54–57.
Hall, Richard. "Dilemma of the Black Cop." *Life,* September 18, 1970, pp. 60–70.
"Harassed Black Police Leader Wins $125,000, Reinstatement in Chicago." *Jet,* October 13, 1977, p. 16.
Harris, John A. "How Charleston Got Negro Policemen." *New South,* September–October 1950, pp. 7–8.
"Harvey Davis Named New Top Cop in Springfield, Illinois." *Jet,* November 15, 1993, p. 27.
Haynes, Karima A. "How Good Are Women Cops?" *Ebony,* September 1993, pp. 64–68.
Herbert, Solomon J. "The Fruits of L.A.: New Chief, New Approach." *Black Enterprise,* October 1992, p. 22.
"Here and There." *Colored American Magazine,* February 1903, pp. 284–285.
Hewins, J. Thomas. "Crime among Negroes." *Southern Workman,* September 1909, pp. 475–477.
Hindman, Robert E. "A Survey Related to the Use of Female Law Enforcement Officers." *The Police Chief,* April 1975, pp. 58–59.
Hines, Burleigh. "No More 'Two-Gun Pete.'" *The Chicagoan,* February 1974, pp. 77–80.
"Houston, Texas Gets 1st Woman Officer." *Jet,* July 30, 1953, p. 8.
"How to Recruit Black Cops." *Newsweek,* October 2, 1972, p. 53.
"If You're Brown." *Black Enterprise,* January 1982, pp. 46–47.
"Indiana Cops Jim Crowed at Cafe, Arrest Owner." *Jet,* October 29, 1953, p. 10.
"Inspector of Police." *Ebony,* August 1956, pp. 60–64.
Jackson, Ida Joyce. "Do Negroes Constitute a Race of Criminals?" *Colored American Magazine,* April 1907, pp. 252–255.
Jacobs, Paul. "The Los Angeles Police: A Critique." *Atlantic Monthly,* December 1966, pp. 95–101.
Jenkins, Herbert T. "Police, Progress and Desegregation in Atlanta." *New South,* June 1962, pp. 10–13, 16.
Johnson, Allen. "How Good Are the Police." *New Orleans Magazine,* June 1990, pp. 32–38, 69–70.
Johnson, Charles S. "Negro Police in Southern Cities." *Public Management,* March 1944, p. 79.
Johnson, Wallis W. "Man in the Middle: The Black Policeman." *Civil Rights Digest,* Summer 1970, pp. 23–27.

Jones, Regina. "Women in Law Enforcement." *The Crisis,* August–September 1991, pp. 18–19, 26, 38.
Katz, Allan. "Policing an Atypical City: A Short History of the New Orleans Police Department." *New Orleans Magazine,* June 1990, pp. 39, 66–68.
"Key Detroit Policeman Takes Sudden Leave." *Jet,* November 4, 1976, p. 6.
Keyes, Edward. "Could You Be a Cop's Wife?" *Cosmopolitan,* February 1971, pp. 109–113.
"King Demands Negro Policemen." *Christian Century,* October 23, 1963, p. 1294.
Kmer, Henry. "They Also Served: Blacks in the Defense of New Orleans." *New Orleans Magazine,* January 1972, pp. 65–72.
"Lady Cops." *Ebony,* September 1954, pp. 26–32.
Landrum, Lynn. "The Case for Negro Police." *New South,* February 1947, pp. 5–6.
"Lawsuit Results in More Blacks on Frederick, MD., Police Department." *Jet,* January 25, 1993, p. 28.
Lawyer, David N. Jr. "The Dilemma of the Black Badge." *The Police Chief,* November 1968, pp. 22–25.
Leary, Mary Ellen. "The Trouble with Troubleshooters." *Atlantic Monthly,* March 1969, pp. 94–99.
Leavy, Walter. "Can Black Mayors Stop Crime?" *Ebony,* December 1983, pp. 116–122.
———. "Hail to the Chiefs." *Ebony,* November 1982, pp. 115–120.
Lee, Elliott D. "Blacks in Blue." *Black Enterprise,* February 1982, pp. 87–90.
"Lee Brown Is Appointed Police Chief of Houston." *Jet,* March 29, 1982, p. 7.
"Lee Brown Sworn In as Nation's New Drug Czar." *Jet,* July 19, 1993, p. 10.
"Lee Brown's New York Blues." *Newsweek,* October 8, 1990, p. 33.
Levinson, Marc R. "Affirmative Action: Is It Just a Numbers Game?" *Police Magazine,* March 1982, pp. 8–27.
Lewin, Julie. "Future Cop." *Parade Magazine,* March 21, 1982, pp. 4–5.
"Lexington, Kentucky Gets 1st Negro Police Sergeant." *Jet,* January 7, 1960, p. 7.
"Lieutenant General B. O. Davis, Jr. Is Praised, Cited at Ceremony." *Jet,* February 19, 1970, p. 5.
Link, Terry S. "Black and White in Blue." *San Francisco Magazine,* June 1970, pp. 16–19, 34.
Lowe, Frederick H. "Policing the Police: Spotlight Focus on Black Top Cops." *NorthStar News and Analysis,* May 1992, p. 5.
McCray, John H. "South Carolina Police Chief Praises Work of Negro Officers." *New South,* November 1946, pp. 3–5.
McGrath, Noreen. "Panel on Police Education Accused of Elitism." *Chronicle of Higher Education,* February 13, 1979, p. 17.
McNair, Marcia. "A Career in Law Enforcement." *Essence,* February 1984, p. 30.
McWilliams, Carey. "Second Thoughts." *The Nation,* November 17, 1979, p. 487.
Marshall, Thurgood. "The Gestapo in Detroit." *The Crisis,* August 1943, pp. 232–233, 246–247.
"Mayor: A Tale of Two Cities." *Newsweek,* October 15, 1973, p. 35.
"Mayor Names Negro Minister Police Chief in Illinois." *Jet,* May 28, 1959, p. 9.
"Miami Klan Tries to Scare Negro Vote." *Life,* May 15, 1939, p. 27.
"Miami Police Chief Quits over Row with City Execs." *Jet,* August 8, 1988, p. 33.
"Miami's Finest." *Jet,* January 28, 1985, p. 24.
Michelmore, Peter. "From Outcast to Supercop." *Reader's Digest,* November 1992, pp. 179–186.
Miller, Kelly. "Crime among Negroes." *Southern Workman,* September 1909, pp. 472–475.
"Mobile Appoints First Negro Policemen." *Jet,* March 11, 1954, p. 9.
"Montgomery Fires Last of 5 Negro Cops." *Jet,* May 14, 1959, p. 8.
Moore, Trudy S. "Lady Cop Patrols Streets on Weekdays and Preaches on Sundays." *Jet,* July 20, 1992, pp. 34–37.
Morton, Carol. "Black Cops: Black and Blue Ain't White." *Ramparts,* May 1972, pp. 20–25.
"NAACP Pushes Probe of Bias in Philly Police Department." *The Crisis,* September 1971, pp. 231–232.

"Name Negro Police Lieutenant in West Palm Beach." *Jet,* February 18, 1960, p. 9.
"Name 23 New Negro Chicago Police Sergeants." *Jet,* January 19, 1961, p. 4.
Narine, Dalton. "Top Cops: More and More Black Police Chiefs Are Calling the Shots." *Ebony,* May 1988, pp. 130–136.
"National Study Reports White Cops' Beatings of Blacks Reveal 'Dirty Secrets of Racism.'" *Jet,* May 3, 1993, p. 18.
"A Negro Country Constabulary." *Southern Workman,* May 1906, p. 259.
"Negro Crime Rate." *Opportunity,* June 1927, p. 160.
"Negro Employment in Miami." *New South,* May 1962, pp. 6–10.
"Negro Gets No. 3 Spot in Detroit Police Dept." *Jet,* November 2, 1967, p. 5.
"Negro Police Auxiliary Make Good in Macon." *Southern Frontier,* March 1943, p. 2.
"Negro Police Captains." *The Messenger,* July 1919, pp. 9–10.
"Negro Police in Southern Cities." *New South,* October 1947, p. 1.
"Negro Police in the South, 1952." *New South,* September 1952, pp. 6–7.
"Negro Police in the South, 1953." *New South,* October–November 1953, pp. 6–7.
"'Negro Police Officers in Los Angeles,' by One of Los Angeles' Negro Police Officers, Who, For Obvious Reasons Remains Anonymous." *The Crisis,* August 1934, pp. 242 and 248.
"Negro Police Successful in South." *Jet,* November 15, 1951, p. 8.
"Negro Policemen." *The Crisis,* April 1962, pp. 219–222.
"Negro Policemen Are Needed in Southern Cities." *Southern Frontier,* March 1943, p. 2.
"Negro Policemen in Southern Cities." *New South,* September 1949, p. 1.
"Negro Sergeant Is Shot and Killed by Policeman." *Southern Frontier,* April 1942, p. 1.
"The New Black Police Chiefs." *Time,* February 18, 1985, pp. 84–85.
"New Men for Atlanta and Detroit." *Time,* January 14, 1974, pp. 13–14.
"New Orleans Gets First Black Police Superintendent." *Jet,* January 21, 1985, p. 30.
"New Orleans Removes Controversial Monument." *Jet,* August 16, 1993, p. 18.
"New York Black Cops File Suit over Sergeant's Exam." *Jet,* September 5, 1994, p. 27.
"New York Deputy Police Commissioner Takes Oath." *Jet,* February 18, 1954, p. 5
"New York Gets First Negro Police Captain." *Jet,* February 12, 1953, p. 9.
"New York Names First Negro Police Inspector." *Jet,* October 29, 1953, p. 3.
"Newark: The Promise of Survival." *The Nation,* December 14, 1974, pp. 619–622.
"NOBLE Honors Lee Brown." *Jet,* August 3, 1987, p. 40.
"N.Y. Has Worst Cop to Resident Ratio for Blacks." *Jet,* November 2, 1992, p. 32.
"Oakland Policeman Becomes Berkeley's New Black Chief." *Jet,* October 6, 1977, p. 4.
"Oklahoma City Suspends Ten Negro Cops." *Jet,* June 25, 1953, p. 7.
"Order Miami's Police Academy to Integrate." *Jet,* February 4, 1960, p. 8.
Osborne, Karen. "Leading the Top Cops." *Black Enterprise,* December 1990, p. 18.
"Over the Edge." *Essence,* March 1990, pp. 60–62, 120–125.
Ovington, Mary White. "Atlanta: A City Nursing Dead Ideals." *Colored American Magazine,* July 1905, pp. 389–390.
"Palmyra's Police Chief." *Ebony,* June 1959, pp. 61–64.
"Past Year Shows Negro Police Gains." *New South,* August–September 1951, p. 12.
Paynter, Bob. "Ollie Stubblefield: Violating the Unspoken Code." *Columbus Monthly,* May 1980, pp. 58–59.
"People." *Jet,* September 13, 1993, p. 20.
"Personal." *The Crisis,* November 1917, p. 40.
Petrie, Phil W. "Do Black Mayors Make a Difference?" *Black Enterprise,* July 1979, pp. 25–32.
"Philadelphia Gets First Negro Police Captain." *Jet,* January 31, 1952, p. 9.
"Philadelphia Gets First Negro Police Inspector." *Jet,* July 22, 1954, p. 4.
"Philly Agrees to Hire More Black Police Officers." *Jet,* September 26, 1983, p. 31.
"Philly Mayor Orders Quota to Hire More Black Cops." *Jet,* April 12, 1982, p. 8.
"Pittsburgh Gets First Black Chief of Police." *Jet,* May 12, 1986, p. 6.
"Plea for a Negro Constabulary." *Southern Workman,* December 1906, pp. 646–648.
Poinsett, Alex. "Atlanta's Winning Fight against Black-on-Black Crime." *Ebony,* June 1976, pp. 66–72.

———. "The Dilemma of the Black Policeman." *Ebony,* May 1971, pp. 123–130.
———. "Houston: Golden City of Opportunity." *Ebony,* July 1978, pp. 132–142.
"Police Administration." *Race Relations,* April 1944, p. 7.
"Police Administration." *Race Relations,* May 1944, p. 7.
"Police Administration." *Race Relations,* April 1945, p. 258.
"Police Administration." *Race Relations,* November 1945, p. 106.
"Police Administration." *Race Relations,* December 1945, p. 140.
"Police Administration." *Race Relations,* May 1946, p. 303.
"Police Administration and Courts." *Race Relations,* March 1947, p. 235.
"Police Administration and Courts." *Race Relations,* June 1947, pp. 333–334.
"Police Administration, Prisons and Crime." *Race Relations,* August–September 1944, p. 11.
"Police Chief Changes Detroit's Crime Image." *The National Leader,* August 25, 1983, p. 21.
"Police Practices in Alabama." *New South,* June 1964, pp. 3–18.
"Police Story: Two Hard Towns." *Time,* September 19, 1977, pp. 29–30.
"Police Veteran Appointed Head of Cleveland's Fourth District Detective Bureau." *Jet,* January 27, 1986, p. 25.
"Policing the Police: Former State Solon Heads St. Louis Police Board." *Ebony,* May 1973, pp. 42–50.
"Portsmouth's Police Chief." *Ebony,* April 1963, pp. 144–147.
Poston, Ted. "Law and Order in Norfolk." *New Republic,* October 7, 1940, pp. 472–473.
Price, Margaret. "South Finding Negro Police Valuable, SRC Poll Shows." *New South,* October 1947, p. 2.
———. "Survey Shows Increase of Negro Policemen in South." *New South,* September 1948, p. 8.
"Quincy, Illinois Police Department, 1874." *Police Magazine,* May 1983, inside cover.
"Racism in the Raw in Suburban Chicago." *Time,* October 17, 1988, pp. 25–26.
Raffauf, Mike. "Jackson v. Inman." *Creative Loafing,* August 24, 1974, clipping.
"Retired D.C. Deputy Chief Selected to Return as Chief." *Jet,* December 7, 1992, p. 8.
Riley, Earl E. "Historical Notes." *Law and Order,* April 1976, p. 61.
Robinson, Louie. "SWAT in Control." *Ebony,* July 1976, pp. 88–96.
Rubinstein, Richard E., and Stephan M. Kaplan. "Black and Blue in Chicago." *New Republic,* April 6, 1968, pp. 19–21.
Ryan, Michael. "How to Catch a Crook." *Parade Magazine,* September 2, 1990, pp. 12–14.
"St. Paul Names First Black Police Chief." *Jet,* August 3, 1992, p. 56.
"Savannah, Georgia." *New South,* May 1947, p. 7.
"Sentiment of the Northern Press on the Recent Criminal Outbreak in Atlanta." *Colored American Magazine,* November 1906, pp. 335–342.
"Sgt. Tells House Panel Blacks on Capitol Police Force Are Job Bias Victims." *Jet,* April 16, 1990, p. 37.
"Social Progress." *The Crisis,* August 1919, p. 206.
"Some Race Related Deaths in the United States, 1955–1965." *New South,* November 1965, pp. 12–15.
"South Africa: Blacks on Parade." *The Economist,* November 29, 1986, pp. 33–34.
"Southern Police Chiefs Comment (on Negro Police)." *New South,* October–November 1953, pp. 7–8.
"SRC's Work and Plans." *New South,* December 1946, pp. 4–7.
"Stanley Robinson: Murderer or FBI Scapegoat?" *Encore American and Worldwide News,* December 8, 1975, pp. 14–17.
Star, Jack. "Chicago Shows a Way to Police Reform." *Look,* October 9, 1965, pp. 43–49.
Stokes, Carl B. "My First Year in Office." *Ebony,* January 1969, pp. 116–122.
"Stop the Cop Killers." *The Crisis,* April 1972, p. 114.
Stuart, Cynthia Gould. "The Changing Status of Women in Police Professions." *The Police Chief,* April 1975, pp. 61–62.
"Survey Shows Negro Police 'Do Good Job' in South." *Jet,* May 14, 1953, p. 10.

"Suspend Negro Cop for Jailing White Woman." *Jet*, April 2, 1953, p. 10.
Sykes, Leonard. "Black and Blue from Caring in Chicago." *The National Leader*, April 7, 1983, pp. 18–19.
"Syracuse, N.Y. Agrees to Hire More Black Officers." *Jet*, May 8, 1980, p. 47.
"Tapscott Takes Charge of Richmond, Virginia Police." *Jet*, July 31, 1989, p. 32.
"Tennessee Negro Police Guilty of Rights Violation." *Jet*, November 20, 1952, p. 12.
Tharp, Mike, and Dorian Friedman. "New Cops on the Block." *U.S. News and World Report*, August 2, 1993, pp. 22–25.
"30-Year Veteran Neal Named to Top Police Job in Philadelphia." *Jet*, September 7, 1992, p. 4.
Thompson, Cordell S. "How Race Crisis Splits Black, White Policemen: Blacks Dedicated to Protecting against Brutality from All." *Jet*, October 16, 1969, pp 14–19.
"Three Mayors Speak of Their Cities." *Ebony*, February 1974, pp. 35–42.
"The Tide of Repression." *The Crisis*, May 1970, p. 181.
"Tough Cop Eldrin Bell Named New Police Chief in Atlanta." *Jet*, September 10, 1990, p. 29.
Triplett, Peggy. "Women in Policing." *The Police Chief*, December 1976, pp. 46–49.
"Troubles of a Black Policeman." *Literary Digest*, January 27, 1912, pp. 177–179.
Tyson, Remer. "Detroit Hangs in There: Mayor Young a Year Later." *The Nation*, March 1, 1975, pp. 237–240.
"Veteran New York Cop Is Named City's First Black Commissioner of Police." *Jet*, November 28, 1983, p. 12.
"Violence Solves Problems? TV Says Yes; Public Safety Chief Says No." *Jet*, December 30, 1976, p. 44.
Viorst, Milton. "Black Mayor, White Power Structure." *New Republic*, June 27, 1975, pp. 9–11.
"Virginia to Elect First Black Woman Sheriff." *Jet*, August 23, 1993, p. 8.
Washington, Linn Jr. "The City of Brotherly Love: The Sleeping Giant v. the White Crusader." *Encore American and Worldwide News*, November 20, 1978, pp. 12–17.
Washington, Sylvester. "Two-Gun Pete." "Why I Killed 11 Men." *Ebony*, January 1950, pp. 51–57.
"What Is the Objection to Negro Policemen?" *Southern Frontier*, January 1944, p. 3.
"White Cop Refuses to Ride with Negroes, Suspended." *Jet*, March 12, 1953, p. 8.
"White Policemen in Harlem." *The Crisis*, January 1945, pp. 16–17.
"Whitlock Named 1st Black Harrisburg Police Chief." *Jet*, December 19, 1988, p. 16.
Williams, Margo. "What Happens When the Police Department Goes from White to Black: The Changing Face of the Detroit Police Department." *The Crisis*, December 1991, pp. 15–17 and 27.
"Wilson Appointed Police Chief of Jackson, Miss." *Jet*, February 17, 1992, p. 8.
"Windy City Cops Greet Mayor." *Jet*, July 5, 1979, p. 15.
"Woman behind the Badge." *Ebony*, April 1982, pp. 124–128.
"Women Cops on the Beat." *Time*, March 10, 1980, p. 58.
Wright, R. R. Jr. "Negro Criminal Statistics." *Southern Workman*, May 1911, pp. 291–307.
———. "Negroes in the North: The Northern Negro and Crime." *Southern Workman*, March 1910, pp. 137–142.
"Wright Named New Police Chief of Gary, Indiana." *Jet*, March 28, 1994, p. 8.

Reports

"Affirmative Action Report." City of Houston, Civil Service Department, January 1974.
Annual Report of the Board of Metropolitan Police for the Year Ending September 30, 1869. New Orleans, 1870.
Atlanta Police Department, *Annual Reports*. Atlanta, Georgia, 1945–1965 and 1974.
Beard, Eugene; Lee P. Brown; and Lawrence E. Gary. *Final Report: Attitudes and Perceptions of Black Police Officers of the District of Columbia Metropolitan Police Department*. Washington, D.C.: Howard University Institute for Urban Affairs and Research, 1976.

Buchanan, James S. "Minority Recruiting: A Move toward a Better Community." St. Louis Police Department Recruiting Division, 1977.

Chicago Police Department. *Annual Reports.* Chicago, Illinois, 1877, 1895, 1898, 1920, and 1923.

Chicago's Black Population: Selected Statistics. City of Chicago Department of Development and Planning, May 1975.

Citizens' Police Committee. *Chicago Police Problems.* Chicago: University of Chicago Press, 1931.

Cleveland Police Department. *Annual Reports.* Cleveland, Ohio, 1895, 1900–1903, 1906–1915, and 1927–1930.

Division of Police, Columbus, Ohio. *Annual Reports.* Columbus, Ohio, 1930–1972.

"Equal Opportunities for Minorities within the Bureau of Police Services in Atlanta: An Analysis." Atlanta City Council Public Safety Committee Report, July 1974.

Hindelang, Michael J.; Michael R. Gottfredson; and Timothy J. Flanagan. *Sourcebook of Criminal Justice Statistics, 1980.* Washington, D.C.: Government Printing Office, 1981.

Houston Police Department. *Annual Reports.* Houston, Texas, 1925–1931.

Human Relations in Chicago. Report for the Year 1946 of the Mayor's Commission on Human Relations. Chicago, 1946.

International Association of Chiefs of Police. *A Survey of the Police Department of Miami, Florida.* Miami: IACP Field Services Division, 1962.

Locke, Hubert G. *The Impact of Affirmative Action and Civil Service on American Police Personnel Systems.* U.S. Department of Justice, Law Enforcement Assistance Administration. Washington, D.C.: Government Printing Office, 1979.

Los Angeles Police Department. *Annual Reports.* Los Angeles, California, 1913–1922 and 1974–1975.

Margolis, Richard J. *Who Will Wear the Badge?: A Study of Minority Recruitment Efforts in Protective Services.* A Report of the United States Commission on Civil Rights. Washington, D.C.: U.S. Government Printing Office, 1971.

Masotti, Louis H., and Jerome Corsi. *Shoot-Out in Cleveland: Black Militants and the Police, July 23, 1968.* Report to the National Commission on the Causes and Prevention of Violence. New York: Frederick A. Praeger, 1969.

Miami Police Department. *Annual Reports.* Miami, Florida, 1953, 1964–1971.

The People of Chicago. Five Year Report, 1947–1951, of the Chicago Commission on Human Relations. Chicago, 1952.

Police-Community Relations in Montgomery, Alabama. A Report of the U.S. Commission on Civil Rights. Washington, D.C.: U.S. Government Printing Office, 1986.

"Police Recruitment and Personnel Polices: New Goals for the Seventies." A Report Prepared for the Boston Police Department. Boston: Learning and Planning Associates, October 1971.

Race Relations in Chicago. Report of the Mayor's Commission on Human Relations for 1945. Chicago, 1945.

Report of the National Advisory Commission on Civil Disorders. Otto J. Kerner, Chairman. Washington, D.C.: Government Printing Office, 1968.

"Report of the Personnel Board of Minority and Majority Sworn Personnel." January 10, 1974, submitted by Clara Nelson. Atlanta, Georgia.

"Report to the Civil Service Board of Minority and Majority Sworn Personnel." April 4, 1974, submitted by Clara C. Nelson. Atlanta, Georgia.

Report to the Honorable Lewis Cutrer, Mayor, City of Houston, The Houston Murder Problem: Its Nature, Apparent Causes and Probable Cure. Henry Allen Bullock, Chairman, Mayor's Negro Law Enforcement Committee. Houston, Texas, 1961.

St. Louis Metropolitan Police Department. *Annual Reports.* St. Louis, 1901–1932 and 1974.

San Francisco Police Department. *Annual Reports.* San Francisco, California, 1936–1970.

Search and Destroy: A Report of the Commission of Inquiry into the Black Panthers and the Police. Roy Wilkins and Ramsey Clark, Chairmen. New York: Metropolitan Applied Research Center, 1973.

Towards a New Potential: A Progress Report. Washington, D.C.: Police Foundation, 1974.

Census Reports

Hall, Charles, ed. *Negroes in the United States, 1920–1932.* New York: Arno Press and the New York Times, 1969.

U.S. Department of Commerce, Bureau of the Census. *Negro Population of the United States, 1790–1915.* Washington, D.C.: U.S. Government Printing Office, 1918.

U.S. Department of Commerce, Bureau of the Census. *Tenth Census of the United States.* (1880) microform.

U.S. Department of Commerce, Bureau of the Census. *Twelfth Census of the United States.* (1900) microform.

U.S. Department of Commerce, Bureau of the Census. *Sixteenth Census of the United States.* Volume II Characteristics of the Population. Washington, D.C.: U.S. Government Printing Office, 1943.

Yearbooks

Atlanta Centennial Yearbook, 1837–1937. Atlanta: Gregg Murphy, 1937.

"Benjamin Ward." *Current Biography Yearbook,* 597–601. New York: H. W. Wilson Company, 1988.

Boris, Joseph, ed. *Who's Who in Colored America.* New York: Who's Who in Colored America Corporation, 1928–1929.

Cantwell, Edward. "A History of the Charleston Police Force." *Charleston Yearbook,* 3–19. Charleston, South Carolina, 1908.

Guzman, Jesse Parkhurst, ed. *Negro Year Book, 1941–1946.* Tuskegee, Alabama: Tuskegee Institute Department of Records and Research, 1947.

———. *Negro Year Book, 1952.* New York: Wm. H. Wise and Company, 1952.

"Kenneth A. Gibson." *Current Biography Yearbook,* 149–152. New York: H. W. Wilson Company, 1971.

Negro Year Book, 1918–1919. Tuskegee, Alabama: Tuskegee Institute, 1919.

Work, Monroe N., ed. *Negro Year Book, 1921–1922.* Tuskegee, Alabama: Negro Year Book Publishing Company, 1922.

———. *Negro Year Book, 1925–1926.* Tuskegee, Alabama: Negro Year Book Publishing Company, 1926.

———. *Negro Year Book, 1931–1932.* Tuskegee, Alabama: Negro Year Book Publishing Company, 1932.

———. *Negro Year Book, 1937–1938.* Tuskegee, Alabama: Negro Year Book Publishing Company, 1938.

1975 Atlanta Bureau of Police Services Yearbook. Atlanta, 1975.

Yearbook: 1949–1951. City of Charleston, South Carolina, 1952.

Newspaper Clipping Files

Associated Negro Press Clipping File. Claude A. Barnett Papers, Chicago Historical Society, Chicago, Illinois.

Mrs. Patrick H. Campbell Scrapbook of Clippings. Houston Metropolitan Research Center, Houston, Texas.

Hampton University Newspaper Clipping File. Peabody Collection, Hampton University Library, Hampton, Virginia.

Moorland-Spingarn Research Center Clipping File. Howard University, Washington, D.C.

Negro History Clippings, July 24, 1928 to January 14, 1966. Houston Metropolitan Research Center, Houston, Texas.

Schomburg Newspaper Clipping File. Schomburg Center for Research in Black Culture, New York Public Library, New York, New York.

Tuskegee University Newspaper Clipping File. Washington Collection, Tuskegee University Library, Tuskegee, Alabama.

Court Cases

United States of America, et al. v. City of Chicago et al. United States Court of Appeals for the Seventh District, No. 76-1344, January 11, 1977.

United States of America v. The City of Miami, Florida, et al. United States District Court of Southern Florida, No. 75-3096-CIV-JE, March 31, 1977.

Lynn Coleman et al. vs. Frank J. Schaefer, Cleveland Lodge Fraternal Order of Police, et al., Petition for Money, Declaratory Judgment, and Further Relief at Law and Equity. County of Cuyahoga, Court of Common Pleas, October 20, 1969.

Officers for Justice, et al. v. The Civil Service Commission, et al. U.S. District Court for the Northern District of California, Civil Action No. C-73-0657, November 14, 1977.

Police Officers for Equal Rights, et al., v. The City of Columbus, et al. U.S. District Court for the Southern District of Ohio, Eastern Division, Civil Action No. C-2-78-394, August 28, 1983.

The Shield Club, et al. v. The City of Cleveland. U.S. District Court Northern District of Ohio, Eastern Division, Civil Action No. C 72-1088, September 27, 1976.

Newspapers (Selected Issues)

Atlanta Daily World
Baltimore Afro-American
Chicago Defender
Cleveland Call and Post
Cleveland Gazette
Columbus Call and Post
Columbus Dispatch
Dallas Express
Dallas Morning News
Houston Forward Times
Houston Informer
Los Angeles Sentinel
Miami Times
New Orleans Tribune
Philadelphia Tribune
Pittsburgh Courier
New York Times
San Antonio Register
San Francisco Sun Reporter
Washington Post

Police Publications

Atlanta Police Department. "Promotional System," proposed affirmative action plan submitted to the Law Enforcement Assistance Administration, December 28, 1973.

Chicago Police Department. *Chicago Police Star.* Bicentennial Edition. July 1976.

Cleveland Police Department. "General Davis, New Safety Director, Urges Courtesy." *Guardian,* January–February 1970, p. 1.

"Davis, Coffey and the C. P. P. A. . . . Let's Keep It That Way." *Blue Line,* July 1970, p. 11.

"Detective Ira Cooper Promoted to Detective Sergeant." *St. Louis Police Journal,* March 7, 1923, p. 9.

"Lt. Ira L. Cooper." *St. Louis Police Journal,* December 1965, p. 8.

"Meetings of the Executive Committee of the Police Relief Association." *St. Louis Police Journal,* July 9, 1924, p. 8.
National Black Police Association Newsletter, Summer 1982.
Officers for Justice Journal, September 1982 and First Quarter 1983.
Officers for Justice Peace Officers Association. *Why the Officers for Justice.* San Francisco, 1968.
"Some 'Quirements' Lacking." *St. Louis Police Journal,* December 28, 1912, p. 7.
"Three Negro Specials Appointed," *St. Louis Police Journal,* June 8, 1912, p. 6.

Miscellaneous

Atlanta NAACP et al. *Wanted: Negro Police for Negro Districts in Atlanta.* Atlanta: Atlanta Daily World and others, 1937.
Bodenhamer, David J. "The Efficiency of Criminal Justice in the Antebellum South." In *Criminal Justice History: An International Annual* 3, 81–96. Westport, Connecticut: Meckler Publishing Company, 1982.
Brown, Lee P. "Community Policing: A Practical Guide for Police Officials." *Perspectives on Policing* 12 (September 1989): 1–12.
———. *The Death of Police-Community Relations.* Occasional Paper of the Howard University Institute of Urban Affairs and Research. Volume 1. Washington, D.C., 1973.
Brown, Lee P., ed. *The Administration of Criminal Justice: A View from Black America.* Occasional Paper of the Howard University Institute of Urban Affairs and Research, Volume 2. Washington, D.C., 1974.
City of Cleveland Council. "A Resolution Honoring Lynn R. Coleman," No. 2214–74, November 18, 1974.
Cole, Donald A.; George G. Kellingerg; Charles M. Friel; and Hazel B. Kerper. "The Negro Law Enforcement Officer in Texas." *Criminal Justice Monograph.* Volume 1. Huntsville, Texas: Sam Houston State University, Institute of Contemporary Corrections and the Behavioral Sciences, 1969.
Dulaney, W. Marvin. "Blacks as Policemen in Columbus, Ohio, 1895–1945." In *Blacks in Ohio History,* ed. Rubin F. Weston, 10–16. Columbus: Ohio Historical Society, 1976.
Ficklen, John R. "History of Reconstruction in Louisiana (through 1868)." Johns Hopkins University Studies in History and Political Science 28 Baltimore: Johns Hopkins University Press, 1910.
Foner, Eric. *"The Tocsin of Freedom": The Black Leadership of Radical Reconstruction.* 31st Annual Robert Fortenbaugh Memorial Lecture. Gettysburg, Pennsylvania: Gettysburg College, 1992.
Jordan, Laylon W. "Police Power and Public Safety in Antebellum Charleston: The Emergence of a New Police, 1800–1860." In Sam M. Hines and George W. Hopkins, eds., *South Atlantic Urban Studies* 3 (1979): 122–140.
Marchiafava, Louis A. "The Houston Police, 1878–1948." *Rice University Studies* 63 (Spring 1977).
Williams, Hubert, and Patrick V. Murphy. "The Evolving Strategy of Policing: A Minority View." *Perspectives on Policing* 13 (January 1990): 1–16.

Oral History Interviews

Adams, George, and Davis, Otis, vice-president and president, respectively, of the Miami Community Police Benevolent Association. Interview by author, October 21 and 30, 1977, Miami, Florida. Audiotape.
Alston, Harvey, retired inspector of the Columbus Police Department. Interview by author, November 10, 1973, Columbus, Ohio. Transcript.

Battle, Wilbert K.; Byrd, Jesse; and Sanders, Prentice, members of the Officers for Justice. Interview by author, December 18, 1977, San Francisco, California. Audiotape.

Bell, Eldrin, deputy director, Atlanta Bureau of Police Services. Interview by author, August 10, 1977, Atlanta, Georgia. Transcript.

Bolden, Edward, retired captain of the St. Louis Police Department. Interview by author, July 11, 1977, St. Louis, Missouri. Transcript.

Bowser, Robert, president, Afro-American Patrolmen's League. Interview by author, August 4, 1977, Atlanta, Georgia. Audiotape.

Bracey, William, district commander, New York City Police Department. Interview by author, January 19, 1978, New York City. Audiotape.

Brant, Jesse, police officer, Columbus Police Department. Interview by author, October 12, 1973, Columbus, Ohio. Transcript.

Broome, Homer F., commander, Los Angeles Police Department. Interview by author, November 30, 1977, Los Angeles, California. Audiotape.

Broomfield, Tyree, lieutenant colonel, Dayton Police Department. Interview by author, June 17, 1977, Washington, D.C. Transcript.

Buchanan, James H., sergeant, St. Louis Police Department. Interview by author, July 7, 1977, St. Louis, Missouri. Audiotape.

Carraway, Gay, captain, St. Louis Police Department. Interview by author, July 14, 1977, St. Louis, Missouri. Audiotape.

Clayton, Mrs. Jean, retired policewoman, Cleveland Police Department. Interview by author, September 10, 1977, Cleveland, Ohio. Audiotape.

Coleman, Lynn R., retired police officer, Cleveland Police Department. Interview by author, September 17, 1977, Cleveland, Ohio. Transcript.

Cuffie, Charles, police officer, Atlanta Bureau of Police Services. Interview by author, August 5, 1977, Atlanta, Georgia. Audiotape.

Dangerfield, Troy, police officer, San Francisco Police Department. Interview by author, December 19, 1977, San Francisco, California. Audiotape.

Dickson, Clarence, major, Miami Police Department. Interview by author, October 26, 1977, Miami, Florida. Audiotape.

Dixon, Claude, major, Atlanta Bureau of Police Services. Interview by author, August 5, 1977, Atlanta, Georgia. Audiotape.

Duty, Margie, policewoman, Houston Police Department. Interview by author, November 9, 1977, Houston, Texas. Transcript.

Eaves, A. Reginald, director of public safety. Interview by author, August 11, 1977, Atlanta, Georgia. Audiotape.

Eddings, Benjamin, retired police officer, Columbus Police Department. Interview by author, December 7, 1973, Columbus, Ohio. Transcript.

Guillory, Julius, assistant chief of police, Opelousas Police Department. Interview by Harry Gardner, May 15, 1977, Opelousas, Louisiana. Transcript.

Hargrove, Jimmy, police officer, New York City Police Department. Interview by author, January 17, 1978, New York City. Transcript.

Hongisto, Richard, chief of police, Cleveland Police Department. Interview by author, February 1, 1978, Cleveland, Ohio. Transcript.

Hopson, Richard, police officer, Columbus Police Department. Interview by author, October 12, 1973, Columbus, Ohio. Transcript.

Humphrey, Raymond, sergeant, Houston Police Department. Interview by author, November 10, 1977, Houston, Texas. Audiotape.

Ingram, Robert, sergeant, Miami Police Department. Interview by author, October 24 and 25, 1977, Miami, Florida. Audiotape.

James, Harold, president, Guardians Civic League. Interview by author, January 12, 1978, Philadelphia, Pennsylvania. Transcript.

Jarrett, Mary, lieutenant, Detroit Police Department. Interview by author, August 26, 1977, New Orleans, Louisiana. Transcript.

Jenkins, Herbert T., retired chief of police, Atlanta Police Department. Interview by author, August 8, 1977, Atlanta, Georgia. Transcript.
Johnson, Mackie C., police officer, Detroit Police Department. Interview by author, August 26, 1977, New Orleans, Louisiana. Transcript.
Johnson, Marion, president, Oscar Joel Bryant Association. Interview by author, November 29, 1977, Los Angeles, California. Audiotape.
Johnson, William, and Respass, Harold, retired members of the Guardians, New York City Police Department. Interview by author, January 18, 1978, New York City. Audiotape.
Jordan, Robert, police officer, St. Louis County Police Department. Interview by author, January 29, 1978, en route from Chicago, Illinois, to St. Louis, Missouri. Transcript.
Landrum, Leroy "Buster," retired police officer, Galveston Police Department. Interview by author, January 7, 1987, Galveston, Texas. Transcript.
Lomax, Leo, police officer, Chicago Police Department. Interview by author, October 6, 1977, Chicago, Illinois. Audiotape.
McNeal, Theodore, retired president of the St. Louis Board of Police Commissioners. Interview by author, July 20, 1977, St. Louis, Missouri. Audiotape.
Mack, Boise, police officer, Cleveland Police Department. Interview by author, September 10 and 11, 1977, Cleveland, Ohio. Audiotape.
Martin, Herbert S., retired police lieutenant, Washington Metropolitan Police Department. Interview by author, June 2, 1977, Washington, D.C. Transcript.
Nash, Jesse, retired police sergeant and former president of the Miami Community Police Benevolent Association. Interview by author, October 31, 1977, Miami, Florida. Audiotape.
Nolan, Samuel, deputy police superintendent, Chicago Police Department. Interview by author, September 26, 1977, Chicago, Illinois. Audiotape.
Pomares, Joyce, assistant to the chief of police, Houston Police Department. Interview by author, November 2 and 3, 1977, Houston, Texas. Transcript.
Proctor, Herbert, police officer, Chicago Police Department. Interview by author, October 6, 1977, Chicago, Illinois. Transcript.
Reece, Eugene, president of the St. Louis Ethical Police Society. Interview by author, July 19, 1977, St. Louis, Missouri. Audiotape.
Reeves, Garth C. Sr., editor of the *Miami Times* newspaper. Interview by author, October 27, 1977, Miami, Florida. Audiotape.
Saffold, Howard, president of the Afro-American Patrolmen's League. Interview by author, January 25, 1978, Chicago, Illinois. Audiotape.
Saunders, Herman, sergeant, St. Louis Police Department. Interview by author, July 18, 1977, St. Louis, Missouri. Audiotape.
Scott, C. A., editor and publisher of the *Atlanta Daily World* newspaper. Interview by author, August 4, 1977, Atlanta, Georgia. Audiotape.
Seay, Norman, former police committee chairman of the Congress of Racial Equality. Interview by author, July 15, 1977, St. Louis, Missouri. Audiotape.
Smith, Leroy A., retired major, Miami Police Department. Interview by author, October 25, 1977, Miami, Florida. Transcript.
Sparks, Johnny L., captain, Atlanta Bureau of Police Services. Interview by author, August 10, 1977, Atlanta, Georgia. Audiotape.
Stringfellow, E. J., city marshal, City of Houston. Interview by author, January 6, 1987, Houston, Texas. Transcript.
Tapia, Arturo, police officer, San Francisco Police Department. Interview by author, December 20, 1977, San Francisco, California. Audiotape.
Taylor, James A., retired sergeant, St. Louis Police Department. Interview by author, July 12 and 13, 1977, St. Louis, Missouri. Audiotape.
Thomas, Adrian, retired police officer, St. Louis Police Department. Interview by author, July 17, 1977, St. Louis, Missouri. Audiotape.

Triplett, Peggy, former assistant to the commissioner, New York City Police Department. Interview by author, August 26, 1977, New Orleans, Louisiana. Transcript.

Walker, May, police officer, Houston Police Department. Interview by author, January 6, 1987, Houston, Texas. Transcript.

Walker, William O., editor and publisher of the *Cleveland Call and Post* newspaper. Interview by author, September 13, 1977, Cleveland, Ohio. Transcript.

Waller, Edward, retired police officer, Columbus Police Department. Interview by author, November 20, 1973, Columbus, Ohio. Transcript.

Ware, Mitchell, deputy superintendent, Chicago Police Department. Interview by author, October 5, 1977, Chicago, Illinois. Audiotape.

Warren, Adkins, lieutenant colonel, St. Louis Police Department. Interview by author, July 11, 1977, St. Louis, Missouri. Audiotape.

Watson, James, police officer, Columbus Police Department. Interview by author, March 3, 1974, Columbus, Ohio. Transcript.

White, Ralph V., retired police officer, Miami Police Department. Interview by author, October 31, 1977, Miami, Florida. Audiotape.

Williams, Earl, detective, Houston Police Department. Interview by author, November 9, 1977, Houston, Texas. Transcript.

Williams, Henry, inspector, San Francisco Police Department. Interview by author, December 19, 1977, San Francisco, California. Audiotape.

Williams, Rodney, police officer, San Francisco Police Department. Interview by author, December 21, 1977, San Francisco, California. Audiotape.

Young, A. V., president of the Afro-American Police Officers Association and former president of the Texas Negro Peace Officers' Association. Interview by author, November 10, 1977, in Houston, Texas; August 25, 1978, in Chicago, Illinois; and January 5 and 6, 1987, in Houston, Texas. Audiotapes and transcripts.

Speeches

Brown, Lee P. "Police Use of Deadly Force." Address to the Sixth Annual Convention of the National Black Police Association, Chicago, Illinois, August 25, 1978.

Days, Drew S., Assistant Attorney General, U.S. Department of Justice, Civil Rights Division. Address to the National Order of Black Law Enforcement Executives (N.O.B.L.E.), Atlanta, Georgia, June 12, 1977. Transcript.

McNeil, Genna Rae. "African American Hopes and Tragic Realities." Lecture delivered at the Twenty-sixth Annual Walter Prescott Webb Lectures, the University of Texas at Arlington, Arlington, Texas, March 14, 1991. Photocopy.

INDEX

W. Marvin Dulaney is Director of the Avery Research Center for African American History and Culture and of the African American Studies Program at the College of Charleston. He is coeditor of *Essays on the American Civil Rights Movement.*